LABOUR AND
SOCIAL HISTORY THESES

LABOUR AND
SOCIAL HISTORY THESES

American, British and Irish university theses and dissertations
in the field of British and Irish labour history,
presented between 1900 and 1978

COMPILED BY
Victor F. Gilbert

MANSELL PUBLISHING LIMITED

ISBN 0 7201 1647 3

Mansell Publishing Limited, 6 All Saints Street, London N1 9RL

First published 1982

© Victor F. Gilbert, 1982

Distributed in the United States and Canada by
The H. W. Wilson Company, 950 University Avenue, Bronx, New York 10452.

British Library Cataloguing in Publication Data

Labour and social history theses.
    1. Dissertations, Academic—Great Britain
    2. Dissertations, Academic—Ireland
    3. Dissertations, Academic—United States
    4. Labor and laboring classes—Great Britain—
History—Bibliography
    I. Gilbert, Victor F.
016.331'09   Z7164.L1

ISBN 0-7201-1647-3

Printed and bound in Great Britain at The Pitman Press, Bath

CONTENTS

INTRODUCTION

The aim of this work is to provide, as comprehensively as possible, a classified list of theses and dissertations presented at North American, British and Irish universities between 1900 and 1978 in the field of British and Irish labour history. The large number of relevant theses has made the need to establish a bibliographical control over them increasingly urgent. This need has been expressed by the Society for the Study of Labour History, for whose members this index was originally intended. My broad treatment of labour history reflects the wide interests of the members of the Society as shown in the pages of its *Bulletin*. Thus I have not limited myself to the political and trade union movements but have included such fields of social history as housing, public health and poverty which have affected working-class life. This coverage reflects the increasing interest in British labour history and the broadening approach to the study of labour history in the last twenty years. My hope is that this reference work will reveal the extent of research in labour history and guide the research worker embarking on his selected field of study to the research already carried out.

For theses that have been presented since 1978 the user should refer to the annual lists of theses and dissertations on British labour history that appear in each Autumn issue of the *Bulletin of the Society for the Study of Labour History*.

The category of dissertation (not full theses but special studies presented in partial fulfilment for higher degrees) has been difficult to cover comprehensively, and I would be grateful for details of any such dissertations not included in this work. Some of these dissertations may not have been officially deposited in main university libraries and in consequence copies may be more difficult to locate.

Sources

Dissertations on British history, 1815–1914: an index to British and American theses by S. Peter Bell (1974) proved an excellent work to commence this compilation.

For British theses, two recent publications have greatly helped retrospective searching: *Retrospective index to theses of Great Britain and Ireland, 1716–1950. Vol. 1: Social sciences and humanities* edited by R. R. Bilboul and F. L. Kent (1975) and *History theses, 1901–1970: historical research for higher degrees in the universities of the United Kingdom* compiled by P. M. Jacobs (1976). Since 1951 the ASLIB publication of *Index to theses accepted for higher degrees by the universities of Great Britain and Ireland and the Council for National Academic Awards* has been the standard checklist. It is important that the user checks in the current issue of the ASLIB *Index* to note the conditions for borrowing and consultation at the deposit libraries. Added to the ASLIB *Index* is *Historical research for university degrees in the United Kingdom. Part 1: Theses completed*, published annually by the Institute of Historical

Research, University of London. This is even more useful with its detailed index and more rapid and regular publication.

North American coverage has been limited to doctoral theses only, and the following sources have been drawn upon:

Dissertation abstracts international (including the retrospective index volumes, 1939–1969).

Index to American doctoral dissertations

Dissertations in history: an index to dissertations completed in history departments of United States and Canadian universities edited by W. F. Kuehl. Vol. 1: 1873–1960 (1965) and Vol. 2: 1961–1970 (1972)

Canadian graduate theses, 1919–1967: an annotated bibliography (covering economics, business and industrial relations) by W. D. Wood, L. A. Kelly and P. Kumar (1970)

Arrangement

The material is divided into subjects and arranged alphabetically (*see* Contents list). Some subject categories are further subdivided where appropriate. The Contents list also provides a subject approach to the material. Within each subject the items are arranged alphabetically by author.

The following two symbols should be noted:

* = dissertation, not full thesis, in partial fulfilment of the conditions for the award of a higher degree.

DA = *Dissertation Abstracts* followed by volume number and page number of the entry. From 1969 *Dissertation Abstracts* divided into *A* and *B* series. *A* series cover Social Sciences and Humanities.

There are four indexes. Reference is to item numbers.

Acknowledgements

I wish to express my warmest appreciation of the help given to me in so many ways. In particular, I acknowledge with many thanks the encouragement and guidance given to me by Professor Sidney Pollard, Dr David Martin, John Halstead, Professor Royden Harrison and Colin Holmes.

The financial help given by the University of Sheffield Research Fund towards the costs of preparing the typescript of this work for publication is also gratefully acknowledged. Mrs Eileen Nixon's great patience and excellent typing brought clarity and order out of the unpromising material of the original manuscript. However, any sins of commission and omission are my own responsibility and I must apologise for any eccentricities in the numbering of the entries.

Once again I must express my grateful appreciation of the forebearance of my wife and family as our home was inundated by those little white slips of paper for so many months.

Finally, I wish to dedicate the work to my father whose long years of unassuming service to the National Union of Railwaymen and the Labour Party gave me my first insights into the trade union and labour movement.

V. F. Gilbert
Sheffield, 1981

ABSENTEEISM

1. AYOUB, A.M.H.
   Absenteeism among manual women workers in engineering: a case study.
   M.Sc., Manchester (Univ. of Manchester Institute of Science and Technology), 1969-70.

2. FROGGATT, P.
   Short-term absence from industry: a statistical and historical study.
   Ph.D., Queen's University, Belfast, 1966-67.

CASUAL LABOUR

3. JONES, G. Stedman
   Some social consequences of the casual labour problem in London, 1860-90 with particular reference to the East End.
   D.Phil., Oxford, 1970.

4. OREN, L.E.
   The problem of casual labour and the origins of the Welfare State in England, 1899-1914.
   Ph.D., Yale, 1974. DA 36 0490A

CHARTISM /see also RADICALISM/
   /To a large extent based upon Bibliography of the Chartist movement, 1837-1976 edited by J.F.C. Harrison and Dorothy Thompson./

5. AIZENMAN, R.
   A re-evaluation of the third Chartist movement.
   M.A., Calgary, Alberta, 1968.

6. ASHTON, O.R.
   The Chartist movement in mid-Wales, 1837-1858.
   M.A., Wales (Swansea), 1971.

7. BEBB, C.S.
   The origins of Chartism in Dundee.
   B.Phil., St. Andrews, 1977.

8. BENNETT, H.J.R.
   Social aspects of the Chartist movement.
   M.A., Birmingham, 1927.

9. BOSTON, R.J.
   Chartist legacy: British Chartists in America, 1839-1890.
   M.A., Wisconsin, 1969.

10. No entry

11. CEPLAIR, L.S.
    Area and agitator: a study of Feargus O'Connor and the Lancashire cotton district, 1838-1842.
    M.A., Wisconsin, 1969.

12. CONKLIN, R.J.
    Thomas Cooper, The Chartist, 1805-1892.
    Ph.D., Columbia, 1936.

13. EPSTEIN, J.A.
    Feargus O'Connor and the English working class radical movement, 1832-1841: a study in national Chartist leadership.
    Ph.D., Birmingham, 1977.

14. FAULKNER, H.U.
    Chartism and the Churches: a study in democracy.
    Ph.D., Columbia, 1916.

15. FEARN, H.
    Chartism in Suffolk.
    M.A., Sheffield, 1952.

16. FYSON, R.C.M.
    Chartism in North Staffordshire, 1836-1842.
    M.A.*, Lancaster, 1975.

17. GEERING, K.
    George White: a nineteenth-century workers' leader and the Kirkdale phenomenon.
    M.A., Sussex, 1975.

18. GLASGOW, E.L.H.
    Feargus O'Connor: Irishman and Chartist.
    M.A., Manchester, 1950.

19. GLASGOW, E.L.H.
    The life and works of Feargus O'Connor.
    Ph.D., Manchester, 1951.

20.   JOHN, A.V.
       The Chartists of industrial South Wales, 1840-1868.
       M.A., Wales (Swansea), 1971.

21.   JONES, R.A.
       Knowledge Chartism: a study of the influence of Chartism on nineteenth century
       educational development in Great Britain.
       M.A., Birmingham, 1938.

22.   KEMNITZ, T.M.
       Chartism in Brighton.
       D.Phil., Sussex, 1969.

23.   McLELLAN, N.J.
       Chartism and the Churches with special reference to Lancashire: an account of the
       Churches and social reform in the Chartist period.
       Ph.D., Edinburgh, 1947.

24.   MARTIN, C.E.
       Female Chartism: a study in politics.
       M.A., Wales (Swansea), 1974.
              /Considers the role of women in the Chartist movement; including a study
               of Female Chartist Associations.7

25.   MATHER, F.C.
       The machinery of public order in the Chartist period.
       M.A., Manchester, 1948.

26.   NEIMAN, F.
       W.J. Linton, 1812-1897.
       Ph.D., Harvard, 1938.

27.   O'HIGGINS, R.
       Ireland and Chartism: a study of the influence of Irishmen and the Irish question on
       the Chartist movement.
       Ph.D., Trinity College, Dublin, 1959.

28.   PLUMMER, A.
       The life of James Bronterre O'Brien.
       B.Litt., Oxford, 1929.

29.   RAMAGE, E.
       Chartism in English literature, 1839-1876.
       Ph.D., Wisconsin, 1939.

30.   REID, N.
       Chartism in Stockport.
       M.A., Hull, 1974.

31.   RICHARDSON, K.E.
       The life and times of Thomas Attwood.
       Ph.D., Nottingham, 1965.

32.   SCHOYEN, A.R.
       George Julian Harney.
       Ph.D., London, 1951.

33.   SELF, G.M.
       The Chartist incident on Kennington Common critically examined in the light of the
       Home Office papers at the Public Record Office.
       M.A., McGill, 1938.

34.   SLOSSON, P.W.
       The decline of the Chartist movement.
       Ph.D., Columbia, 1916.

35.   TRAWICK, B.B.
       The works of Gerald Massey.
       Ph.D., Harvard, 1942.

36.   VAMPLOW, W.
       Barnsley, the right eye of Yorkshire: a study of local Chartism.
       B.Sc.*, Southampton, 1964.

37.   VIRTUE, J.B.
       Carlyle's Chartism.
       Ph.D., Yale, 1935.

38.   WILLIAMS, Myfanwy
       The Chartist movement in Wales.
       M.A., Wales (Bangor), 1919.

39.   WILSON, A.
       The Chartist movement in Scotland.
       D.Phil., Oxford, 1951.

40. WILSON, J.S.
The debate over Chartism, 1854-1952.
M.A., Columbia, 1953.

41. WRIGHT, L.C.
Scottish Chartism and its economic background.
Ph.D., Edinburgh, 1951.

CHILD AND JUVENILE LABOUR

42. BEHLMER, G.K.
The child protection movement in England 1861-90.
Ph.D., Stanford, 1977.
DA 39 1031A

43. GILL, C.J.
Education and industrialism: a study of the way in which changes in industrial organisation have led to changes in the use of child labour and to the growth in England of a system of education based on compulsory school attendance.
M.A., Liverpool, 1938.

44. GILLAN, D.J.
The effect of industrial legislation on the social and educational condition of children employed in coal mines between 1840 and 1876 with special reference to Durham County.
M.Ed., Durham, 1968.

45. OWEN, A.D.K.
Problems of juvenile employment.
M.Com., Leeds, 1929.

46. PETHERICK, F.R.
The movement for the abolition of child labour in the mines of England.
Ph.D., Boston, 1954.

47. SCARF, J.W.
The employment of juveniles and young persons in the West Riding wool textile industry with some reference to the effect of the raising of the school-leaving age and release for part-time further education.
D.Phil., Oxford, 1947.

48. STOCKDALE, K.F.
Some aspects of juvenile employment in Leeds.
B.A.*, Leeds, 1930.

CHRISTIAN SOCIALISM /see also RELIGION7

49. ALLEN, P.R.
Charles Kingsley: the broad Church background to his thought.
Ph.D., Toronto, 1965.
DA 28 0662A

50. ALLEN, R.E.
Charles Kingsley and the Industrial Revolution.
Ph.D., Missouri, 1955.
DA 16 1680

51. ANDERSON, T.R.
Christian Socialism reconsidered.
Ph.D., Union Theological Seminary, 1967.
DA 28 1511A

52. BACKSTROM, P.N.
John Malcolm Forbes Ludlow, a little known contributor to the cause of the British working man in the 19th century.
Ph.D., Boston, 1960.
DA 21 0859A
        /Christian Socialism: Co-operative movement7

53. BALDWIN, S.E.
Charles Kingsley, novelist and reformer.
Ph.D., Cornell, 1925.

54. BOOTH, H.F.
The knowledge of God and the practice of society in Frederick Denison Maurice.
Ph.D., Boston University Graduate School, 1963.
DA 24 0863A

55. BUTLER, B.J.
Frederick Lewis Donaldson and the Christian Socialist movement.
M.Phil., Leeds, 1970.

56. BYROM, T.B.
The novels of Charles Kingsley.
B.Litt., Oxford, 1967.

57.   COX, J.W.
God manifesting Himself: a study of some central elements in the theology of F.D. Maurice.
Ph.D., Cambridge, 1960-61.

58.   EVANS, I.
Christian Socialism: its rise and development, its economic and social results and its
relation to the working class movements.
M.A., Wales (Aberystwyth), 1912.

59.   GRIERSON, P.S.
The place of F.D. Maurice in recent theology.
B.D., Leeds, 1974.

60.   GRUBB, D.S.
Kingsley's Alton Locke: propaganda and the device of fiction.
Ph.D., Michigan, 1967.
DA 28 2646A

61.   HARTLEY, A.J.
Literary aspects of Christian Socialism in the work of F.D. Maurice and Charles Kingsley.
Ph.D., King's College, London, 1963.

62.   HOLLANDER, R.R.
The theology and social philosophy of Anglican Christian Socialism: the roots and mission
of the Church Socialist League, 1906-1924.
Ph.D., Washington, 1974.
DA 35 2174A

63.   JONES, P.d'A.
Christian Socialism in Britain and the U.S.A.
Ph.D., London, 1964.

64.   KETCHUM, R.H.
Frederick Denison Maurice: an assessment of his contributions to 19th century English
education.
Ph.D., Syracuse, 1969.
DA 30 5262A

65.   LACEB, M.
The evolution of Charles Kingsley's political and social thought.
M.Phil., Leeds, 1968.

66.   LEVITAS, R.A.
A sociological analysis of Christian Socialism, 1848-54.
Ph.D., Sheffield, 1974.

67.   LINDSAY, D.W.
The political thought of F.D. Maurice.
M.Litt., Durham, 1968-69.

68.   McCLAIN, F.M.
Maurice as moralist: the ethical teaching of Frederick Denison Maurice.
Ph.D., Cambridge, 1969.
DA 33 2485A

69.   MARTIN, R.B.
An edition of the correspondence and private papers of Charles Kingsley, 1819-56.
B.Litt., Oxford, 1951.

70.   MEADE, P.C.
F.D. Maurice: a critical account of his writings and their intellectual background.
M.Litt., Cambridge, 1955.

71.   MORRIS, J.V.
The political and social novels of Charles Kingsley.
M.A., Wales, 1921.

72.   PARKYN, J.
The political thought of some of the founders of Christian Socialism.
M.A., London, External, 1962.

73.   PERCIVAL, S.W.
Charles Dickens and Charles Kingsley as social critics.
M.A., Manchester, 1947.

74.   PINNOW, J.L.
Carlyle's influence on Charles Kingsley's life and writings.
Ph.D., Colorado, 1973.
DA 34 1865A

75.   PORTER, J.F.
The place of Christ in the thought of F.D. Maurice.
Ph.D., Columbia, 1959.
DA 20 3869A
        /His activity in the Christian Socialist movement is put in the perspective
        of his Christocentric social ethic./

76. POSTLES, D.
The influence of Frederick Denison Maurice on modern theology.
M.A., Birmingham, 1964-65.

77. SAXBY, D.L.
Charles Kingsley: his religious and social ideas: the critique of an age.
Ph.D., Princeton, 1965.
DA 26 4100A

78. SMITH, A.C.
Frederick Denison Maurice.
M.A., Sheffield, 1950.

79. SPENCE, M.
Charles Kingsley and education.
M.A., Bristol, 1945.

80. STOKES, F.C.
Godliness, cleanliness and art: the priorities of Charles Kingsley's novels of purpose.
Ph.D., Illinois, 1972.
DA 34 0742A

81. WEST, H.W.
The social and religious thought of Charles Kingsley and his place in the Christian
Socialist School of 1848-54.
Ph.D., Edinburgh, 1947.

CLASS-STRUCTURE AND ATTITUDES

82. BAADER, H.G.
Class and status as viewed by feudal aristocrat and peasant.
Ph.D., California, Berkeley, 1965.
DA 26 3891
/Study of English, French and German society from 12th to 14th centuries.7

83. BICKFORD, C.P.
The improving principle: changing attitudes towards social mobility in England,
1700-1860.
Ph.D., Connecticut, 1971.
DA 32 2590A

84. COMINOS, P.T.
The late Victorian revolt, 1859-95.
D.Phil., Oxford, 1958.

85. DAVIES, J.H.
The social structure and economy of south-west Wales in the late nineteenth century.
M.A., Wales (Aberystwyth), 1967.

86. FOSTER, J.O.
Capitalism and class-consciousness in earlier nineteenth century Oldham.
Ph.D., Cambridge, 1967.

87. GRAY, R.Q.
Class structure and the class formation of skilled workers in Edinburgh, c.1850-c.1900.
Ph.D., Edinburgh, 1973.

88. KIRK, N.
Class and fragmentation: some aspects of working-class life in south-east Lancashire
and north-east Cheshire, 1850-1870.
Ph.D., Pittsburgh, 1974.
DA 36 1036A

89. LAWLESS, J.T.
Disraeli's concepts of English social class.
Ph.D., St. Louis, 1967.
DA 28 3115A

90. LE BEAU, S.S.
Pride and prejudice: the 1867 Parliament's image of the English working classes.
Ph.D., Pittsburgh, 1971.
DA 32 3214A

91. MASSEY, G.M.
"Embourgeoisement" and the working class: a critique.
Ph.D., Indiana, 1975.
DA 36 2439A
/A comparative study of U.S.A., Britain, Germany and France in the 1950s
and an analysis of Marxist theory.7

92. MEJIA, A.
The upper class in late Victorian and Edwardian England: a study of the formation and
perpetuation of class bias.
Ph.D., Stanford, 1968.
DA 29 2187A

93.   PRYCE, W.T.R.
       The social and economic structure of north-east Wales, 1750-1890.
       Ph.D., C.N.A.A., 1971.

94.   SHEARING, H.A.
       The social structure and development of London, c.1800-30.
       D.Phil., Oxford, 1955.

95.   SHERIDAN, Sister M.Q.
       John Stuart Mill's concept of class.
       Ph.D., St. Louis, 1967.
       DA 28 3126A

96.   SMITH, R.J.
       The social structure of Nottingham and adjacent districts in the mid-nineteenth century:
       an essay in quantitative social history.
       Ph.D., Nottingham, 1968.

97.   THOMPSON, P.G.
       Social-class placement of working-class males in England: the relative importance of
       mobility values and mobility resources of the family.
       Ph.D., Wisconsin, 1970.
       DA 31 3062A
               /Contemporary sociological study.7

98.   TILLER, K
       Working class attitudes and organizations in three industrial towns, 1854-1875.
       Ph.D., Birmingham, 1975.
               /Halifax, Wigan, Kidderminster.7

CO-OPERATIVE MOVEMENT

99.   DARVILL, P.A.
       The contributions of co-operative retail societies to welfare within the social
       framework of the north-east coast area.
       M.L.H., Durham, 1954-55.

100.   DOYLE, D.J.
       Rochdale and the origin of the Rochdale Society of Equitable Pioneers.
       Ph.D., St. John's University, 1972.
       DA 33 2855A

101.   FAY, C.R.
       Co-operation at home and abroad: a description and analysis.
       D.Sc., London, 1909.

102.   FIELDEN, M.J.
       Industrial producer co-operation in Great Britain: three case studies.
       M.A., Sheffield, 1973.
               /Leicester Co-operative Boot & Shoe Manufacturing Co. Ltd., Leicester
                Co-operative Printers, Rowen (Onllwyn) Ltd.7

103.   HIMEIMY, I.A. EI-R.
       The development and organisation of the Scottish co-operative movement.
       Ph.D., Edinburgh, 1955.

104.   JENKIN, G.B.
       Production in the consumer's co-operative movement.
       M.Com., Birmingham, 1934.

105.   JONES, D.C.
       The economics of British producer co-operatives.
       Ph.D., Cornell, 1974.
       DA 35 4808A

106.   KINLOCH, J.A.
       History of the Scottish Co-operative Wholesale Society.
       Ph.D., Strathclyde, 1976.

107.   LANE, P.J.
       Distribution and classification of co-operative societies in Ireland.
       M.A., National University of Ireland, 1953-54.

108.   MARS, H.
       Efficiency of capital raising, investment and financial administration in consumers'
       co-operative production.
       M.Com., Birmingham, 1937.

109.   MILDER, D.A.
       A study of retail innovation in the United Kingdom Co-operative Movement.
       B.L.H., Oxford, 1964.

110.   RAGHAILLAIGH, M.
       Recent aspects of the co-operative movement in Ireland.
       M.A., National University of Ireland, 1929.

111. REMPE, P.L.
Sir Horace Plunkett and the politics of Irish agriculture, 1890-1914.
Ph.D., State University of New York at Stoney Brook, 1976.
<u>DA</u> <u>37</u> 7261A
/Agricultural co-operatives/

112. RODDOCK, J.W.
Economics of the consumers' co-operative movement.
M.Sc., L.S.E., 1939.

113. ROSS, N.S.
The development of consumers' co-operation on the north-east coast area (1860-80).
Ph.D., Durham, 1939.

114. SYMONS, W.G.
Control and management in co-operative retail societies.
M.Com., Birmingham, 1936.

CRIME AND PUNISHMENT

115. DEMOTTE, C.M.
The dark side of town: crime in Manchester and Salford, 1815-1875.
Ph.D., Kansas, 1977.
<u>DA</u> <u>38</u> 4299A

116. FAIRS, G.H.
Criminal transportation: its theory and practice with special reference to Australia.
M.A., Bristol, 1932.

117. HAY, C.D.
Crime, authority and the criminal law: Staffordshire, 1750-1800.
Ph.D., Warwick, 1975.

118. LINEBAUGH, P.
Tyburn: studies about the relationship between crime and the labouring poor in the first half of eighteenth century London.
Ph.D., Warwick, 1975.

119. MUNSCHE, P.B.
The game laws in England, 1671-1831.
Ph.D., Toronto, 1978.
<u>DA</u> <u>39</u> 4423A

120. OLDHAM, W.
The administration of the system of transportation of British convicts, 1763-1793.
Ph.D., King's College, London, 1933.

121. PHILIPS, D.J.
Crime and authority in the Black Country, 1835-60: a study of prosecuted offences and law enforcement in an industrialising area.
D.Phil., Oxford, 1974.

122. SCHUPF, H.W.
The perishing and dangerous classes: effort to deal with the neglected vagrant and delinquent juvenile in England, 1840-75.
Ph.D., Columbia, 1971.
<u>DA</u> <u>32</u> 1455A

123. SMITH, A.E.
The transportation system in the seventeenth century with special reference to the West Indies.
D.Phil., Oxford, 1933.

124. STACK, J.A.
Social policy and juvenile delinquency, 1815-1875.
Ph.D., Iowa, 1974.
<u>DA</u> <u>35</u> 2197A

125. WINSLOW, C.P.
Sussex smuggling: a case study of 18th century crime.
Ph.D., Washington, 1973.
<u>DA</u> <u>34</u> 2541A
/"Rural poor main participants: part of the general resistance of the poor to efforts to destroy older 'moral economy'"./

DISABLED PERSONS

126. KIM, H.S.
Employment of disabled persons in Britain: a study of the legal framework and some problems of administration.
M.A.(Econ), Manchester, 1972-73.

127. PHILLIPS, N.
The Disabled Persons (Employment) Act, 1944: a study of its administration with special reference to the north-west region of the Ministry of Labour and National Service.
M.A.(Econ), Manchester, 1954-55.

128.   RIVIERE, M.
       Rehabilitation of the disabled: with special reference to the administration of the
       Disabled Persons (Employment) Act, 1944.
       D.Phil., Oxford, 1954-55.

       EDUCATION

       For fuller coverage of this field you should refer to:

(a)   HURT, J.S.
       Education and the working classes: bibliographical essay in <u>Bulletin of the Society for</u>
       <u>the Study of Labour History</u> <u>30</u>, 42-54 and <u>31</u>, 20-44 (1975).

(b)   <u>Theses and dissertations in the history of education presented at British and Irish</u>
       <u>universities, 1900-1976;   compiled by V.F. Gilbert and Colin Holmes</u>
       (History of Education Society, 1979.)

              EDUCATIONAL POLICIES AND INFLUENCES

129.   BARKER, R.S.
       The educational policies of the Labour Party, 1910-1961.
       Ph.D., L.S.E., 1968.

130.   BILSKI, R.
       The relation between ideologies and policies in the debate about comprehensive schools.
       Ph.D., Glasgow, 1971-72.

131.   BURGEVIN, J.D.
       Politics and education: case study of a pressure group: the National Association of
       Labour Teachers.
       Ph.D., Syracuse, 1969.
       <u>DA</u> <u>30</u> 3509A

132.   CRADDOCK, S.R.
       The origins of comprehensive education in Sheffield.
       M.Ed.*, Sheffield, 1974.

133.   DEAN, D.W.
       The political parties and the development of their attitude to educational problems,
       1918-1942.
       M.Phil., King's College, London, 1968.

134.   DOBSON, J.L.
       The contribution of Francis Place and the Radicals to the growth of popular education,
       1800-1840.
       Ph.D., Durham (Newcastle), 1959.

135.   FEARN, E.
       Role of political parties and pressure groups in comprehensive secondary reorganisation
       in four local authority areas: Chesterfield, Doncaster, Rotherham and Sheffield.
       Ph.D., Leeds, 1978.

136.   FENWICK, I.G.K.
       Organised opinion and the comprehensive school: a study of some educational groups and
       the policy-making process for education in England.
       Ph.D., Manchester, 1967-68.

137.   FLETCHER, B.
       The Labour Government and education, 1964-70.
       M.Ed.*, Sheffield, 1978.

138.   HARGREAVES, D.
       The Labour Party and higher education, 1964-1970.
       M.A., Lancaster, 1975.

139.   HOWELLS, R.B.
       A study of the emergence after 1945 of the comprehensive principle and secondary school
       organisation in Anglesey, Montgomeryshire, Denbighshire and Carmarthenshire.
       M.A., Wales (Swansea), 1966.

140.   ISAAC-HENRY, K.
       The politics of comprehensive education in Birmingham, 1957-67.
       M.Soc.Sc., Birmingham, 1969-70.

141.   JACKSON, H.D.
       Attempts to obtain the provision of popular education in the period 1807-33, with
       particular reference to the work of Whitbread, Brougham and Roebuck.
       M.Ed., Durham, 1967.

142.   JONES, J.C.
       The Labour movement in relation to State secondary education, 1902-1924.
       M.Ed., Leicester, 1966.

143.   LAFORGE, M.W.
       Labour and education in England, 1895-1924.
       Ph.D., Syracuse, 1967.
       <u>DA</u> <u>28</u> 0478A

144. LEWIS, J.W.
An examination of the influences of nineteenth century Radicals by 1870 on educational theory and practice.
M.A., Birmingham, 1951.

145. McCANN, W.P.
Trade Unionist, Co-operative and Socialist organisations in relation to popular education, 1870-1902.
Ph.D., Manchester, 1959-60.

146. MILLER, T.W.G.
A critical and empirical study of the emergence, development and significance of the comprehensive secondary school in England with special reference to certain educational and social effects.
Ph.D., Birmingham, 1958.

147. PARKINSON, M.H.
The Labour Party and the organisation of secondary education, 1918-65.
M.A., Manchester, 1968.

148. RICHMOND, R.
The Conservative Party's national policy on comprehensive education, 1944-71.
M.Ed., Durham, 1975.

149. ROBERTSON, A.B.
Discussion of education in Parliamentary debates, 1830-1870.
M.Ed., Newcastle, 1967.

150. SCHOFIELD, J.
The Labour Movement and educational policy, 1900-1931.
M.Ed., Manchester, 1963-64.

151. WARD, L.O.
An investigation into the educational ideas and contributions of the British political parties, 1870-1918.
Ph.D., King's College, London, 1970.

152. WILKINSON, M.K.
The development of Parliamentary opinion in respect to education, 1832-1870.
M.A., Wales, 1925.

EDUCATIONAL THOUGHT AND INFLUENCES

153. BLUNDEN, M.A.
The educational and political work of the Countess of Warwick.
M.A., Exeter, 1966.

154. BRENNAN, E.J.T.
The influence of Sidney and Beatrice Webb in English education, 1892-1903.
M.A., Sheffield, 1959.

155. BROOKS, J.R.
R.H. Tawney and the reform of English education.
Ph.D., Wales (Bangor), 1975.

156. CREWES, F.R.
An evaluation of the contribution to education of Rev. John Scott Lidgett with special reference to his work at the Bermondsey settlement.
M.A., London, External, 1974.

157. POOLE, M.G.
A critical analysis of the educational thought of Harold Laski.
Ph.D., Oklahoma, 1967.
DA 28 0479A

158. SALT, J.
Isaac Ironside and education in the Sheffield region in the first half of the nineteenth century.
M.A., Sheffield, 1960.

159. THOMAS, D.H.
John Scott Lidgett, 1854-1953 and the education of the people.
Ph.D., King's College, London, 1959.

/see also sections on Robert Owen and Christian Socialism/

WORKING-CLASS EDUCATION AND WORKERS' EDUCATION

160. ABELL, V.A.
Independent working class education: stages in the rise and fall of an ideal.
M.Ed.*, Sheffield, 1974.

161. ATKINSON, J.D.
Working-class attitudes to education in Nottingham, 1836-1870.
M.Phil., Nottingham, 1977.

162. COSSLETT, J.A.
Opinions regarding the theory and practice of imparting information to the lower orders, 1830-1862.
M.Phil., King's College, London, 1977.

163. DAVIES, A.M.
Education for working-class children in Barnsley during the nineteenth century with particular reference to the Barnsley School Board.
M.Ed., Durham, 1969.

164. DONNELLY, R.
The Co-operative College, 1919-1969.
M.Ed., Glasgow, 1974.

165. ELLIS, A.C.O.
Influences on the growth of literacy in Victorian working-class children.
M.A., Liverpool, 1970.

166. EVANS, L.W.
The works schools of the Industrial Revolution in Wales.
Ph.D., Wales, 1963.

167. FRITH, S.W.
Education, industrialisation and social change: the development of elementary schooling in nineteenth century Leeds: a case study in historical sociology.
Ph.D., University of California, Berkeley, 1976.
DA 38 1047A

168. FROST, M.B.
The development of provided schooling for working class children in Birmingham, 1781-1851.
M.Litt, Birmingham, 1978.

169. FROW, R.
Independent working class education with particular reference to South Lancashire, 1909-1930.
M.Ed., Manchester, 1968.

170. GRAHAM, T.B.
Some aspects of working-class adult education in nineteenth century Carlisle.
M.Phil., Nottingham, 1971-72.

171. HAINES, S.
Thoughts for the labouring classes: a study of the response of the Society for Promoting Christian Knowledge Tract Committee to social and economic conditions in England from 1820 to 1830.
M.A., Sussex, 1975.

172. HALDANE, I.R.
Workers' education: a psychological survey.
Ph.D., Birkbeck College, London, 1962-63.

173. HARRIS, F.B.
The Liverpool School Board day industrial schools.
M.Ed., Liverpool, 1977.

174. HEBRANK, H.G.
Manchester and the struggle for non-denominational education, 1841-1870.
Ph.D., Minnesota, 1976.
DA 37 7576A

175. LAQUEUR, T.W.
The English Sunday School and the formation of a respectable working class, 1780-1850.
Ph.D., Princeton, 1973.
DA 34 7157A

176. LEVY, P.C.
A nobler humanity: a study of the influences of poverty and community on the self-education of working-class men born in Britain, 1750-1850.
Ph.D., York (Canada), 1976.
DA 37 7911A

177. MONIES, M.G.S.
The impact of the Education (Scotland) Act 1872 on Scottish working class education up to 1899.
Ph.D., Edinburgh, 1974.

178. PEERS, S.
      The education and training of the professional and commercial worker in the Greater
      Dortmund and South Lancashire areas.
      M.Ed., Manchester, 1968-69.

179. ROBERTS, J.H.
      The National Council of Labour Colleges and working class education in Scotland,
      1919-1963.
      M.Sc., Edinburgh, 1971.

180. RUSSELL, K.V.
      The educational achievements and aspirations of trade unionists at a steel works since
      1944.
      M.Ed., Leicester, 1967.

181. SANDERSON, J.M.
      The basic education of labour in Lancashire, 1780-1939.
      Ph.D., Cambridge, 1966.

182. SHAW, M.E.
      The childhood of the working class in the Leeds area, 1830-1871.
      M.Phil., London, 1975.

183. STEELE, I.D.
      A study of the education of the working-class in Stockport during the nineteenth century.
      M.A., Sheffield, 1968.

184. WILDMAN, R.A.
      A social history of Scottish working-class education, 1800-1872 with particular
      reference to Glasgow.
      Ph.D., Edinburgh, 1977.

EDUCATION OF THE "POOR"

185. BABLER, A.M.
      Education for the destitute: a study of London ragged schools 1844-74.
      Ph.D., Northern Illinois University, 1978.
      DA 39 4771A

186. BAKER, G.F.
      The care and education of children in union workhouses of Somerset, 1834-1870.
      M.A., London, External, 1960.

187. BLOOMER, R.G.
      The Ragged School movement before 1870, with special reference to some Lancashire
      Ragged Schools.
      M.Ed., Manchester, 1968.

188. CLARK, E.A.G.
      The Ragged School Union and the education of the London poor in the nineteenth century.
      M.A., London, External, 1968.

189. DASH, M.D.
      The evolution of Hanley ragged schools.
      Dip. Advanced studies in Educ.*, Keele, 1974.

190. DUKE, F.
      The education of pauper children: policy and administration, 1834-1855.
      M.A., Manchester, 1968.

191. GORDON, P.
      The Endowed Schools Acts and the education of 'poor' children, 1869-1900.
      M.Sc., L.S.E., 1965.

192. GWILLIAM, H.W.
      The provision of education for the poor in the City of Worcester during the eighteenth
      and nineteenth centuries.
      Dip.Ed.*, Birmingham, 1966.

193. HUGHES, D.B.
      The education of pauper children in Monmouthshire, 1834-1929.
      M.A., Wales (Cardiff), 1966.

194. MARTIN, F.M.
      Elementary education in the Poor Law Union of Runcorn from 1870-1903.
      M.Ed., Durham, 1970.

195. O'BRIEN, T.
      The education and care of workhouse children in some Lancashire Poor Law Unions,
      1834-1930.
      M.Ed., Manchester, 1975.

196. OLSON, B.V.
      Philanthropic educational programs for children of the poor: a study of objectives and
      in methodology within the context of eighteenth century British society.
      Ph.D., New York, 1975.
      DA 36 2073A

197.   PHILLIPS, R.J.
       E.C. Tufnell, 1806-1886.
       Ph.D., Sheffield, 1973.

198.   PURDY, J.
       The care and education of pauper children in North East Cumberland during the
       nineteenth century.
       M.Ed., Newcastle, 1973.

199.   ROSS, A.M.
       The care and education of pauper children in England and Wales, 1834 to 1896.
       Ph.D., University College, London, 1955.

200.   WEBSTER, D.H.
       The Ragged School movement and the education of the poor in the nineteenth century.
       Ph.D., Leicester, 1973.

201.   WILEY, G.T.
       Educating the children of England's laboring poor, 1850-1865.
       Ph.D., Case Western Reserve, 1965.
       DA 27 0738A

ADULT EDUCATION: EVENING CLASSES

202.   BRYAN, E.A.
       The development of the organisation of rate-aided evening schools in Leicester, 1871-1925.
       M.Ed., Leicester, 1971.

203.   JOHNSON, F.
       Evening education in England, with special reference to London.
       Ph.D., King's College, London, 1937.

204.   JONES, B.G.
       The development of non-vocational adult education in evening institutes, 1919-1939.
       M.Ed., Nottingham, 1969.

205.   PERCY, K.A.
       The development of rate aided evening schools for adults, 1870-1902.
       M.A., Nottingham, 1969.

206.   SOMPER, S.
       The London School Board and the development of evening education, 1870-1893.
       M.A., King's College, London, 1954.

207.   TURNER, M.
       The miners' search for self improvement: the history of evening classes in the
       Rhondda Valley from 1862 to 1914.
       M.A., Wales (Cardiff), 1967.

ADULT EDUCATION

England: National Studies

208.   BOOTH, D.J.
       The emergence, development and prospects of the Workers' Educational Association with
       special reference to the Southern District and the New Milton W.E.A., Branch.
       M.Phil., Southampton, 1974.

209.   BRENNAN, P.D.
       Adult education in the Roman Catholic Church, the Church of England and the religious
       Society of Friends.
       M.Ed., Manchester, 1970-71.

210.   BUNTINE, M.A.
       Adult education: a survey from the beginning of the nineteenth century.
       Ph.D., Edinburgh, 1925.

211.   COOK, R.J.
       Adult education in England and Germany: a comparative study.
       M.A., Institute of Education, London, 1954-55.

212.   DEWAR, J.M.
       An assessment of the ideas of F.D. Maurice and Sir Richard Livingstone in adult education.
       B.Phil., Hull, 1973.

213.   ELLIOTT, S.F.
       Tuition by correspondence: a study of growth in Britain principally during the period
       1870-1914.
       M.Ed., Leicester, 1974.

214.   KELLY, T.
       George Birkbeck, pioneer in adult education.
       Ph.D., Liverpool, 1957.

215.   KENNERLEY, A.
       The education of the merchant seaman in the nineteenth century.
       M.A., Exeter, 1978.

216.   KING, E.J.
       The relationship between adult education and social activities in English industrial
       society.
       Ph.D., London, 1955.

217.   STOTT, J.
       A history of the development of adult education in England.
       M.A., Liverpool, 1930.

England: Regional Studies

218.   ASHURST, T.B.
       Liberal education in York since 1815, with special reference to provision for non-
       vocational adult education.
       M.Ed., Durham, 1972.

219.   COHEN, R.L.
       The influence of Jewish radical movements on adult education among Jewish immigrants
       in the East End of London, 1881-1914.
       M.Ed., Liverpool, 1977.

220.   HAKKEN, D.J.
       Workers' education: the reproduction of working class culture in Sheffield, England and
       'Really Useful Knowledge'.
       Ph.D., American University (Washington D.C.), 1978.
       DA 39 3674A

221.   HANNA, I.
       A socio-psychological survey of the student membership of adult education classes in
       Leeds and changes in the adult education student population since 1945.
       M.A., Leeds, 1964.

222.   HARRISON, J.F.C.
       Social and religious influences in adult education in Yorkshire between 1830 and 1870.
       Ph.D., Leeds, 1955.

223.   HEMMING, J.P.
       The history of adult education in Huddersfield and district between 1851 and 1884.
       M.Ed., Manchester, 1967.

224.   HUDSON, H.L.
       Adult education in the county of Cornwall: its development and present position.
       M.A., King's College, London, 1946.

225.   LOWE, R.A.
       The development of adult education in the Potteries with special reference to the
       founding of a university in the area.
       M.A.(Ed.), Keele, 1966.

226.   McGREGOR, J.
       The history of adult and technical education in Skipton-in-Craven during the nineteenth
       century.
       M.Ed., Leeds, 1949.

227.   MILLER, H.C.
       Adult education in North Staffordshire· its history and development.
       M.Ed., Manchester, 1928.

228.   PRICE, H.J.
       Adult education in Bristol during the nineteenth century.
       M.A.(Educ.), Bristol, 1965.

229.   ROGERSON, G.
       Elements of working-class adult education in Sheffield in the nineteenth century.
       M.Phil., Nottingham, 1975.

230.   SMITH, A.G.
       A history of adult education in Derby, 1769-1907.
       M.A., Sheffield, 1977.

231.   STEEPLE, T.W.
       A history of adult and further education in nineteenth century Rotherham and district.
       M.Phil., Nottingham, 1977.

232.   STEPHENS, M.D.
       Adult education in nineteenth century Cornwall.
       M.Ed., Leicester, 1969.

233.   STEPHENS, W.B.
       The development of adult education in Warrington during the nineteenth century.
       M.A., Exeter, 1958.

Scotland

234. BARCLAY, J.B.
Adult education in S.E. Scotland.
Ph.D., Edinburgh, 1960.

235. GRIFFIN, J.
The development of adult education in Scotland.
Ph.D., St. Andrew's, 1953-54.

236. McKINLEY, A.D.
Rural adult education in East Lothian.
M.Ed., Edinburgh, 1974.

Wales

237. EASTWOOD, D.A.
The full man: the history of adult education in Cardiff, 1860-1960.
M.Ed., Cardiff, 1969-70.

238. OWEN, O.P.
Adult and further education in Carmarthenshire, 1759-1870.
M.Ed., Manchester, 1970.

University Extension Movement and Extra-Mural Education

239. GORDON, H.
The early development of the University extension movement under the influence of James Stuart.
M.A., Sheffield, 1941.

240. JEPSON, N.A.
A critical analysis of the origin and development of the Oxford and Cambridge extension movement between 1873 and 1902 with special reference to the West Riding of Yorkshire.
Ph.D., Leeds, 1955.

241. PASHLEY, B.W.
Role definition and fulfilment in English adult education· a study of certain aspects of university and working class adult education, 1900-1950.
M.A., Liverpool, 1965-66.

Adult Residential Colleges

242. BLUMLER, J.G.
The effects of long-term residential education in post-war Britain, with particular reference to Ruskin College, Oxford.
D.Phil., Oxford, 1961-62.

243. O'LEARY, M.P.
The history and influence of Plater College, Oxford.
M.Ed., Liverpool, 1968.

244. ROWE, K.
The development and changing roles of adult residential colleges in Britain.
M.A.(Ed.), Keele, 1970-71.

Education in the Armed Forces

245. BEREFORD, R.S.
The development since 1943 of the policy for the non-specialist education of Army officers in science and technology.
B.Litt., Oxford, 1970.

246. BOWYER-BOWER, T.A.
The development of educational ideas and curricula in the army during the eighteenth and nineteenth centuries.
M.Ed., Nottingham, 1954.

247. BROOK, R.
The Queen's army schoolmistresses, 1840-1968.
M.Phil., London, 1971.

248. HANCOCK, S.T.R.
The history of adult education in the army from 1800 to 1939.
M.Ed., Manchester, 1949.

249. HAWKINS, T.H.
History of education in the British army to 1939.
M.Ed., Leeds, 1945.

250. JACK, D.R.
A history of the Royal Dockyard Schools with particular reference to the Portsmouth school.
M.A., London, External, 1969.

251. LOVE, C.P.
The Army's Formation Colleges: an educational answer to some of the problems of demobilisation and resettlement, 1944-1951.
M.Ed., Bristol, 1975.

252. McGREGOR, J.
The development of adult education in the army with special reference to the organisation of civilian aid in army education since 1914.
Ph.D., Leeds, 1954.

253. MORAN, J.E.
The Royal Army Educational Corps.
M.Ed., Liverpool, 1970.

254. OWEN, F.S.
The contribution of British universities to education in the armed forces, 1949-1960.
M.A.(Educ.), Bristol, 1965.

255. SULLIVAN, F.B.
The origin and development of education in the Royal Air Force, 1918-1946.
M.A.(Educ.), Bristol, 1965-66.

256. SULLIVAN, F.B.
The origin and development of education in the Royal Navy from 1702 to 1902.
Ph.D., Reading, 1974.

MECHANICS' INSTITUTES

257. BOWERS, C.L.
The development of mechanics' institutes in the south-west of England during the first half of the nineteenth century.
M.A., London, External, 1971.

258. CHADWICK, A.F.
The Derby Mechanics' Institute, 1825-1880.
M.Ed., Manchester, 1971.

259. EVANS, T.
The Mechanics' Institutes of South Wales.
Ph.D., Sheffield, 1966.

260. HEMMING, J.P.
The Mechanics' Institute movement in the textile districts of Lancashire and Yorkshire in the second half of the nineteenth century.
Ph.D., Leeds, 1974.

261. HEYDON, R.J.
The origin and development of Glasgow mechanics' institutions.
M.Ed., Glasgow, 1968.

262. INKESTER, I.
Studies in the social history of science in England during the Industrial Revolution, c.1790-1850.
Ph.D., Sheffield, 1977.
         (includes a section on Mechanics' Institutes especially in Derby & Sheffield)

263. PHYTHIAN, M.E.
The Mechanics' Institutes in Lancashire and Yorkshire before 1851.
Ph.D., Manchester, 1932.

264. POPPLE, J.
The origin and development of the Yorkshire Union of Mechanics' Institutes.
M.A., Sheffield, 1960.

265. SMITH, J.V.
The Dundee Watt Institution, 1824-49.
B.Phil., Dundee, 1973.

266. TURNER, C.M.
The development of Mechanics' Institutes in Warwickshire, Worcestershire and Staffordshire, 1825-1890: a regional survey.
M.Ed., Leicester, 1966.

267. TYLECOTE, M.
The mechanics' institute movement in Lancashire and Yorkshire, 1824-1850 with special reference to the institutions at Manchester, Ashton-under-Lyne and Huddersfield.
Ph.D., Manchester, 1930.

268. WILLIAMS, J.H.
The Crewe Mechanics' Institutions, 1843-1913.
M.Ed., Manchester, 1969.

269. WILSON, M.D.
The history of the Leeds Mechanics' Institute: a social and educational perspective, 1824-1870.
M.A.*, Lancaster, 1972.

270. WILSON, R.C.
The objectives and achievements of the Chester Mechanics' Institution and the
Macclesfield Society for Acquiring Useful Knowledge.
M.Ed., Manchester, 1968.

EDUCATIONAL, MEDICAL AND WELFARE SERVICES

271. ADAMS, D.F.
The historical antecedents, 1834-1906, of the Education (Provision of Meals) Act, 1906.
Ph.D., L.S.E., 1954.

272. ANDREWS, L.I.
The Education (Provision of Meals) Act, 1906: a study of the Education (Provision of
Meals) Act, 1906, against its social, political and economic background.
M.A., Institute of Education, London, 1966.

273. HOWARD, J.C.
The development of the educational welfare services in Doncaster, 1870-1950 with special
reference to the provision of meals and medical facilities.
M.Ed.*, Sheffield, 1976.

274. KIRBY, R.M.
The health and welfare of children in Beverley in relation to national developments,
1902-1944.
M.Ed.*, Sheffield, 1978.

275. MAXWELL, J.D.
The school boards and pupil welfare, 1873-1919.
M.Litt., Strathclyde, 1974.

WORKING-CLASS PARENTS AND EDUCATION

276. ARCHER, M.S.
The educational aspirations of English working class parents: their formation and their
influence upon children's school achievement.
Ph.D., L.S.E., 1966-67.

277. TOOMEY, D.M.
Changes in working class life and parents' attitudes towards their sons' education and
career.
M.A., Kent, 1969-70.

EMPLOYERS AND EMPLOYERS' ORGANISATIONS

278. BRADBURN, W.
The development of capitalist employers in industry during the Industrial Revolution.
M.A., Manchester, 1914.

279. GOSPEL, H.F.
Employers' organisations: their growth and function in the British system of industrial
relations in the period, 1918-1939.
Ph.D.(Econ), L.S.E., 1974.

280. JONES, M.
The organisations of industrial employers in England in the early nineteenth century.
M.A., Manchester, 1933.

281. WILLIAMS, L.J.
The Monmouthshire and South Wales Coal Owners' Association, 1873-1914.
M.A., Wales (Aberystwyth), 1958.

282. YARMIE, A.H.
The captains of industry in mid Victorian Britain· a study of their social, industrial
and political attitudes towards labour.
Ph.D., London, 1975.

EMPLOYMENT

283. ARISTIDOU, I.
Trends in capital, employment and output in the British manufacturing industry, 1900-62.
Ph.D., London, 1966.

284. ASHTON, D.J.L.
New town policy and the employment of annual workers in the London new towns, 1956-64.
M.Sc., Bradford, 1970-71.

285. BLACK, W.
Employment in the linen industry.
Ph.D., Queen's University, Belfast, 1955-56.

286. COLFER, J.M., D.C. DOOLAN & D.F. O'FARRELL
The development of industries in Eire since 1924 with special reference to
(a) employment and (b) the national income and its distribution.
M.Econ.Sc., National University of Ireland, 1944.

287.   CRAVEN, T.
An analysis of seasonal and cyclical movements in employment in the British motor vehicle industry over the period 1949-1969.
M.B.A., Queen's University, Belfast, 1971-72.

288.   CROSS, D.A.E.
The geographical aspects of some industrial and other occupational changes and developments in the basin of the Hampshire Avon.
M.A., London, External, 1960.

289.   EVANS, T.R.
A study of some social effects of recent changes in the employment structure of the Kidwelly district.
M.A., Wales, 1957-58.

290.   FARMER, T.J.
The provision of new job opportunities in areas of South Wales affected by colliery closures.
M.Sc., Bath, 1971-72.

291.   FLYNN, N.
The structure of employment in new industries in the northern region since 1948.
M.A., Newcastle, 1975.

292.   FROST, M.E.
Regional employment change in Great Britain 1952-68 with special reference to the influence of government policy in the northern region.
Ph.D.(Econ.), L.S.E., 1974.

293.   HAYES, A.E.
A study of employment in coal mining and agriculture in the Wrexham area.
M.A., Liverpool, 1945.

294.   HODGSON, J.
Changes in the structure of employment in the northern region of England, 1921-71.
M.A., Newcastle, 1975.

295.   McNIE, W.M.
Long run local employment multiplier effects in Great Britain, 1921-51.
Ph.D., Cambridge, 1972.

296.   MARTINUZZI, L.S.
The history of employment in the British Post Office.
B.Litt., Oxford, 1952.

297.   MOYES, A.
Post-war changes in the distribution of employment and population in North Staffordshire.
M.A., Keele, 1970-71.

298.   O'NEILL, J.P.
Employment trends in Saorsta't Eireann.
M.A., National University of Ireland, 1937.

299.   RICHARDS, M.A.
A study of statistics of population and occupations in the counties, urban and rural districts of Wales, 1901-31.
M.Sc., Wales, 1942.

300.   ST.CYR, E.B.A.
The cyclical behaviour of employment and factor income shares in British manufacturing industry, 1955-64.
Ph.D., Manchester, 1966-67.

301.   SMART, M.W.
The determination of labour market areas in Great Britain.
M.Phil., L.S.E., 1971.

302.   SMITH, P.
Employment linkages in the Coventry sub-region of the West Midlands.
Ph.D., Birmingham, 1971-72.

303.   SPENCE, N.A.
Spatial dynamics of English regional employment change, 1951 and 1961.
Ph.D., L.S.E., 1974.

304.   THOMAS, W.K.
Industry and employment in Metropolitan Kent, 1945-60.
Ph.D.(Econ.), L.S.E., 1972.

305.   TOPPING, J.F.
A survey of industrial trends in employment in the West Riding of Yorkshire since 1921.
M.Com., Leeds, 1946.

306.   WALKER, R.G.
Population and employment growth in the London and Glasgow new towns, 1951-64.
Ph.D., Birmingham, 1968-69.

EMPLOYMENT SERVICE

307.   CANNER, H.E.
The juvenile employment service in Manchester, 1910-1939.
M.Ed., Manchester, 1958-59.

308.   COOK, G.
Development and administrative control of the Youth Employment Service since 1939.
M.A.(Econ.), Manchester, 1964-65.

309.   DAWSON, J.M.
The juvenile employment service.
M.A., Bedford College, London, 1948.

310.   PROBERT, G.J.
The growth and development of the Cardiff Youth Employment Service from 1912 to the present day.
M.Ed., Wales (Cardiff), 1969-70.

311.   WARRINGTON, S.
A national employment service: Great Britain's experience.
M.Sc., London, External, 1947.

EMIGRATION AND MIGRATION

312.   ADAMS, W.F.
Ireland and emigration to the New World from 1815 to the famine.
Ph.D., Yale, 1929.

313.   BALFOUR, R.A.C.S.
Emigration from the Highlands and Western Islands of Scotland to Australia during the nineteenth century.
M.Litt., Edinburgh, 1974.

314.   BASTIN, R.
Cunard and the Liverpool emigrant traffic, 1860-1900.
M.A., Liverpool, 1971.

315.   BERTHOFF, R.T.
British immigrants in industrial America.
Ph.D., Harvard, 1952.

316.   BURCHELL, R.A.
British immigration to California before 1870.
B.Litt., Oxford, 1969.

317.   CADFAN, N.H.
Hanes a llenyddiath cychoyniad a datblygiad mudiad y wladfa gymreig yn Mhatagonia.
(The history and literature of the origin and development of the Welsh colony in Patagonia.)
M.A., Wales, 1942.

318.   CAMERON, H.M.W.
Wilmot Horton's experimental emigration to Upper Canada: his management of the emigration and his evaluation of the prospects and progress of his settlers.
B.Litt., Oxford, 1972.

319.   CAMERON, J.M.
A study of the factors that assisted and directed Scottish emigration to Upper Canada, 1815-1855.
Ph.D., Glasgow, 1970-71.

320.   CARR, D.R.
Factors influencing migration from the U.K. to the U.S.A. 1860-1914.
Ph.D., Pennsylvania State, 1974.
DA 35 3275A

321.   CARROTHERS, W.A.
Emigration from the British Isles, 1815-1921.
Ph.D., Edinburgh, 1921.

322.   CLEMENTS, R.V.
English trade unions and the problem of emigration, 1840-80.
B.Litt., Oxford, 1954.

323.   CROWLEY, F.K.
British migration to Australia, 1860-1914.
D.Phil., Oxford, 1951.

324.   DICKSON, R.J.
An investigation into the causes, extent and character of emigration from the Northern parts of Ireland to colonial America with particular reference to the activities in Ireland of promoters of American lands.
Ph.D., Belfast, 1949.

325.   DILLON, M.F.
       Irish emigration, 1840-1855.
       Ph.D., California, Los Angeles, 1940.

326.   EBBAGE, F.
       British emigration in the nineteenth century.
       B.Com.*, Leeds, 1923.

327.   EDWARDS, P.M.
       The Scottish role in Midlands America with particular reference to Wyoming, 1865-1895.
       Ph.D., St.Andrews, 1971-72.

328.   GRAHAM, I.C.C.
       Scottish emigration to North America, 1707-1783.
       Ph.D., Illinois, 1955.
       DA 15 2180

329.   HARRIS, M.
       British migration to Western Australia, 1829-50.
       Ph.D., L.S.E., 1934.

330.   HAYDEN, A.A.
       Governmental assistance to immigration to New South Wales, 1856-1900.
       Ph.D., Wisconsin, 1959.
       DA 20 1005

331.   HOWARD, A.G.
       Emigration from the British Isles to New Zealand· a select bibliography with reference
       to other literature on colonisation and emigration.
       Dip.Lid.*, London, 1964.

332.   JOHNSON, S.C.
       A history of emigration from the United Kingdom to North America, 1763-1912.
       D.Sc., London, 1913.

333.   JOHNSTON, H.J.M.
       The emigration policies and experiments of the British Government after the Napoleonic
       Wars, 1815-1830.
       Ph.D., King's College, London, 1970.

334.   JONES, D.L.
       The backgrounds and motives of Scottish emigration to the United States of America in
       the period 1815-1861, with special reference to emigrant correspondence.
       Ph.D., Edinburgh, 1970.

335.   JONES, M.A.
       The role of the United Kingdom in the transatlantic emigrant trade, 1815-1875.
       D.Phil., Oxford, 1956.

336.   KEEP, G.R.C.
       The Irish migration to North America in the second half of the nineteenth century.
       Ph.D., Trinity College, Dublin, 1951.

337.   KENNEDY, R.E.
       Irish emigration, marriage and fertility.
       Ph.D., California, Berkeley, 1967.
       DA 29 0333A

338.   LAW, D.T.S.
       Emigration and the flight from the land, 1901-51.
       M.A., National University of Ireland, 1952-53.

339.   LOCKHART, A.
       Some aspects of emigration from Ireland to the North American colonies, 1660-1775.
       M.Litt., Trinity College, Dublin, 1971-72.

340.   MACDONAGH, O.O.G.M.
       A history of Irish emigration during the great famine.
       M.A., Trinity College, Dublin, 1946.

341.   MACDONAGH, O.O.G.M.
       Irish overseas emigration and the State during the great famine.
       Ph.D., Cambridge, 1952.

342.   MADGWICK, R.B.
       The quality of immigration into eastern Australia before 1851.
       D.Phil., Oxford, 1935.

343.   MALCHOW, H.L.
       The late-Victorian movement for state emigration, 1869-1902.
       Ph.D., Stanford, 1972.
       DA 33 4311A

344.   MARTIN, D.
       Migration within and emigration from the six counties of Northern Ireland between 1911
       and 1937.
       M.A., Queen's University, Belfast, 1977.

345.   MILLER, K.A.
       Emigrants and exiles: the Irish exodus to North America from colonial times to the First
       World War.
       Ph.D., University of California, Berkeley, 1976.
       DA 38 0978A

346.   MOREHOUSE, F.
       Emigration from the United Kingdom to America, 1840-1850.
       Ph.D., Manchester, 1926.

347.   NOLAN, N.G.
       The Irish emigration: a study in demography.
       Ph.D., National University of Ireland, 1936.

348.   PAGE, M.G.
       A study of emigration from Great Britain, 1802-60.
       Ph.D., L.S.E., 1931.

349.   RICHARDS, C.J.F.
       British immigration into Canada, 1832-1873.
       M.A., Manitoba, 1963.

350.   ROBERTS, E.K.R.R.
       A contribution to the study of emigration from North Wales to the U.S.A. 1800-1850.
       M.A., Liverpool, 1931.

351.   SCHRIER, A.
       Ireland and the American emigration 1850-1900.
       Ph.D., North Western, 1956.
       DA 17 0615

352.   SHEPPERSON, W.S.
       British views of emigration to North America, 1837-1860.
       Ph.D., Western Reserve, 1951.

353.   SHOULDICE, F.J.
       Emigration, 1900-1950.
       M.A., National University of Ireland, 1952-53.

354.   TURNBULL, M.R.M.
       The colonisation of New Zealand by the New Zealand Company (1839-1843).
       B.Litt., Oxford, 1951.

355.   WAINWRIGHT, M.D.
       Agencies for the promotion or facilitation of emigration from England to the United
       States of America, 1815-1861.
       M.A., Bedford College, London, 1951.

356.   WALPOLE, K.A.
       Emigration to British North America under the early Passenger Acts, 1803-1842.
       M.A., London, 1929.

357.   WERTIMER, S.
       Migration from the United Kingdom to the Dominions in the inter-war period with special
       reference to the Empire Settlement Act of 1922.
       Ph.D., L.S.E., 1952.

358.   WHITCOMB, J.D.
       Emigration to South Africa, 1820-1840.
       M.A., Birmingham, 1953.

MIGRATION, RURAL DEPOPULATION, POPULATION CHANGES AND MOBILITY

359.   ALLEN, A.T.
       Population changes in Worcestershire (south of the Birmingham conurbation) and
       Gloucestershire, 1851-1951.
       M.Sc., Wales, 1961.

360.   BLACKLEDGE, R.
       Population and settlement growth in the south Yorkshire coalfield.
       M.A., Birmingham, 1951.

361.   BLEWETT, R.
       Migration and the growth of small industrial towns in the middle Calder Valley in the
       nineteenth century.
       M.Phil., King's College, London, 1974.

362.   BOWES, I.
       Cleveland and Teesside: a geographical study of population and occupational changes
       since 1800.
       M.A., Bedford College, London, 1948.

363.   BRAMWELL, R.D.
       Nineteenth century changes in the distribution of population in the small Staffordshire
       coalfield.
       M.A., Birmingham, 1935.

364.   BUNCE, M.F.
An examination of some factors reflecting population changes in rural communities in an
area of the north-east Midlands of England, 1861-1911, with special reference to the
impact of agricultural depression.
Ph.D., Sheffield, 1970.

365.   BUNKER, R.C.
Some aspects of the population growth and structure in the Warwickshire coalfield since
1800.
M.A., Birmingham, 1952.

366.   CAROE, L.
Urban change in East Anglia in the 19th century.
Ph.D., Cambridge, 1966.

367.   CHANDLER, T.J.
Population changes and industrial growth in Leicestershire since the late 18th century.
M.Sc., London, 1955.

368.   CONNELL, K.H.
The population of Ireland from 1780 to 1846 and the social and economic factors
associated with its increase.
Ph.D., London, External, 1948.

369.   COUSENS, S.H.
The regional variations in the fall of population in Ireland, 1846-61, following the
great Irish famine.
Ph.D., Cambridge, 1958.

370.   CROFT, J.J.
The geographical variations of rural population change in eastern Nottinghamshire 1811-
1911 with particular reference to the correlative effect of this variation of changes
in agriculture, rural industry and transport.
M.A., Leeds, 1961.

371.   CUNNINGHAM, S.E.
Changes in the pattern of rural settlement in northern Essex between 1650 and 1850.
M.A., Manchester, 1968.

372.   DAVIES, D.J.
The conditions of the rural population of England and Wales, 1870-1928 in relation to
migration and its effects in age and sex selection, income and standards of living,
changes in social organisation.
Ph.D., Wales (Aberystwyth), 1931.

373.   DAVIES, V.C.
Some geographical aspects of the depopulation of rural Wales since 1841.
Ph.D., London, External, 1955.

374.   EL-RAYAH, M.E.M.
The internal migration of labour in Ireland, 1841-1911.
M.A., Queen's University, Belfast, 1961.

375.   GALLAGHER, S.R.
The flight from the land (Ireland).
M.A., National University of Ireland, 1952-53.

376.   GURNEY, R.
Population change and population structure, 1807-1861, in the Peak District of Derbyshire.
Ph.D., London, 1970.

377.   HANNAN, D.F.
Factors involved in the migration decisions of Irish rural youth.
Ph.D., Michigan State, 1967.
DA 28 4286A
        (Sociological contemporary study.)

378.   HARE, A.E.C.
Labour migration: a study in the mobility of labour.
Ph.D., L.S.E., 1933.

379.   HEADS, J.
The internal migration of population in England and Wales, 1851-1911.
M.Sc., Cambridge, 1956.

380.   HEWITT, F.
Population and urban growth in east Bristol, 1800-1914.
Ph.D., Bristol, 1966.

381.   HILLIER, D.
Patterns of migration in north-eastern Scotland, 1863-1961.
Ph.D., Aberdeen, 1974.

382.   HOWELL, E.J.
Movements of mining population in the anthracite mining area of South Wales, 1861 to
the present day.
M.Sc., Wales (Swansea), 1938.

383.   JENKINS, J.E.C.
       Population in Central Wales: changes in number and distribution, 1801-1831.
       M.A., King's College, London, 1937.

384.   JONES, M.
       Changes in industry, population and settlement on the exposed coalfield of south
       Yorkshire, 1840-1908.
       M.A., Nottingham, 1967.

385.   JONES, P.N.
       Aspects of the population and settlement geography of the South Wales coalfield,
       1850-1926.
       Ph.D., Birmingham, 1965.

386.   JONES, R.
       Rural depopulation in Wales, 1881-1901: an enquiry into its extent, nature, causes and
       consequences, with a brief discussion of some of the more important remedies.
       M.A., Queen's University, Belfast, 1911.

387.   KIM, S.H.
       The effects of migration from the countryside to the towns on the social lives, conditions,
       and habits of English workers during the Industrial Revolution as revealed by specified
       autobiographical evidence.
       M.A., Manchester, 1964.

388.   LAMB, V.M.
       Migration in Great Britain since 1927 with special reference to the industrial revolution.
       B.Litt., Oxford, 1939.

389.   LAWTON, R.
       Population migration to and from Warwickshire and Staffordshire, 1841-1901.
       M.A., Liverpool, 1950.

390.   LEVER, W.F.
       Population change and its relation to employment, housing and the provision of services
       in the cotton-weaving towns of north-east Lancashire.
       D.Phil., Oxford, 1970-71.

391.   LEVINE, D.C.
       The demographic implications of rural industrialisation: a family reconstitution study
       of two Leicestershire villages, 1600-1857.
       Ph.D., Cambridge, 1974.

392.   LOBBAN, R.D.
       The migration of Highlanders into Lowland Scotland (c.1750-1890) with particular
       reference to Greenock.
       Ph.D., Edinburgh, 1970.

393.   LUKE, W.R.
       Changes in the distribution of population since 1800.
       M.A., London, External, 1939.

394.   MACDONALD, D.F.
       Population movements in Scotland, 1770-1850.
       D.Phil., Oxford, 1933.

395.   McGUINESS, T.W.
       Changes of population in West Cornwall with rise and decline of mining.
       M.Sc., Birkbeck College, London, 1938.

396.   McGUINESS, T.W.
       Population changes in Cornwall in relation to economic resources.
       Ph.D., King's College, London, 1944.

397.   McQUILLAN, K.F.
       Modernization and internal migration: the cases of nineteenth century England and France.
       Ph.D., Princeton, 1978.
       DA 39 2567A

398.   MORGAN, W.G.
       The mobility of labour in the principal industries of Somerset, 1923-33.
       M.A., Wales, 1934.

399.   NALSON, J.S.
       The mobility of farm families in an upland area of N.E. Staffs.: a study of the locational
       and social origins of the farm population and its movement within and between agricultural
       and other occupations.
       Ph.D., Manchester, 1961-62.

400.   ORRIN, J.E.S.
       A study of the changes in the geographical distribution of industry and population in
       England and Wales during the twentieth century.
       M.A., Wales, 1932.

401.   PARSONS, E.C.
       The geographical and industrial mobility of the labour force in Great Britain between
       1924 and 1935.
       B.Litt., Oxford, 1951-52.

402. PITFIELD, D.E.
      Labour migration and the regional problem in Britain 1920-1939.
      Ph.D., Stirling, 1973.

403. RATHURE, A.H.
      The role of agricultural labour in the depopulation trends in rural Scotland, 1945-63.
      B.Litt., Glasgow, 1968-69.

404. REDFORD, A.
      Labour migration in England, 1800-1850.
      Ph.D., Manchester, 1922.

405. RILEY, K.C.
      Changes in the population distribution in the Tern 'basin' of north-east Shropshire with
      special reference to the Wellington-Oakengates conurbation, 1801-1951.
      M.A., London, 1958.

406. SLEEPER, R.D.
      Inter-industry labour mobility in Britain since 1959.
      D.Phil., Oxford, 1972.

407. TAYLOR, R.C.
      Implications of migrations from the Durham coalfield: an anthropological study.
      Ph.D., Durham, 1966-67.

408. VINCE, S.W.E.
      The rural population of England and Wales, 1801-1951.
      Ph.D., London, External, 1955.

409. WALSHAW, R.S.
      Population movements in the British Isles since 1921.
      M.A., Liverpool, 1937.

410. WHITELEY, N.M.
      Survey of the effects of the 1939-45 war and of the immigration of former city dwellers
      in a Midland township.
      M.Com., Birmingham, 1948.

411. WILLIAMS, M.I.
      A sociological and statistical study of the population of the Vale of Glamorgan during
      the first half of the nineteenth century.
      M.A., Wales, 1939.

412. WITHERICK, M.E.
      Stages in the growth of urban settlement in central Cornwall.
      Ph.D., Birmingham, 1963.

413. WOOD, E.R.G.
      A study of changes in the distribution and density of population in Worcestershire,
      1841-1931.
      M.A., Birmingham, 1950.

FABIANS

414. CLARK, W.R.
      The literary aspects of Fabian Socialism.
      Ph.D., Columbia, 1951.
      DA 12 615

415. HOBSBAWM, E.J.E.
      Fabianism and the Fabians, 1884-1914.
      Ph.D., Cambridge, 1951.

416. HOWARD, S.L.
      The new Utilitarians?: studies in the origins and early intellectual associations of
      Fabianism.
      Ph.D., Warwick, 1977.

417. HOWLAND, R.D.
      Fabian thought and social change in England from 1884 to 1914.
      Ph.D., L.S.E., 1942.

418. IKOKU, S.G.
      Fabianism as the climax of the new Liberalism.
      M.Sc., London, External, 1949.

419. McBRIAR, A.M.
      Fabian doctrine and its influence in English politics.
      D.Phil., Oxford, 1949.

420. McCARRAN, Mary M. Sister
      Fabianism in the political life of Britain, 1919-1931.
      Ph.D., Catholic University of America, 1952.

421. REED, D.J.
      The Fabian historians: a socialist interpretation of English history.
      Ph.D., Chicago, 1958.

422.   RICCI, D.M.
The conceptual foundations of Fabian Socialism.
Ph.D., Harvard, 1968-69.

423.   SCHNEIDER, F.D.
The Fabian Society and the British Empire.
M.A., Stanford, 1947.

424.   WILBUR, W.C
The origins and development of Fabian Socialism to 1890.
Ph.D., Columbia, 1953.
DA 14 0104

FACTORY AND MINES' INSPECTION

425.   CASSELL, A.J.
Her Majesty's Inspectors of Mines, 1843-1862.
M.Sc.(Econ.), Southampton, 1962.

426.   DJANG, T.K.
Factory inspection in Great Britain.
Ph.D., L.S.E., 1940.

427.   HAMPEL, J.A.
Leonard Horner, 1785-1864.
Ph.D., Chicago, 1968-69.

428.   HOLMES, C.
The life and work of H.S. Tremenheere.
M.A., Nottingham, 1964.

FACTORY AND MINES LEGISLATION AND FACTORY SYSTEM

429.   BAYLIS, G.M.
The factory system and the Factory Acts, 1802-1850.
M.A., Birmingham, 1930.

430.   BRAENDGAARD, A.T.
Occupational health and safety legislation and working class political action: a
historical comparative analysis.
Ph.D., North Carolina, 1974.   DA 36 0506A
(Comparison between England, Germany, Pennsylvania and Wisconsin.)

431.   EASTEAL, B.M.
Responses to the factory system, 1840-44.
M.A., Birmingham, 1973-74.

432.   ELOVITZ, P.H.
"Airy and salubrious factories" or "dark satanic mills"?· some early reactions to the
impact of the Industrial Revolution on the condition of the English working classes.
Ph.D., Rutgens, 1969.
DA 30 5375A

433.   FLIGHT, A.T.
Legislation relating to mining in the 19th century (1840-67).
Ph.D., London, 1937.

434.   GOTTLIEB, A.Z.
The regulation of the coal-mining industry in Illinois with special reference to the
influence of British miners and British precedents, 1870-1911.
Ph.D., London, 1975.

435.   HARRISON, A.
English factory legislation considered with regard to its economic effects and methods
of administration.
D.Sc., London, 1903.

436.   MANNING, F.E.
Sir Robert Peel the elder and early factory legislation.
M.A., Bristol, 1932.

437.   MESS, H.A.
Factory legislation and its administration, 1891-1924.
Ph.D., London, 1926.

438.   NIXON, M.J.
The emergence of the factory system in the Staffordshire pottery industry.
Ph.D., Aston, 1976.

439.   ROBSON, A.P.W.
The factory controversy, 1830-1853.
Ph.D., Bedford College, London, 1958.

440.   SINCLAIR, R.C.
Judicial interpretation of the Factories Acts: a critical appraisal.
LL.M., Queen's University, Belfast, 1969-70.

441.   SORENSON, L.R.
       The English factory inspectors and the development of factory legislation, 1833-1844.
       Ph.D., Illinois, 1947.

442.   THOMAS, M.W.
       The development of factory legislation from 1833-47: a study of legislative and
       administrative evolution.
       Ph.D., University College, London, 1948.

443.   WARD, J.T.
       The factory movement, c.1830-1850.
       Ph.D., Cambridge, 1957.

FOLK-LORE

444.   McKELVIE, D.
       Some aspects of oral, social and material tradition in an industrial urban area.
       Ph.D., Leeds, 1963.
               (Based on field work in industrial West Riding of Yorkshire chiefly
                in Bradford area.)

445.   MELLORS, D.D.
       Folklore and traditions of the railway industry with special reference to Doncaster.
       M.A., Leeds, 1968.

446.   MESSENGER, B.T.
       Folklore of the Northern Irish linen industry, 1900-1935.
       Ph.D., Indiana, 1975.
       DA 36 1018A

FRIENDLY SOCIETIES

447.   BARNETT, D.C.
       Friendly societies and other forms of social insurance in England, 1780-1850.
       M.A., Nottingham, 1961.

448.   BRODIE, R.R.
       Some aspects of a fall in the rate of mortality as affecting the financial position
       of friendly societies and sickness funds.
       Ph.D., London, External, 1932.

449.   BUSHROD, W.T.
       The development of the great affiliated friendly societies from their humble and often
       obscure origins in the 18th century.
       M.A., Manchester, 1924.

450.   GOSDEN, P.H.J.H.
       The development of friendly societies in England, 1815-1875.
       Ph.D., Birkbeck College, London, 1959.

451.   SHIPLEY, S.
       Metropolitan friendly societies in the 1820s.
       M.A., Warwick, 1975.

HOUSING

452.   BAXTER, M.D.
       Housing policies and standards in England and Wales, 1875-1969.
       M.Litt., Cambridge, 1973.

453.   BULL, W.H.
       Working-class housing in Glasgow, 1866-1912.
       M.Litt., Strathclyde, 1973.

454.   BURROWS, H.R.
       Studies in social science: Pt.1.   The housing problem in Bristol.
       M.Com., Leeds, 1932.

455.   CARROLL, W.D.
       Local authority housing in Dundee, 1919-1939.
       B.Phil., Dundee, 1969.

456.   CHORLEY, S.I.
       The location and form of corporation housing in Glasgow, 1960-1970.
       M.Sc., Strathclyde, 1971-72.

457.   DALE, J.A.
       Public housing, England and Wales, 1919-1969.
       Ph.D., L.S.E., 1977.

458.   ELEISH, M.G.E.
       A comparative study of housing methods and policy in Britain and Egypt since the First
       World War.
       Ph.D., Edinburgh, 1955-56.

459.   ENGLANDER, D.
       The Workmen's National Housing Council, 1898-1914.
       M.A.*, Warwick, 1972-73.

460. FERGUSON, N.A.
      Working class housing in Bristol and Nottingham, 1868-1919.
      Ph.D., Oregon, 1971.
      DA 32 3202A

461. FORSTER, C.A.
      The historical development and present day significance of bye-law housing morphology
      with particular reference to Hull, York and Middlesbrough.
      Ph.D., Hull, 1969.

462. GASKELL, S.M.
      Housing estate development, 1840-1918 with particular reference to Pennine towns.
      Ph.D., Sheffield, 1974.

463. GOODGER, J.M.
      The slums of Salford with particular reference to living conditions and slum clearances.
      M.Sc., Salford, 1972-73.

464. GOODWIN, P.A.T.
      Housing needs and planning policy in Greater London, 1945-71.
      M.Sc., Edinburgh, 1970-71.

465. HARTLEY, O.A.
      Housing policy in four Lincolnshire towns, 1919-59.
      D.Phil., Oxford, 1969.

466. HOGAN, W.C.
      The housing movement in Ireland.
      M.Econ.Sc., National University of Ireland, 1942.

467. HOGARTH, A.H.
      The present position of the housing problem in and around London.
      D.M., Oxford, 1908.

468. HOLE, W.W.
      The housing of the working classes in Britain, 1850-1914: a study of the development
      of standards and methods of provision.
      Ph.D., L.S.E., 1915.

469. HOLMES, A.R.
      Some effects of the slum clearance schemes of the London County Council.
      M.Sc., L.S.E., 1947.

470. JACKSON, J.T.
      Housing and social structures in mid-Victorian Wigan and St. Helens.
      Ph.D., Liverpool, 1977.

471. JACKSON, K.
      Working class housing and standards in the 19th century.
      Ph.D., Kent, 1978.

472. JACKSON, M.A.
      Richard Assheton Cross and the Artizan's Dwelling Act of 1875: a study in Conservative
      social reform.
      Ph.D., City University of New York, 1970.
      DA 31 2845A

473. JENNINGS, J.H.
      Geographical aspects of the local authority house building programme in England and
      Wales, 1919-1939.
      D.Phil., Ulster, 1972-73.

474. JORDAN, J.R.
      Housing problems at the end of the First World War with special reference to the work
      of the Ministry of Reconstruction.
      M.A., Kent, 1972.

475. KUNZE, N.L.
      English working-class housing: a problem of social control (in the 1880s).
      Ph.D., California, Los Angeles, 1971.
      DA 32 3925A

476. LICHTEN, N.A.
      The legal and administrative principles relating to slum clearance· their history and
      practice.
      M.A., Liverpool, 1959-60.

477. McCUTCHEON, R.
      High flats in Britain, 1945 to 1971· factors affecting their use by local authorities
      and some of the implications.
      M.Sc., Sussex, 1972.

478. McHUGH, J.
      The Labour Party and the politics of housing, 1918-1963.
      M.Sc., Salford, 1975.

479. MACINERNEY, A.M.
      Public authority housing in an urban community.
      M A., National University of Ireland, 1964-65.

480. McKEE, J.J.
      Working class housing in Glasgow between the wars, 1919-1939.
      M.Litt., Strathclyde, 1977.

481. McVAIL, E.M.
      An enquiry into the housing of seasonal workers in Scotland.
      M.D., Glasgow, 1915.

482. MALCOLMSON, P.E.
      The Potteries of Kensington: a study of slum development in Victorian London.
      M.Phil., Leicester, 1970.

483. MALLIER, A.T.
      Housing in Coventry· the development of municipal action, 1890-1908.
      M.Soc.Sc., Birmingham, 1970.

484. MARTIN, M.
      A study of the relationship between homelessness and housing policy at both national
      and local levels in England and Wales since 1948.
      M.A.(Econ.), Manchester, 1968-69.

485. MASSAY, P.G.
      An explanatory study of the housing of West Indian immigrants in Bradford.
      M.A., Bradford, 1972.

486. MATHIAS, P.
      The Liverpool Corporation Estate: a study of the development of housing in the Moss Lake
      Fields area of Liverpool, 1800-1875.
      M.A., Liverpool, 1957.

487. NUGENT, P.D.
      A typology of planned worker communities in the United States and Great Britain,
      1820-1920.
      Ph.D., Illinois at Urbana-Champaign, 1976.
      DA 37 6654A
              /'Employer built' communities including utopian schemes and company towns._7

488. ORBACH, L.F.
      "Homes for heroes": a study in the politics of British social reform, 1915-1921.
      Ph.D., Columbia, 1967.
      DA 28 1771A
              (Addison and the housing programme.)

489. ORSER, P.E.
      The Local Government Board and the housing problem, 1871-1919.
      Ph.D., Northwestern, 1974.
      DA 35 3653A

490. PASSMORE, R.S.
      The mid-Victorian urban mosaic: studies in functional differentiation and community
      development in three urban areas, 1841-1871.
      Ph.D., Sheffield, 1975.
              /Sheffield, Leeds and the Potteries._7

491. RHODES, G.W.
      Housing developments in Leeds, 1919-1939, a survey of housing progress in Leeds, with
      particular reference to the manner in which inter-war Housing Acts were implemented by
      the local authority, especially in relation to the rent provisions.
      M.A., Leeds, 1954.

492. RICHARDS, J.H.
      Fluctuations in house building in the South Wales coalfield, 1851-1954.
      M.A., Wales, 1956-57.

493. RODGER, R.G.
      Scottish urban house-building, 1870-1914.
      Ph.D., Edinburgh, 1976.

494. SABATINO, R.A.
      The housing policy of the British Labour Government, 1945-49.
      Ph.D., Pennsylvania, 1952.
      DA 13 1012

495. SCHIFFERES, S.
      Tenants' struggles in the 1930s.
      M.A.*, Warwick, 1972-73.

496. SHOEBRIDGE, P.J.
      The nature and location of post-war housing development in the coalfield area of
      County Durham.
      Ph.D., Durham, 1969-70.

497. SMITH, A.
An examination of government housing policy, 1915-65.
Dip.Public Admin., London, 1968.

498. SMITH, L.D.W.
Textile factory settlements in the early Industrial Revolution with particular reference
to housing owned by cotton spinners in the waterpower phase of industrial production.
Ph.D., Aston, 1976.

499. STAFFORD, F.A.
Housing policies and the coloured immigrant: a study of North Westminster.
M.Sc., Edinburgh, 1969-70.

500. STEFFEL, R.V.
Housing for the working classes in the East End of London, 1890-1907.
Ph.D., Ohio State, 1969.
DA 30 1512A

501. STRINGER, E.
The housing pattern in North Tyneside since 1945 with special reference to Newcastle-
upon-Tyne.
M.A., Durham, 1971-72.

502. TARN, J.N.
Housing in urban areas, 1840-1914.
Ph.D., Cambridge, 1962.

503. TREEN, C.
Building and estate development in the northern outer townships of Leeds, 1781-1914.
Ph.D., Leeds, 1977.

504. TURNER, F.L.
The movement to provide improved working-class housing in England, 1840-1860.
Ph.D., North Carolina, 1960.
DA 21 1933A

505. WILDING, P.R.
Government and housing: a study on the development of social policy, 1906-1939.
Ph.D., Manchester, 1969-70.

506. WILSON, L.F.
The state and the housing of the English working class with special reference to
Nottingham, 1845-1914.
Ph.D., California, Berkeley, 1970.
DA 32 0902A

507. WOHL, A.S.
The housing of the artisans and labourers in nineteenth century London, 1815-1914.
Ph.D., Brown, 1967.
DA 28 0610A

508. ZOOND, V.
Housing legislation in England, 1851-1867, with special reference to London.
M.A., London, 1932.

IMMIGRANTS AND MINORITIES

509. AURORA, G.S.
Indian workers in England: a sociological and historical survey.
M.Sc.(Econ.), L.S.E., 1960.

510. BAYME, S.G.
Jewish leadership and anti-Semitism in Britain, 1898-1918.
Ph.D., Columbia, 1977.
DA 38 0425A

511. BLUME, H.S.B.
A study of anti-Semitic groups in Britain, 1918-1940.
M.Phil., Sussex, 1971.

512. BUCKMAN, J.
The economic and social history of alien immigrants to Leeds, 1880-1968.
Ph.D., Strathclyde, 1968.

513. COLBENSON, P.D.
British Socialism and anti-semitism 1884-1914.
Ph.D., Georgia State, 1977.
DA 39 0403A

514. DESAI, R.H.
The social organisation of Indian migrant labour in the United Kingdom with special
reference to the Midlands.
M.A., School of Oriental and African Studies, London, 1960.

515. DE WITT, J.
Indian workers' associations in Britain.
Ph.D., Chicago, 1971-72.

516.   DIMMOCK, G.W.
       Racial hostility in Britain with particular reference to the disturbances in Cardiff
       and Liverpool in 1919.
       M.A.*, Sheffield, 1976.

517.   FOSSICK, S.
       Factors affecting the distribution of coloured immigrants in industry in Birmingham.
       M.Soc.Sc., Birmingham, 1965-66.

518.   FREEMAN, G.P.
       British and French policies on immigration and race relations, 1945-1974.
       Ph.D., Wisconsin-Madison, 1975.
       DA 36 6915A

519.   GAINER, B.
       The alien invasion: the origins of the Aliens Act (1905).
       Ph.D., Cambridge, 1969.

520.   GARRARD, J.A.
       The political left wing (the Liberals and emergent Labour Party) and the issue of alien
       Jewish immigration, 1880-1910.
       M.Sc., Manchester, 1965.

521.   GARTNER, L.P.
       The Jewish immigrant in England, 1870-1914.
       Ph.D., Columbia, 1957.
       DA 17 1539

522.   GRANATH, A.
       The Irish in mid-nineteenth century Lancashire, 1830-71.
       M.A., Lancaster, 1975.

523.   HICKEY, J.V.
       The origin and growth of the Irish community in Cardiff.
       M.A., Wales, 1959.

524.   JACKSON, J.A.
       The Irish in London: a study of migration and settlement in the past 100 years.
       M.A., London, 1958.

525.   KERR, B.M.
       Irish immigration into England, 1789-1838.
       B.Litt., Oxford, 1939.

526.   LOWE, W.J.
       The Irish in Lancashire, 1847-1871.
       Ph.D., Trinity College, Dublin, 1975.

527.   LUNN, K.J.
       The Marconi scandal and related aspects of British anti-semitism, 1910-14.
       Ph.D., Sheffield, 1978.

528.   McDONAGH, A.M.
       Irish immigrants and labour movements in Coatbridge and Airdrie, 1891-1931.
       B.A.*, Strathclyde.

529.   MAY, J.
       The British working class and the Chinese, 1870-1911: with particular reference to the
       Seamen's strike of 1911.
       M.A*, Warwick, 1972-73.

530.   PATTERSON, S.C.
       Immigrants in industry.
       Ph.D., L.S.E., 1970.

531.   RYAN, W.
       Assimilation of Irish immigrants in Britain.
       Ph.D., St. Louis, 1973.
       DA 35 3139A

532.   SUSSER, B.
       The Jews of Devon and Cornwall from the Middle Ages to the early 20th century.
       Ph.D., Exeter, 1978.

533.   THOMAS, R.E.
       The assimilation of Jamaican transport workers in England.
       Ph.D., Yale, 1973.
       DA 34 3588A

534.   TREBLE, J.H.
       The place of the Irish Catholics in the social life of the North of England, 1829-51.
       Ph.D., Leeds, 1969.

535.   VOLZ-LEBZELTER, G.C.
       Political anti-semitism in England, 1918-1939.
       D.Phil., Oxford, 1977.

536.   WALDENBERG, L.M.
       The history of Anglo-Jewish responses to immigation and racial tension, 1950-70.
       M.A., Sheffield, 1972.

537.   WRIGHT, P.L.
       The coloured worker in British industry with special reference to the Midlands and North
       of England.
       Ph.D., Edinburgh, 1965-66.

IMPERIALISM

538.   ALLISON, G.R.
       Imperialism and appeasement: a study of the ideas of the Round Table group.
       Ph.D., Harvard, 1965.

539.   AUSTIN, J.R.
       The Liberal Party and South Africa, 1868-1880.
       Ph.D., Bradford, 1974.

540.   BEHRMAN, C.F.
       The mythology of British imperialism, 1880-1914.
       Ph.D., Boston, 1965.
       DA 26 2705

541.   BLANCH, M.D.
       Nation, empire and the Birmingham working class, 1899-1914.
       Ph.D., Birmingham, 1975.

542.   BRODHEAD, F.M.
       Social imperialism and the British youth movement 1880-1914.
       Ph.D., Princeton, 1978.
       DA 39 5672A

543.   CARROLL, J.J.
       The government of Jamaica, 1900-13 with special reference to the role of Sir Sydney Olivier.
       Ph.D., Queen Mary College, London, 1973.

544.   CONWAY, J.J.
       The Round Table: a study in Liberal imperialism.
       Ph.D., Harvard, 1951.

545.   CRANGLE, J.V.
       The decline and survival of British anti-imperialism, 1878-1885.
       Ph.D., South Carolina, 1970.
       DA 31 1722A

546.   CROWDER, D.D.
       Labour, Britain and Empire.
       Ph.D., Colorado, 1975.
       DA 36 3083A

547.   DAVIES, D.I.
       Labour and politics in Africa, 1950-1968.
       Ph.D., Essex, 1971-72.

548.   DEAN, D.W.
       The contrasting attitudes of the Conservative and Labour parties to problems of empire
       during the period 1922 to 1936.
       Ph.D., London, 1974.

549.   DUNAE, P.A.
       Popular juvenile literature, 1880-1914, viewed as an expression of the 'New Imperialism'
       and as a method of inculcating contemporary youth with an enthusiasm for the Empire.
       Ph.D., Manchester, 1976.

550.   EDWARDS, R.W.
       Liberal Imperialism, 1885-1906.
       M.A., Wales (Bangor), 1957.

551.   ELLINWOOD, D.C.
       Lord Milner's "Kindergarten", the British Round Table group, and the movement for
       imperial reform, 1910-1915.
       Ph.D., Washington, 1962.
       DA 22 4334

552.   FIDUCCIA, M.R.
       Rudyard Kipling· a study of popular education during an imperialist era.
       Ph.D., Loyala University of Chicago, 1977.
       DA 37 7575A

553.   HENDERSON, I.
       The attitudes and policy of the main sections of the British Labour movement to
       Imperial issues, 1899-1924.
       B.Litt., Oxford, 1965.

554. HIND, R.J.
      The views on imperial affairs of Henry Labouchère and his activities in this connection,
      1880-1886.
      Ph.D., London, External, 1967.

555. HYAM, R.
      The African policy of the Liberal Government, 1905-9.
      Ph.D., Cambridge, 1967.

556. KLEIN, G.A.
      Sir Henry Campbell-Bannerman and the Liberal Imperialists, 1899-1903.
      Ph.D., Ohio State, 1969.
      DA 31 0701A

557. KOSS, S.E.
      "His Master's Voice": John Morley at the India Office.
      Ph.D., Columbia, 1966.
      DA 27 0730A

558. McCULLOUGH, E.
      Labour's policy on Africa, 1900-1951: the theory and practice of trusteeship.
      Ph.D., McGill, 1970-71.

559. MATTHEW, H.C.G.
      Liberal Imperialists, 1895-1905.
      D.Phil., Oxford, 1970.

560. MORROW, M.I.
      The origins and early years of the British Committee of the Indian National Congress,
      1885-1907.
      Ph.D., London, 1977.

561. MUNN, G.H.
      Thought on race as part of the ideology of British imperialism, 1894-1904.
      B.Litt., Oxford, 1976.

562. NACHOD, D.E.
      Liberalism and imperialism: the ideological foundations of anti-imperialist sentiment
      in Great Britain, 1898-1914.
      Ph.D., Harvard, 1972.

563. NIMOCKS, W.S.
      Lord Milner's "Kindergarten" and the origins of the Round Table movement.
      Ph.D., Vanderbilt, 1965.
      DA 26 2168

564. NWDRAH, K.K.D.
      Humanitarian pressure groups and British West Africa, 1895-1911.
      Ph.D., London, 1966.

565. OCHS, G.M.
      The Labour Party and the constitutional reform for India.
      Ph.D., Illinois, 1960.
      DA 21 3080
              (Period 1900-1939)

566. PORTER, B.J.
      Radical and labour attitude to Empire, 1896-1914.
      Ph.D., Cambridge, 1967.

567. PRICE, R.N.
      The Boer War and the British working class, 1899-1902: a study in working class
      attitudes and reactions to imperialism.
      D.Phil., Sussex, 1965.

568. PYRAH, G.B.
      The imperial policy of the Liberal Party: the settlement of South Africa, 1902-10.
      Ph.D., Leeds, 1952.

569. REYNOLDS, P.G.
      Race, nationality and empire: aspects of mid-Victorian thought 1852-72.
      Ph.D., Queen's University at Kingston (Canada), 1978.
      DA 39 5675A

570. SCOTT, G.
      Wilfred Scawen Blunt: anti-imperialist.
      B.Litt., Oxford, 1961-62.

571. SEMMEL, B.
      Imperialism and social reform in Great Britain, 1900-1914.
      Ph.D., Columbia, 1955.
      DA 16 0743

572. SIMPSON-HOLLEY, L.B.
      The attitude of British Labour Members of Parliament towards the Empire, 1895-1914.
      Ph.D., Southampton, 1971.

573.   SPRINGHALL, J.
        Youth and empire: a study of the propagation of imperialism to the young in Edwardian
        Britain.
        D.Phil., Sussex, 1968.

574.   STURGIS, J.L.
        The ideas and activities of John Bright in relation to the Empire, 1843-1889.
        M.A., London, 1963.

575.   TROTTER, D.J.B.
        John Morley and the Empire before 1886.
        M.A., Manchester, 1967.

576.   TSIANG, T.F
        Labour and Empire: a study of the reaction of British labour, mainly as represented in
        Parliament, to British Imperialism since 1880.
        Ph.D., Columbia, 1923.

577.   VIJAY, K.I.
        British opinion and Indian independence: a study of some British pressure groups which
        advanced the cause of Indian independence.
        M.Phil., L.S.E., 1971.

578.   WULIGER, R.
        The idea of economic imperialism with special reference to the life and works of
        E.D. Morel.
        Ph.D., L.S.E., 1953.

INDUSTRIAL RELATIONS

579.   ANTHONY, P.D.
        Joint consultation: its meaning and purpose in a nationalized industry.
        M.Sc.(Econ.), Wales (Cardiff), 1969-70.

580.   ANTHONY-JONES, W.J.
        Labour relations in the South Wales coal mining industry, 1926-1939.
        Ph.D., Wales (Aberystwyth), 1959.

581.   BANKS, R.F.
        Labour relations in the baking industry in England and Wales since 1860, with special
        reference to the impact of technical and economic change on union administration and
        bargaining procedure.
        Ph.D., L.S.E., 1965.

582.   BARTLETT, A.F.
        Industrial conciliation and arbitration in the United Kingdom - other than emergency
        and special legislation.
        L.L.M., Queen's University, Belfast, 1970-71.

583.   BLAIN, A.N.J.
        Industrial relations in the United Kingdom airlines: a study of pilots and managements.
        Ph.D., L.S.E., 1970.

584.   BOROVIAK, D.L.
        Institutionalization of capital-labour relations in Western Europe.
        Ph.D., Washington, 1972.
        DA 33 6977A
                (Britain, France and Sweden used as case studies.)

585.   BROADLEY, O.
        The colliery consultative committee.
        M.A., Liverpool, 1959-60.

586.   BROOKE, M.Z.
        Frederick Le Play and the problems of human relations in industry.
        M.A., Manchester, 1964-65.

587.   CHARLES, R.F.
        National consultation and co-operation between trade unionists and employers in Britain
        1911-39.
        D.Phil., Oxford, 1970.

588.   CHILD, J.
        A history of industrial relations in the printing trades of Great Britain.
        D.Phil., Oxford, 1953.

589.   CHILD, J.
        British management, thought and education: their interpretation of industrial
        relationships.
        Ph.D., Cambridge, 1967.

590.   CHOUDHRI, S.U.R.
        The British worker's attitude towards industrial unrest.
        M.Sc., Tech., Manchester, 1964-64.

591.   CLARKE, J.F.
        Labour relationships in engineering and shipbuilding on the north-east coast in the second
        half of the nineteenth century.
        M.A., Newcastle, 1966.

592.   COATES, R.L.
       An analysis of joint consultation in terms of political democracy with particular
       reference to British European Airways.
       B.Litt., Oxford, 1971.

593.   CROUCHER, R.
       Shop stewards and Communists in British engineering, 1935-1946.
       Ph.D., Warwick, 1977.

594.   EDWARDS, R.
       Industrial relations and organisational change in the Post Office.
       M.Sc., Strathclyde, 1970-71.

595.   EVANS, E.W.
       A history of industrial relations in the South Wales coal industry to 1912.
       Ph.D., Wales (Aberystwyth), 1955.

596.   FAIRHURST, D.W.
       Industrial relations in a municipal passenger transport undertaking in Liverpool,
       1955-1971.
       M.A., Liverpool, 1973-74.

597.   FOX, A.
       Industrial relations in Birmingham and the Black Country, 1860-1914.
       B.Litt., Oxford, 1952.

598   (No entry)

599.   GARNER, R.J.
       A study of the work of the Standing Joint and Burnham Committees, 1919-1971.
       M.Ed., Leicester, 1975.

600.   GARNHAM, R.I.
       Industrial relations in the hosiery industry.
       Ph.D., Nottingham, 1976.

601.   GIDWELL, D.
       Industrial relations and the wages structure in the coal mining industry.
       M.Sc.(Econ.), Wales (Cardiff), 1974.

602.   GILL, H.S.
       Industrial relations in the United Kingdom Atomic Energy Authority.
       Ph.D., Bradford, 1968.

603.   GOH, S.T.H.
       Statutory provisions for the settlement of collective industrial disputes in England
       and Australia and India.
       B.Litt., Oxford, 1970-71.

604.   GRIFFIN, A.R.
       The development of industrial relations in the Nottinghamshire coalfields, 1550-1930.
       Ph.D., Nottingham, 1964.

605.   HALVERSON, G.C.
       Development of labour relations in the British railways since 1860.
       Ph.D., London, 1952.

606.   HANKINSON, J.A.
       An examination of the historical and present structure of industry and industrial
       relationships in the cotton textiles and men's tailoring industries, to determine the
       reasons for the variations in the respective current bargaining methods.
       M.A., Liverpool, 1957-58.

607.   HARGREAVES, J.J.
       Labour conditions in the road transport industry.
       B.Litt., Oxford, 1938.

608.   HICK, J.H.
       The implications of the Whitley reports.
       M.Soc.Sc., Birmingham, 1973-74.

609.   HOPKINS, T.N.
       The operation of the National Reference Tribunal in the coal industry since 1943.
       M.A., Wales (Aberystwyth), 1961-62.

610.   HORN, C.A.
       The development of industrial management in the United Kingdom.
       Ph.D., Loughborough, 1970-71.

611.   HUDDLESTON, J.
       Industrial relations in the distributive trades with special reference to the Co-
       operative Movement.
       M.A., Leeds, 1938.

612.   JACKSON, N.W.
       The development of the North Western Provincial Whitley Council for the administrative,
       professional, technical and clerical services of local authorities, 1921-50.
       M.A.(Admin.), Manchester, 1951.

613. JACKSON, T.E.A.K.
      Industrial relations in road transport.
      Ph.D., Manchester, 1946.

614. JONES, E.H.
      A study of industrial relations in the British tinplate industry, 1874-1939.
      M.A., Wales (Aberystwyth), 1941.

615. KAY, C.
      Industrial relations in the boot and shoe industry.
      B.A., Leeds, 1952.

616. LIDDALL, M.E.
      Experiments in the maintenance of industrial peace.
      B.A., Bristol, 1923.

617. LUDFORD, I.
      Industrial unrest.
      M.Com., Birmingham, 1918.

618. McCORMICK, B.J.
      Labour relations in the catering industry with special reference to the operation of
      the Catering Wages Act, 1943.
      M.A.(Econ.), Manchester, 1956-57.

619. McGIVERING, J.C.
      Personnel management in large manufacturing firms in Liverpool.
      M.A., Liverpool, 1959-60.

620. MUTTALIB, M.A.
      On the Whitley Councils in the British civil service.
      Ph.D., L.S.E., 1960.

621. PORTER, J.H.
      Industrial conciliation and arbitration, 1860-1914.
      Ph.D., Leeds, 1968.

622. QUINN, K.P.J.
      Industrial Relations Act, 1946.
      M.A., National University of Ireland, 1952-53.

623. REES, W.D.
      The practical functions of joint consultation considered historically and in the light
      of some recent experiences in South Wales.
      M.Sc., London, External, 1963.

624. REISS, M.
      Compulsory arbitration as a method of settling industrial disputes with special
      reference to British experience since 1940.
      B.Litt., Oxford, 1964.

625. ROBERTS, R.
      An investigation into workshop relations at the Saunders Valve Co., during a period of
      change.
      M.Sc., Bath, 1971-72.

626. ROBERTSON, N.
      A study of the development of labour relations in the British furniture trade.
      B.Litt., Oxford, 1955.

627. ROWLANDS, M.B.
      Masters and men in the small metallurgical trades of the West Midlands, 1660-1760.
      Ph.D., Aston, 1972.

628. SHARP, I.G.
      A study of the practice and procedure of arbitration and conciliation as a voluntary
      principle in some British industries with an account of state action in the field.
      Ph.D., L.S.E., 1940.

629. STITT, J.W.
      Whitley Councils: their conception and adoption during World War I.
      Ph.D., South Carolina, 1976.
      DA 37 6693A

630. STRICK, H.C.
      British newspaper journalism, 1900-1956: a study in industrial relations.
      Ph.D., L.S.E., 1957.

631. TAN-SIM-HONG
      Industrial relations in nationalized road and rail transport with particular reference
      to road haulage.
      M.A., Bristol, 1954.

632. THOMAS, B.M.
      Labour relations in steel: a comparative analysis of Great Britain and the U.S.A.
      M.A., Liverpool, 1961-62.

633.   THOMPSON, A.E.
       Industrial relations in the fuel and power industries with special reference to selected
       undertakings in Midlothia.
       Ph.D., Edinburgh, 1952-53.

634.   THORPE, E.
       Industrial relations and the social structure: a case study of the Bolton cotton-mule
       spinners, 1880-1910.
       M.Sc., Salford, 1969.

635.   TIZARD, J.
       Industrial relations in the British co-operative movement.
       B.Litt., Oxford, 1949.

636.   TURPIN, D.A.R.
       Personnel practices, work systems and conditions in the motor industry.
       M.Sc., Edinburgh, 1969-70.

637.   WARD, H.
       The development of the coal industry for 1900 with particular reference to the
       Doncaster area and the aspect of industrial relations.
       B.A.*, Leeds, 1949.

638.   WILLIAMS, C.G.
       The process of negotiation in the railway industry under nationalisation.
       M.A., Manchester, 1958-59.

COLLECTIVE BARGAINING

639.   DYSON, R.F.
       The development of collective bargaining in the cotton spinning industry, 1893-1914.
       Ph.D., Leeds, 1971.

640.   HAWKINS, K.H.
       Current trends in collective bargaining in British industry with special
       reference to productivity bargaining.
       B.Litt., Oxford, 1971-72.

641.   HAWKINS, K.H.
       The reform of collective bargaining in British industry.
       M.Sc., Bradford, 1971.

642.   KENNEDY, G.
       Productivity bargaining: a case study of a petroleum refinery, 1964-71.
       M.Sc., Strathclyde, 1971-72.

643.   LYMAN, E.H.
       The legal status of collective bargaining agreements in the United States, the
       United Kingdom and the Republic of Ireland.
       L.L.M., Queen's University, Belfast, 1969-70.

644.   OWEN-SMITH, E.
       Productivity bargaining.
       Ph.D., Loughborough, 1971-72.

645.   REASON, J.P.
       A comparative study of productivity bargaining in the United Kingdom margarine and
       edible fats group of Unilever Ltd.
       M.Sc., Loughborough, 1970-71.

646.   SHUMAN, H.E.
       Local and district collective agreements in the British engineering industry.
       B.Litt., Oxford, 1952-53.

647.   TAFT, C.H.
       Collective bargaining in the British electricity supply industry.
       M.Sc.(Econ.), L.S.E., 1951-52.

648.   WHITE, P.J.
       Productivity bargaining in the Scottish Gas industry.
       M.Sc., Strathclyde, 1971-72.

INDUSTRIAL TRAINING AND APPRENTICESHIP

APPRENTICESHIP

649.   ASHTON, G.L.
       Socialisation into the work role: a study of apprentices.
       M.A., Leicester, 1965-66.

650.   BLANCHARD, S.R.
       Calendar of Dursley and Stroud apprentice indentures in the 17th and 18th centuries.
       Dip.Archive Admin.*, University College, London, 1958.

651.   BLAND, C.S.
       A study in attitudes in industrial apprentices to trade unions, social class and
       politics: an exploratory study into class consciousness.
       Ph.D., L.S.E., 1969.

652.   BLOOR, T.
Trade union job-control through apprenticeship training: the case of the printing industry.
M.A.(Econ.), Manchester, 1964-65.

653.   CLEGG, N.C.
A study of the attitudes of National Coal Board craft apprentices and craftsmen in a
College of Further Education towards home, work, college and aspects of these institutions.
M.Ed., Leeds, 1968-69.

654.   COSTIGAN, H.A.
Education and the apprentice.
M.A., Liverpool, 1938.

655.   DERRY, T.**K**.
The enforcement of a seven years' apprenticeship under the Statute of Artificers.
D.Phil., Oxford, 1931.

656.   DUNLOP, J.
English apprenticeship and child labour: a history.
D.Sc., London, 1912.

657.   LANE, J.
Apprenticeship in Warwickshire, 1700-1834.
Ph.D., Birmingham, 1977.

658.   LYON, J.
Engineering apprenticeships in the Bolton area, 1900-1940.
M.Ed., Manchester, 1967-68.

659.   MOORE, R.C.
The industrial training and education of apprentices.
M.A., Manchester, 1921.

660.   SMITH, S.R.
The apprentices of London, 1640-1660: a study of revolutionary youth sub-cultures.
Ph.D., Vanderbilt, 1971.
DA 32 3936A

661.   WILLIAMS, J.C.
Apprentices and operatives: a study of the facilities for training and guidance
available to the 15 and 16 year old school leaver in Wales.
M.Sc.(Econ.), Wales (Cardiff), 1969-70.

INDUSTRIAL TRAINING

662.   BARKER, R.M.
An evaluation of certain training methods with specific reference to juveniles
entering industry.
M.A., Leeds, 1954.

663.   CALVERT, R.H.B.
An examination of education and training in the coal-mining industry from 1840 to 1947
with special reference to the work and influence of the mines inspectorate.
M.Phil., Nottingham, 1969-70.

664.   DEARLE, N.B.
Industrial training with special reference to the conditions prevailing in London.
D.Sc., London, 1915.

665.   ENTWISTLE, R.
Industrial training policy: a study of influences on government intervention, 1958-62.
M.A.(Econ.), Manchester, 1964-65.

666.   FOLEY, B.J.
The development of, and case for, a positive government training policy in the United
Kingdom.
M.A., Liverpool, 1968-69.

667.   HAY, R.L.
The technical education of the mine worker with special reference to the effect of the
industry on the receptivity of the student.
M.Ed., Durham, 1935.

668.   KING, M.A.
An economic and social analysis of the effects of state aid for industrial training and
professional education with special reference to the Swansea and Aberystwyth district.
M.A., Wales, 1921.

669.   MANCINI, P.V.
The economics of training.
M.Phil., York, 1972.
        (Effects of the Industrial Training Act, 1964 on training in British Industry.)

670.   NAGIB, A.F.
Recent changes in the structure and training of labour in the British engineering industry
and their future trends.
Ph.D., Manchester, 1945.

671. PERRIGO, A.E.B.
      The Industrial Training Act and management training with particular reference to the
      needs of the small firms.
      Ph.D., Aston, 1971-72.

672. PRICE, J.B.
      The role of Government training centres with special reference to North Wales.
      M.A., Liverpool, 1971-72.

673. TEASDALE, J.R.
      Industrial rehabilitation and vocational guidance.
      M.A., Hull, 1966.
            (An assessment of the long term effectiveness of the vocational guidance
             at Hull Ministry of Labour Industrial Rehabilitation Unit.)

INTERNATIONAL AFFAIRS: DEFENCE POLICIES   /see also INTERNATIONALISM AND PACIFICISM and
                                            THE SOVIET UNION AND BRITISH LABOUR.7

674. ARMISTEAD, C.D.
      The formation of British Labour's foreign policy, 1914-1920.
      M.Litt., St. Andrew's, 1970.

675. BAKER, A.J.
      The Labour movement and the international crisis, 1933-1937.
      M.A., Sheffield, 1973.

676. BOYLE, T.
      The Liberal party and foreign affairs, 1893-1905.
      M.Phil., London, 1969.

677. BURRIDGE, T.D.
      The British Labour Party and the 'German Question' during the Second World War, 1939-45.
      Ph.D., McGill, 1973.
      DA 34 4142A

678. DAVIES, J.E.
      The attitude of the British Labour Government towards German rearmament, 1949-51.
      M.Sc.(Econ.), Wales (Aberystwyth), 1969-70.

679. DAVIS, S.
      The British Labour Party and British foreign policy, 1933-1939.
      Ph.D., L S.E., 1950.

680. DELARGY, B.
      The Labour Party and defence, 1933-1939.
      M.A.(Econ.), Manchester, 1959-60.

681. DIAMOND, N.
      The foreign policy of the Labour Party, 1940-51.
      M.Phil., Leeds, 1974.

682. DOREY, A.J.
      Radical Liberal criticism of British foreign policy, 1906-14.
      D.Phil., Oxford, 1965.

683. DRAKE, P.
      Labour and Spain: British Labour's response to the Spanish Civil War with particular
      reference to the labour movement in Birmingham.
      M.Litt., Birmingham, 1978.

684. EDELSTEIN, D.J.
      The failure of consensus: the British Labour Party and unilateralism, 1957-61.
      Ph.D., California, Los Angeles, 1966.
      DA 27 3495A

685. EDWARDS, J.
      The British government and non-intervention in Spain.
      Ph.D., Reading, 1977.

686. FRANCIS, D.H.
      The South Wales miners and the Spanish Civil War: a study in internationalism.
      Ph.D., Wales (Swansea), 1978.

687. GILES, D.D.
      An analysis of the parliamentary opposition to the National Government's foreign policy,
      November 1935 - May 1940.
      Ph.D., Nottingham, 1977.

688. GOLDSTEIN, W.
      The Labour Party and the Middle East crisis.
      Ph.D., Chicago, 1960-61.

689. GORDON, M.R.
      The Labour Party and the reasons accounting for its recurrent conflict over foreign
      policy, 1900-1951 with particular reference to the period between 1945 and 1951. an
      exercise in political culture.
      Ph.D., Harvard, 1966-67.

690.   GRANTHAM, J.T.
       The Labour Party and European unity, 1939-1951.
       Ph.D., Cambridge, 1977.

691.   GROSS, R.H.
       Factors and variations in Liberal and radical opinion on foreign policy, 1885-99.
       D.Phil., Oxford, 1950.

692.   HAWKINS, T.J.D.
       The Labour Party and the decision to withdraw from East of Suez, 1951-68.
       M.Phil., Southampton, 1972-73.

693.   HILL, G.M.
       British Socialism and British foreign affairs, 1880-1900.
       Ph.D., Indiana, 1960.
       DA 21 0606

694   KELLY, C.P.
       The nuclear imperative: an analysis of the British Labour Party's nuclear deterrent policy.
       Ph.D., New York, 1974.
       DA 35 4655A

695.   LANCIEN, D.P.F.
       British left-wing attitudes to the Spanish Civil War.
       B.Litt., Oxford, 1965.

696.   LINDSAY, J.E.
       The failure of Liberal opposition to British entry into World War I.
       Ph.D., Columbia, 1969-70.

697.   LUCAS, G.
       The response of the British Liberal Party and its supporters to Nazi Germany, 1935-8.
       B.Litt., Oxford, 1977.

698.   LUKOWITZ, D.C.
       The defence policy of the British Labour Party, 1933-1939.
       Ph.D., Iowa, 1968.
       DA 29 1850A

699.   MEEHAN, E.J.
       The British 'Left' and foreign policy, 1945-1951.
       Ph.D., L.S.E., 1953-54.

700.   MOORE, R.A.
       The foreign policy image of Aneurin Bevan.
       Ph.D., Columbia, 1961.
       DA 22 3256.

701.   NAYLOR, J.F.
       British Labour's international policy, 1931-1939.
       Ph.D., Harvard, 1964.

702.   POIVAN, J.H.
       The British Labour Party and international sanctions, 1918-1935.
       Ph.D., Rutgers, 1968.
       DA 29 2191A

703.   ROBINS, L.J.
       The Labour Party and the European Economic Community, 1961-1971.
       Ph.D., Southampton, 1973-74.

704.   ROSE, C.R.
       The relation of Socialist principles to British Labour foreign policy, 1945-51.
       D.Phil., Oxford, 1959-60.

705.   SHAPIRO, S.
       The British Labour Party and the Munich crisis.
       M.A., Stanford, 1952.

706.   SHAW, E.D.
       Socialism and foreign policy: the Labour Left and foreign affairs, 1945-1951.
       M.Phil., Leeds, 1974.

707.   SHIBLEY, D.R.
       Ernest Bevin and the Arab League.
       M.A., Stanford, 1957.

708.   SKOP, A.L.
       The British Left and the German Revolution, 1918-1920.
       Ph.D., Catholic University of America, 1969.
       DA 30 2469A

709.   SMITH, A.A.
       The response of British intellectuals to Fascist Italy, 1922-32.
       M.A., Kent, 1975.

710. STERNE, E.C.
The opposition within the Liberal and Labour parties to the foreign policy of the
Liberal Governments, 1906-14.
M.A., Leeds, 1957.

711. STERNE, E.C.
Opposition to Grey's foreign policy and its connection with the demand for open diplomacy.
Ph.D., Cambridge, 1957.

712. WEISSER, H.G.
The British working class and European affairs, 1815-1845.
Ph.D., Columbia, 1965.
DA 26 2172

713. WINNICKI, T.Z.
Labour's foreign policy, 1919-24.
M.Litt., Cambridge, 1950.

INTERNATIONALISM AND PACIFICISM

714. ANDERSON, D.C.
English working class internationalism, 1846-1864.
Ph.D., Oklahoma, 1976.
DA 37 7908A

715. BARKER, R.A.G.
Conscientious objection in Great Britain, 1939-45.
Ph.D., Cambridge, 1978.

716. BARTON, B.L.
The Fellowship of Reconciliation, pacificism, labour and social welfare, 1915-1960.
Ph.D., Florida State, 1974.
DA 35 6048A

717. BARTY, P.F.
The League of Nations Union between the wars: the rise and decline of a British
political pressure group.
Ph.D., Kentucky, 1972.
DA 33 5076A

718. BERKMAN, J.A.
Pacificism in England, 1914-1939.
Ph.D., Yale, 1967.
DA 27 4187A

719. BISCEGLIA, L.R.
Norman Angell: Knighthood to Nobel Prize, 1931-1935.
Ph.D., Ball State, 1967.
DA 28 3102A

720. BRAATOY, B.F.
Labour and war: the theory of labour action to prevent war.
Ph.D., L.S.E., 1934.

721. BUZA, B.G.
The British peace movement from 1919 to 1939.
Ph.D., L.S.E., 1973.

722. CARTER, L.J.
The development of Cobden's thought on international relations, particularly with reference
to his role in the mid-nineteenth century peace movement.
Ph.D., Cambridge, 1971.

723. CEADEL, M.E.
Pacificism in Britain, 1931-39.
D.Phil., Oxford, 1976.

724. EVANS, J.D.
The internationalism in the work and thought of William Ewart Gladstone with reference
to present day theory and practice of internationalism.
M.A., Wales (Cardiff), 1938.

725. EXLEY, R.A.
The Campaign for Nuclear Disarmament, its organisation, personnel and methods in its
first year.
M.A., Manchester, 1959-60.

726. FARRAR, E.
The British Labour Party and international organisations: a study of the Party's policy
towards the League of Nations, the United Nations and Western Union.
Ph.D., L.S.E., 1951-52.

727. FEILDING, R.J.
The elimination of war: an examination of the work of Sir Norman Angell.
M.Phil., Sussex, 1966-67.

728. No entry.

729. FRICK, S.
      Joseph Sturge, Henry Richard and the Herald of Peace: pacific response to the Crimean War.
      Ph.D., Cornell, 1971.
      DA 32 4525A

730. GAVIGAN, P.J.
      Ralph Norman Angell Lane: an analysis of his political career, 1914 to 1931.
      Ph.D., Ball State, 1972.
      DA 33 4300A

731. GOLDSTEIN, R.
      The elimination of war: a study of the writings of Sir Norman Angell in international
      affairs from 1903 to 1939.
      M.A., Wales (Swansea), 1966.

732. JEWELL, F.R.
      Sir Norman Angell: the World War II years, 1940-45.
      Ph.D., Ball State, 1975.
      DA 36 7571A

733. JORDAN, G.H.S.
      The politics of conscription in Britain, 1905-16.
      Ph.D., California, Irvine, 1974.
      DA 35 3639A

734. KENNEDY, T.C.
      The hound of conscience: a history of the No-conscription Fellowship, 1914-1919.
      Ph.D., South Carolina, 1968.
      DA 28 4575A

735. KENNETT, W.A.
      Nationalism and internationalism in English Liberal political thought from J.S. Mill
      to L.T. Hobhouse.
      M.Sc.(Econ.), L.S.E., 1957.

736. KOFF, S.P.
      The anti-war elements in the British Labour Party: 1906-1922.
      Ph.D., Columbia, 1964.
      DA 26 0466A

737. KYBA, J.P.
      British attitudes towards disarmament and rearmament, 1932-5.
      Ph.D., L.S.E., 1967.

738. McCOLLESTER, M.A.B.
      Attitudes to peace and war in the eighteen-forties and the eighteen-nineties: a
      comparison of the two decades.
      M.Litt., Cambridge, 1965.

739. MACKIE, W.E.
      The conscription controversy and the end of Liberal power in England, 1905-1916.
      Ph.D., North Carolina, Chapel Hill, 1966.
      DA 27 2481A

740. MARTIN, D.A.
      A study of the ideology of pacificism and its background with special reference to
      Britain, 1915-1945.
      Ph.D., L.S.E., 1964.

741. MILLER, F.G.
      Norman Angell: peace, politics and the press, 1919-1924.
      Ph.D., Ball State, 1969.
      DA 30 3888A

742. PARKIN, F.I.
      A study of the Campaign for Nuclear Disarmament: the social basis of a political mass
      movement.
      Ph.D., L.S.E., 1966.

743. RAE, J.M.
      The development of official treatment of conscientious objectors to military service,
      1916-1945.
      Ph.D., King's College, London, 1965.

744. RISINGER, E.A.
      Sir Norman Angell: critic of appeasement 1935-40.
      Ed.D., Ball State University, 1977.
      DA 39 0421A

745. ROBBINS, K.G.
      The abolition of war: a study in the ideology and organisation of the peace movement,
      1914-19.
      D.Phil., Oxford, 1965.

746. SAGER, E.W.
      Pacificism and the Victorians: a social history of the English peace movement, 1806 to
      1878.
      Ph.D., British Columbia, 1975.
      DA 36 4683A

747.   SHEPHERD, G.W.
       The theory and practice of internationalism in the British Labour Party with special
       reference to the inter-war period.
       Ph.D., L.S.E., 1952.

748.   SPEAR, S.
       E.D. Morel: the Union of Democratic Control and the Labour Party, 1918-24.
       Ph.D., New York, 1975.
       DA 36 2383A

749.   STIERS, F.C.
       Democratic control of foreign policy: the history of a political demand in Britain
       before and during World War I.
       Ph.D., Washington, 1971.
       DA 32 0899A

750.   STRICKLER, E.
       The organisation of peace through collective security, 1934-1938.
       M.Sc., L.S.E., 1949.

751.   SUPINA, P.D.
       Norman Angell and the years of illusion, 1908-1914.
       Ph.D., Boston University Graduate School, 1971.
       DA 32 2624A

752.   SWARTZ, M.
       The Union of Democratic Control in British politics during World War I.
       Ph.D., Yale, 1969.
       DA 30 3415A

753.   TATE, M.
       Public opinion and the movement for disarmament, 1888-98.
       B.Litt., Oxford, 1935.

754.   THOMIS, M.I.
       The Labour Movement in Great Britain and compulsory military service, 1914-1916.
       M.A., King's College, London, 1959.

755.   UNDERWOOD, J.J.
       British disarmament policy, 1925-1934.
       M.Phil., Leeds, 1977.

756.   WEINROTH, H.S.
       British pacificism, 1906-1916: a study in the ideology and activities of the British
       peace movement during the early years of the twentieth century.
       Ph.D., Cambridge, 1968.

LABOUR: AREA STUDIES

757.   CHRISTIE, P.S.
       Occupations in Portsmouth, 1550-1851.
       M.Phil., C.N.A.A., 1976.

758.   DUGGAN, E.P.
       The impact of industrialization on an urban labour market: Birmingham, England, 1770-1860.
       Ph.D., Wisconsin, 1972.
       DA 33 3133A

759.   SINGELMANN, J.
       The sectoral transformation of the labour force in seven industrialized countries,
       1920-1960. (Incl. England)
       Ph.D., Texas, Austin, 1974.
       DA 35 3140A

760.   STRAKA, W.W.
       Scottish industrial labour during the age of reform, 1792-1832.
       Ph.D., McGill, 1963.

761.   STRAKA, W.W.
       The Scottish industrial labourer during the Anglo-French wars, 1792-1815.
       M.A., McGill, 1960.

762.   WRIGHT, K.
       The Portsmouth area labour market with special reference to H.M. Dockyard, Portsmouth.
       M.Phil., Southampton, 1970-71.

LABOUR: OCCUPATIONAL STUDIES

A. AGRICULTURAL WORKERS AND PEASANTRY

763. ADAMS, M.G.
Agricultural change in the East Riding of Yorkshire 1850-80, with special reference to agricultural labour.
Ph.D., Hull, 1977.

764. ALLAN, D.G.C.
Agrarian discontent under the early Stuarts and during the last decades of Elizabeth.
M.Sc., L.S.E., 1950.

765. BARRON, B.
A study of the following factors: nature of the work, lack of social intercourse, limitation of educational possibilities, migration of population and low social status upon the mental life of the modern English agricultural labourers with special reference to Oxfordshire.
B.Litt., Oxford, 1923.

766. BATES, D.N.
The agricultural labourer in West Oxfordshire (in the nineteenth century).
M.A., Birmingham, 1955.

767. BROWN, J.A.
Agriculture in Lincolnshire during the 'Great Depression' c.1873-1896.
Ph.D., Manchester, 1978.

768. FIELD, R.K.
The Worcestershire peasantry in the later middle ages.
M.A., Birmingham, 1962.

769. FINKELSTEIN, J.
Agricultural depression and social dislocation: England, 1870-1900.
Ph.D., Harvard, 1953.

770. FRASER, J.
George Sturt ("George Bourne") and rural labouring life.
Ph.D., Minnesota, 1961.
DA 22 1996
        (Concentrates on period 1901-1913.)

771. GURDEN, H.
Trade unionism, education and religion: aspects of the social history of Warwickshire agricultural labourers in the 1870s.
M.Phil., Warwick, 1975.

772. HINCKLEY, P.
The condition of the Irish peasantry, 1840-50.
M.A., Leeds, 1917.

773. HOUSTON, G.F.B.
A history of the Scottish farm worker, 1800-1850.
B.Litt., Oxford, 1954.

774. HOWELL, C.A.H.
The economic and social conditions of the peasantry in South East Lancashire, 1300-1700.
D.Phil., Oxford, 1974.

775. HUGHES, E.
The changes in the numbers of agricultural labourers and in their wages and efficiency during the past fifty years ... with special reference to Wales.
M.A., Wales (Aberystwyth), 1909.

776. HYAMS, P.R.
Legal aspects of villeinage between Glanvill and Bracton.
D.Phil., Oxford, 1968.

777. MARSH, B.
The agricultural labour force of England and Wales in 1851.
M.Phil., Kent, 1977.

778. MEJER, E.
Agricultural labour in England and Wales, 1917-1939.
M.Sc.(Agric.), Nottingham, 1951-52.

779. MORGAN, D.H.
Harvesting in the nineteenth century, with special reference to Berkshire, Buckinghamshire and Oxfordshire between 1840 and 1900: being a study of change in corn producing counties as it affected the lives of the rural population in Southern England.
M.A., Warwick, 1971-72.

780. PEDLEY, W.H.
Labour on the land since 1920.
B.Litt., Oxford, 1940.

781.   RAZI, Z.
        The peasants of Halesowen; 1270-1400: a demographic, social and economic study.
        Ph.D., Birmingham, 1976.

782.   SAMPSON, B.
        The British peasant, 1770-1820 as reflected in our literature.
        M.A., London, 1921.

783.   SENIOR, W.H.
        An account of an investigation into the labour force employed on farms.
        M.Sc., Reading, 1929.

784.   SHEEHY, E.J.
        Land and peasantry in Anglo-Irish literature.
        M.A., National University of Ireland, 1932.

785.   SPRINGHALL, L.M.
        The Norfolk agricultural labourer, 1834-84: a study in social and economic history.
        Ph.D., London, 1935.

786.   WILLIAMSON, J.G.
        Peasant holdings on medieval Norfolk: a detailed investigation into the holdings of the
        peasantry in three Norfolk villages in the thirteenth century.
        Ph.D., Reading, 1976.

787.   WILSON, M.A.
        The composition and recruitment of the agricultural labour force and their bearing in
        future supply.
        B.Litt., Oxford, 1949.

788.   YATES, N.
        English agriculture and the labourer, 1840-85 with special reference to the depression
        of the "seventies".
        M.A., Birmingham, 1930.

B.   INDUSTRIAL WORKERS

789.   BAACK, B.D.
        An economic analysis of the English enclosure movement.
        Ph.D., Washington, 1972.
        DA 33 1956A
                (Includes an examination of the significance of enclosure on the position
                of the industrial labour force in England during the industrial revolution.)

790.   DAHRENDORF, R.
        Unskilled labour in British industry.
        Ph.D., L.S.E., 1955-56.

791.   INGRAM, W.H.
        The British workman: being a study of industrial life.
        M.A., Toronto, 1903.

        (a) Mining

792.   ALLEN, B.B.F.
        The pitmen of Tyneside and Weardale: conditions of their life and work in the first half
        of the 19th century.
        M.A., Liverpool, 1920.

793.   BRAYSHAW, M.
        The demography of three West Cornwall mining communities, 1851-71: a society in decline.
        Ph.D., Exeter, 1976.

794.   BROWN, A.J.Y.
        The Scots coal industry, 1854-1886.
        D.Litt., Aberdeen, 1953.

795.   ELLIS, G.M.
        A history of the slate quarrymen in Caernarvonshire in the nineteenth century.
        M.A., Wales (Bangor), 1931.

796.   FISHER, C.
        Social and economic history of the Forest of Dean miners 1800-1900.
        Ph.D., Warwick, 1978.

797.   GREGORY, R.G.
        The miners and politics in England and Wales, 1906-14.
        D.Phil., Oxford, 1963.

798.   HAIR, P.E.H.
        The social history of the British coal miner, 1800-45.
        D.Phil., Oxford, 1955.

799.   HUNT, C.J.
        The economic and social conditions of lead miners in the Northern Pennines in the
        eighteenth and nineteenth centuries.
        M.Litt., Durham, 1968.

800. KELLY, D.M.
The contraction of the coal industry: a labour market study.
Ph.D., Strathclyde, 1970-71.

801. KIRBY, M.W.
Aspects of the coal mining industry in Great Britain in the inter-war period, 1919-1939.
Ph.D., Sheffield, 1971.

802. MACMILLAN, N.S.C.
Coal mining and transport in Kinlyre, 1750-1967.
M.Sc., Strathclyde, 1972.

803. MARSHALL, C.R.
Levels of industrial militancy and the political radicalization of the Durham miners, 1885-1914.
M.A., Durham, 1977.

804. MORGAN, D.T.
Industrial and social conditions in the Wrexham coalfield, 1800-1860.
M.A., Liverpool, 1927.

805. NEVILLE, R.G.
Yorkshire miners, 1881-1926: a study in labour and social history.
Ph.D., Leeds, 1974.

806. RIMLINGER, G.
Labour protest in British, American and German coalmining prior to 1914.
Ph.D., California, 1956.

807. RULE, J.G.
The labouring miner in Cornwall - c.1740-1870.
Ph.D., Warwick, 1971.

808. SLAVEN, A.
Coal mining in the West of Scotland in the 19th century: the Dixon enterprises.
B.Litt., Glasgow, 1967.

809. SLIFER, W.L.
The British coal miners and the Government, 1840-1860.
Ph.D., Pennsylvania, 1931.

810. SPAVEN, P.
The historical micro-comparative study of some mining communities in South Yorkshire 1851-80.
Ph.D., Warwick, 1978.

811. STEWART, W.D.
Some psychological aspects of employment in the coal-mining industry with special reference to the Ayrshire coalfield in Scotland.
B.Litt., Oxford, 1933.

812. WOODHOUSE, M.G.
Rank-and-file movements amongst the miners of South Wales, 1910-26.
D.Phil., Oxford, 1970.

(b) Textile workers

813. BRASSAY, G.Z.
Glasgow cotton spinners, c.1810-1830.
M.Litt., Strathclyde, 1975.

814. BYTHELL, D.
The handloom weavers in the English cotton industry during the Industrial Revolution.
D.Phil., Oxford, 1968.

815. CHARLESWORTH, S.E.
An examination of the weaving industry in Huddersfield, the Colne Valley and the Holme Valley from 1870-1900, with particular reference to the problems of the labour force.
B.A.*, Sheffield, 1974 (Department of Economic and Social History).

816. COLLIER, F.
The family economy of the workers in the cotton industry during the period of the Industrial Revolution, 1784-1833.
M.A., Manchester, 1921.

817. DONY, J.G.
The history of the straw hat and straw platting industries of Great Britain to 1914 with special reference to the social conditions of the workers engaged in them.
Ph.D., L.S.E., 1941.

818. ELBOURNE, R.D.
Industrialization and popular culture: a case study of Lancashire handloom weavers, 1780-1840.
M.Phil., L.S.E., 1974.

819. JORDAN, W.M.
The silk industry in London, 1760-1830 with special reference to the conditons of the wage-earners and the policy of the Spitalfields Acts.
M.A., University College, London, 1931.

820. MURRAY, N.
The handloom weavers in the West of Scotland in the first half of the nineteenth century.
Ph.D., Strathclyde, 1976.

821. SEARBY, P.
Weavers and freedom in Coventry, 1820-1861: social and political traditionalism in an early Victorian town.
Ph.D., Warwick, 1971-72.

822. TAYLOR, G.
The handloom weavers in the Stockport area, 1784-94.
M.A., Manchester, 1922.

823. WALKER, W.M.
Dundee's jute and flax workers, 1889-1923.
Ph.D., Dundee, 1976.

(c) Engineering and manufacturing industries

824. CHALKIDIS, G.
A comparison of changes in labour productivity in manufacturing industries in the United Kingdom and the E.E.C. countries since 1945.
M.Sc., L.S.E., 1962-63.

825. GARRETT, J.L.
The aircraft industry of Greater London with special reference to its location and labour supply.
B.Litt., Oxford, 1955-56.

826. GOODMAN, J.F.B.
A new motor vehicle factory: a socio-economic study of a local labour market and industrial relations.
Ph.D., Nottingham, 1969-70.

827. HICKS, J.R.
The position of the skilled and less skilled workmen in the engineering and building trades, 1914-25.
B.Litt., Oxford, 1927.

828. MANNING, P.A.
The postwar relations of skilled and unskilled labour in the printing, building and engineering industries.
Ph.D., L.S.E., 1933.

829. MATSUMARA, T.
The Flint glassmakers in the classic age of the labour aristocracy, 1850-80.
Ph.D., Warwick, 1976.

830. MATHER, J.D.
A comparative sociological study of foremen in two engineering factories in North West England.
M.A.(Econ.), Manchester, 1959-60.

831. PATON, G.E.C.
The sociological aspects of the growth of technician occupations in British industry.
M.A., Nottingham, 1968-69.

832. STONE, V.C.
A study of some social and industrial problems involved in modern, large-scale employment of labour in unskilled work, based on observation and investigation in a wartime filling factory.
M.A., Liverpool, 1945.

(d) Building workers

833. GROSSMAN, S.
The radicalization of London building workers 1890-1914.
Ph.D., Toronto, 1977.
DA 39 2454A

834. VILES, D.M.
The building trade workers of London, 1835-60.
M.Phil., London, 1975.

(e) Craftsmen

835. FAIRCLOUGH, O.N.F.
Joseph Finney and the clockmakers and watchmakers of 18th century Liverpool.
M.A., Keele, 1976.

(f)   Dock-workers

836.   HILL, S.R.
A comparative occupational analysis of dock foremen and dock-workers in the Port of London.
Ph.D., L.S.E., 1973.

837.   WHITESIDE, N.
The dock decasualisation issue, 1889-1924: public policy and port labour reform.
Ph.D., Liverpool, 1977.

838.   WILSON, D.R.
A social history of workers in H.M. Dockyards during the Industrial Revolution, particularly 1793-1815.
Ph.D., Warwick, 1975.

(g)   Printing industry

839.   CANNON, I.C.
The social situation of the skilled workers: a study of the compositor in London.
Ph.D., L.S.E., 1960-61.

(h)   Railway workers

840.   KINGSFORD, P.W.
Railway labour, 1830-1870.
Ph.D., L.S.E., 1951.

C.   SEAMEN AND FISHERMEN

841.   BYRON, R.F.
Burra fishermen: the social organisation of work in a Shetland community.
Ph.D., University College, London, 1974.

842.   FRICKE, D.H.
The social structure of the crews of British dry cargo merchant ships.
Ph.D., Durham, 1973-74.

843.   McGEOGH, H.
Labour in the merchant service, 1850-1920.
M.Com., Birmingham, 1921.

844.   PRESS, J.P.
The economic and social conditions of British merchant seamen in the first half of the nineteenth century.
Ph.D., Bristol, 1978.

845.   PRIOR, M.L.
Fisher Row: the Oxford community of fishermen and bargemen, 1500-1800.
D.Phil., Oxford, 1976.

D.   CLERICAL WORKERS

846.   ANDERSON, G.L.P.
A study of clerical workers in Liverpool and Manchester, 1850-1914.
Ph.D., Lancaster, 1974.

847.   HUTCHINSON, J.M.
A study of the economic status, trade union affiliations, working conditions and occupational training of clerical workers in Great Britain.
M.A.(Econ.), King's College, Durham, 1963-64.

848.   KLINGENDER, F.D.
The black-coated worker in London.
Ph.D., L.S.E., 1934.

849.   LOCKWOOD, D.
The black-coated worker: a study in class consciousness.
Ph.D., London, External, 1957.

E.   DOMESTIC SERVANTS

850.   AUSTIN, F.O.
Studies in the language of the Clift family correspondence: some grammatical and epistolary features in the letters of an 18th century family of the servant class.
Ph.D., Southampton, 1968-69.

851.   HECHT, J.J.
The domestic servant class in 18th century England.
Ph.D., Harvard, 1948.

852.   PERRY, R.D.
History of domestic servants in London, 1850-1900.
Ph.D., University of Washington, 1975.
DA 37 1159A

853.   RICHARDSON, S.J.
"The servant question": a study of the domestic labour market, 1851-1917.
M.Phil., Bedford College, London, 1967.
     (See also entry no 2537)

F. COMMERCE

854. AVARI, B.J.
British commercial travellers and their organisations, 1850-1914.
M.A., Manchester, 1970.

LABOUR AND MAN-POWER POLICIES

855. DAVIDSON, R.
Sir Hubert Llewellyn Smith and labour policy, 1886-1916.
Ph.D., Cambridge, 1971-72.

856. FARRAR, C.
The manpower policy of the British government, 1945-1950.
Ph.D., L.S.E., 1951-52.

857. FEARNLEY, H.D.
British industrial labor and the transition from freedom to control, 1914-1916.
Ph.D., University of California, Santa Barbara, 1976.
DA 38 0958A

858. GREEN, R.
The evolution of manpower policy in Great Britain from the fifteenth century to the mid-nineteen sixties.
Ph.D., L.S.E., 1971.

859. HARRISON, E.M.
The development of the regional organisation of the Ministry of Labour and National Service.
B.Litt., Oxford, 1951-52.

860. KERSEY, E.R.
Labour organisations and political development: an historic comparative analysis.
Ph.D., Minnesota, 1971.
DA 33 5252A
(Labour policy development for 20 European countries over a 100 year period.)

861. LOWE, R.
The demand for a Ministry of Labour, its establishment and its initial role, 1916-26.
Ph.D., London, 1975.

862. MONTGOMERY, B.G. de
British and continental labour policy: the political labour movement and labour legisla-
tion in Great Britain, France and the Scandinavian countries, 1900-1922.
D.Phil., Oxford, 1923.

863. READ, J.H.S.
British labour and social policies to 1914.
Ph.D., Toronto, 1946.

864. SMITH, C.S.
Planned transfer of labour with special reference to the coal industry.
Ph.D., Bedford College, London, 1960-61.

865. STAINSBY, P.
Manpower planning within the shipbuilding industry.
M.Sc., Strathclyde, 1971-72.

LABOUR AND WORKING-CLASS MOVEMENT: NATIONAL STUDIES

866. ATKINSON, B.J.
The British Labour movement, 1868-1906.
D.Phil., Oxford, 1970.

867. CROWLEY, D.W.
The origin of the revolt of the British labour movement from Liberalism, 1875-1906.
Ph.D., London, 1952.

868. FRASER, J.D.
The impact of the labour unrest, 1910-14, on the British labour movement.
Ph.D., Leicester, 1968.

869. GILLESPIE, F.E.
The political history of the English working classes, 1850-1867.
Ph.D., Chicago, 1923.

870. HARVEY, R.H.
A comparison of the approach towards socialism of British and American labour since 1900.
Ph.D., Stanford, 1924.

871. JOHNSON, P.A.M.
The 1880s: seedbed of the labour synthesis of twentieth century England.
Ph.D., Oklahoma, 1970.
DA 31 5986A

872. LAMB, W.K.
British Labour and Parliament, 1867-93.
Ph.D., L.S.E., 1934.

873.   LIND, J.A.D.
       Foreign and domestic conflict: the British and Swedish labour movements, 1900-1950.
       Ph.D., Michigan, 1973.
       DA 34 5335A

874.   MALLALIEU, W.C.
       The influence of British labour upon politics and legislation, 1875-1900.
       Ph.D., Johns Hopkins, 1925.

875.   MOBERG, D.R.
       George Odger and the English working class movement, 1860-1877.
       Ph.D., L.S.E., 1954.

876.   MORRIS, D.C.
       The history of the Labour movement in England, 1825-52: the problem of leadership
       and articulation of demands.
       Ph.D., L.S.E., 1952.

877.   PALMEGIANO, E.M.
       Henry Broadhurst and working class politics, 1869-1880.
       Ph.D., Rutgers State, 1966.
       DA 27 1766

878.   PRESTON, A.H.
       The relationship of British middle-class intellectuals to the British labour movement
       of the 1880s: a critical analysis.
       M.Phil., London, 1978.

879.   TAYLOR, C.L.
       The emergence of British working class politics.
       Ph.D., Yale, 1962-63.

880.   WARE, E.C.
       The impact of the Irish question on the British labour movement, 1916-21.
       M.A.*, Warwick, 1975-76.

881.   WHEELER, R.G.G.
       George Wheeler and working-class politics, 1859-95.
       M.Phil., Queen Mary College, London, 1969.

882.   YEARLEY, C.K.
       British men and ideas in the American labor movement, 1860-1895.
       Ph.D., Johns Hopkins, 1953.

Ireland

883.   BOYLE, J.W.
       The rise of the Irish labour movement, 1888-1907.
       Ph.D., Trinity College, Dublin, 1961.

884.   CAIN, L.F.
       The Irish Labour movement under the Free State and the Republic.
       Ph.D., Catholic University of America, 1966.
       DA 27 2709A

885.   JUDGE, J.J.
       The labour movement in the republic of Ireland.
       Ph.D., National University of Ireland, 1955-56.

886.   LARKIN, E.J.
       James Larkin and the Irish Labour movement, 1876-1914.
       Ph.D., Columbia, 1957.
       DA 17 1739

887.   MITCHELL, A.H.
       Labour in Irish politics, 1890-1930.
       Ph.D., Trinity College, Dublin, 1967.

Scotland

888.   BURNS, C.M.
       Industrial labour and radical movements in Scotland in the 1790s.
       M.Sc., Strathclyde, 1971.

889.   YOUNG, J.D.
       The evolution of Scottish radical and working-class movements and the revolt from
       Liberalism, 1865-1900.
       Ph.D., Stirling, 1974.

LABOUR AND WORKING-CLASS MOVEMENT

REGIONAL STUDIES

890. ABADIE, H.D.
Sheffield politics, 1885-1900: organisation, ideology and political behaviour.
Ph.D., California, Los Angeles, 1971.
DA 32 3904A

891. BARNSBY, G.J.
The working-class movement in the Black Country, 1815-1867.
M.A., Birmingham, 1965.

892. BROWN, D.
The Labour movement in Wigan, 1874-1967.
M.A., Liverpool, 1969.

893. BROWN, R.
The labour movement in Hull, 1870-1900 with special reference to new unionism.
M.Sc.(Econ.), Hull, 1966.

894. CALCOTT, M.
Northumberland and Durham in the General Elections of 1929, 1931 and 1935.
M.Litt., Newcastle, 1973.

895. CLARK, D.G.
The origins and development of the Labour Party in the Colne Valley, 1891-1907.
Ph.D., Sheffield, 1978.

896. FORD, C.
The political behaviour of the working-class in Coventry, 1870-1900.
M.A.*, Warwick, 1972-73.

897. FOX, K.O.
The emergence of the political Labour movement in the eastern sector of the South Wales coalfield, 1894-1910.
M.A., Wales (Aberystwyth), 1965.

898. GOLDBERG, G.C.
The Socialist and political Labour movement in Manchester and Salford, 1884-1914.
M.A., Manchester, 1975.

899. HARRIS, P.A.
Class conflict, the trade unions and working class politics in Bolton, 1875-1891.
M.A.*, Lancaster, 1971.

900. HASTINGS, R.P.
The Labour movement in Birmingham, 1925-1957.
M.A., Birmingham, 1959.

901. HUNTER, D.
Politics and the working class in Wigan, 1890-1914.
M.A.*, Lancaster, 1974.

902. McLEAN, I.
The Labour movement in Clydeside politics, 1914-22.
D.Phil., Oxford, 1972.

903. MANDRELL, T.R.
The structure and organisation of London trades, wages and prices and the organisation of labour, 1793-1818.
M.Litt., Cambridge, 1972.

904. NEALE, R.A.
Economic conditions and working class movements in Bath, 1800-1850.
M.A., Bristol, 1962.

905. PROTHERO, I.J.
London working-class movements, 1823-1848.
Ph.D., Cambridge, 1967.

906. SHEPPARD, M.
Labour at municipal elections, 1901-13.
M.A.*, Warwick, 1974-75.

907. TAYLOR, E.
The working-class movement in the Black Country, 1863-1914.
Ph.D., Keele, 1974.

908. TODD, N.R.
Comparative studies of Labour movements in Barrow-in-Furness and Lancaster.
M.Litt., Lancaster, 1976.

909. TRODD, G.N.
Political change and the working class in Blackburn and Burnley 1880-1914.
Ph.D., Lancaster, 1978.

LABOUR LAW   (See also TRADE UNIONS: Period studies: mid 19th century and the legal recognition struggle and also FACTORY LEGISLATION)

910.   COX, L.C.
The Trade Disputes Act 1906.
M.A., Wales, 1978.

911.   EDGAR, W.W.
Railway labour legislation in Great Britain and Canada.
M.A., Toronto, 1904.

912.   ELIAS, P.
The legal regulation of trade union democracy and members' rights.
Ph.D., Cambridge, 1974.

913.   EPSTEIN, M.
Trade unions before the courts.
LLM (Law), Dalhousie, 1958.
     (Comparison of Canada, U.K. and U.S.A.)

914.   FISK, W.L.
Twenty years of English labour legislation.
Ph.D., Ohio, 1946.

915.   GRODIN, J.R.
Comparison of British and American law relating to internal trade union affairs.
Ph.D., L.S.E., 1959.

916.   HAMILTON, M.C.
The Irish Labour Court.
M.Econ.Sc., National University of Ireland, 1948.

917.   HASLAM, A.L.
The law relating to combinations.
D.Phil., Oxford, 1929.

918.   HEALY, B.P.J.
The operation of the Trade Disputes Act, 1906 and 1965.
LLM, University College, London, 1966.

919.   HENDY, J.G.
A comparison between certain aspects of the law relating to organisations of workers and limited companies.
LLM, Queen's University, Belfast, 1971-72.

920.   HICKLING, M.A.
The law relating to internal relations of trade unions.
Ph.D., King's College, London, 1958.

921.   KAY, M.R.
The settlement of membership disputes in the trade unions.
Ph.D., Sheffield, 1971.

922.   LIU, C.C.
Trade union law in the United Kingdom, the United States and the Republic of China.
M.Litt., Cambridge, 1949.

923.   McERLEAN, J.R.
The effect of the criminal law and emergency and special legislation on trade disputes in the British Isles.
LLM, Queen's University, Belfast, 1970-71.

924.   MILLER, I.P.
Development of the common law of master and servant in Scotland from the close of the Industrial Revolution period to the present day.
Ph.D., Glasgow, 1965-66.

925.   NJUBA, S.
Legal controls over the structure and internal organisation of trade unions in the United Kingdom of Great Britain and Northern Ireland, the Republic of Ireland and Uganda.
LLM, Queen's University, Belfast, 1969-70.

926.   NORRIE, A.W.
Ideology and labour law: differing explanations of the genesis and growth of an area of law.
M.A.*, Sheffield, 1976 (Faculty of Law).

927.   RIDEOUT, R.W.
The right to membership of trade unions.
Ph.D., University College, London, 1958.

928.   RUBAMA, Y.
The right to strike as a fundamental freedom.
LLM, Queen's University, Belfast, 1969-70.

929. WOODWARD, B.
      The "trade dispute" concept in British labour law.
      LLM, Sheffield, 1970.

930. ZUPKO, R.E.
      Statutes of Labourers in the reign of Edward III.
      Ph.D., Chicago, 1962-63.

      LAND

931. ARONSON, D.M.
      Jesse Collings, agrarian radical, 1850-1892.
      Ph.D., McMaster, 1975.
      DA 36 6253A

932. COX, R.M.
      Land nationalisation.
      M.Phil., University College, London, 1974.

933. DONNELLY, J.S.
      The land and people of 19th century Cork: the rural economy and the land question.
      Ph.D., Harvard, 1971.

934. FAITH, R.J.
      The peasant land market in Berkshire during the later middle ages.
      Ph.D., Leicester, 1962.

935. GOSS, L.W.
      Tenants rights in England: a case study in agricultural reform, 1832-75.
      Ph.D., Oklahoma State, 1972.
      DA 33 6839A

936. HAY, J.M.
      Common right and enclosure: Northamptonshire, 1700-1800.
      Ph.D., Warwick, 1977.

937. JACOBS, W.A.
      The Irish land question and the Land Act of 1881.
      Ph.D., Oregon, 1972.
      DA 33 5093A

938. KENNEDY, B.A.
      The struggle for tenant-right in Ulster, 1829-50.
      M.A., Queen's University, Belfast, 1943.

939. LANE, P.
      The working of the Encumbered Estates Act.
      M.A., Trinity College, Durham, 1969.

940. LYONS, M.J.
      The Liberal reconsideration of property· the debate over the Irish Land Act of 1881.
      Ph.D., Minnesota, 1969.
      DA 31 1201A

941. MACASKILL, J.
      The treatment of "land" in English social and political theory, 1840-85.
      D.Phil., Oxford, 1959.

942. MARTIN, D.E.
      Economic and social attitudes to landed property in England, 1790-1850, with
      particular reference to John Stuart Mill.
      Ph.D., Hull, 1972.

943. MORAN, D.M.
      The origin and status of the allotment movement in Britain with particular
      reference to Swindon, Wiltshire.
      Ph.D., Oregon, 1976.
      DA 37 7970A

944. NUTTALL, E.R.
      The economic objects and results of land legislation in Ireland in the Gladstone era.
      M.A., Wales (Bangor), 1936.

945. PALMER, N.D.
      The Irish Land League crisis, 1879-1881.
      Ph.D., Yale, 1936.

946. PEACOCK, A.J.
      Land reform, 1880-1919: a study of the English Land Restoration League and the
      Land Nationalisation Society.
      M.A., Southampton, 1962.

947. PERREN, R.
      The effects of agricultural depression on the English estates of the Dukes of
      Sutherland, 1870-1900.
      Ph.D., Nottingham, 1967.

948.   PING-TI HO
       Land and state in Great Britain, 1873-1910: a study in land reform movements and
       land policies.
       Ph.D., Columbia, 1953.
       DA 13 0083

949.   STEELE, E.D.
       Irish land reform and English Liberal politics, 1865-70.
       Ph.D., Cambridge, 1963.

950.   WALTON, J.R.
       Aspects of agrarian change in Oxfordshire, 1750-1880.
       D.Phil., Oxford, 1977.

951.   WARD, S.
       Land reform in England and Wales, 1870-1918.
       Ph.D., Reading, 1976.

952.   WILKS, W.I.
       Jesse Collings and the 'back to the land' movement.
       M.A., Birmingham, 1964.

ENCLOSURES AND THE "IMPROVING" MOVEMENT

953.   BLAKE, W.J.
       On the causes and course of the rebellion of 1549 in Devon and Cornwall.
       M.A., London, 1909.

954.   EDWARDS, J.W.
       Enclosure and agricultural improvement in the Vale of Clwyd, 1750-1875.
       M.A., University College, London, 1963.

955.   ELLIOTT, S.
       The enclosure of Stamford open fields.
       M.A., Nottingham, 1965.

956.   ELLIS, J.R.
       The Parliamentary enclosure in Wiltshire.
       Ph.D., Bristol, 1971.

957.   ENDACOTT, G.B.
       The progress of enclosures in the county of Dorset since 1700.
       B.Litt., Oxford, 1938.

958.   HAMMOND, R.J.
       The social and economic circumstances of Ket's rebellion.
       M.A., L.S.E., 1934.

959.   HUNT, H.G.
       The Parliamentary enclosure movement in Leicestershire, 1730-1842.
       Ph.D., London, External, 1956.

960.   JOHNSON, S.A.
       Enclosure and the agricultural landscape of Lindsey from the 16th to the 19th century.
       M.A., Liverpool, 1957.

961.   JONES, E.J.
       The enclosure movement in Anglesey, 1788-1866.
       M.A., Wales, 1924.

962.   JONES, T.I.J.
       The enclosure movement in South Wales during the Tudor and early Stuart periods.
       M.A., Wales, 1936.

963.   KIRK, M.
       Parliamentary enclosure in Bulmer Wapentake.
       M.A., Leeds, 1948.

964.   LOUGHBROUGH, B.
       Some geographical aspects of the enclosure of the Vale of Pickering in the 18th and
       19th centuries.
       M.A., Hull, 1960.

965.   MARTIN, J.M.
       Warwickshire and the Parliamentary enclosure movement.
       Ph.D., Birmingham, 1965.

966.   MORGAN, C.
       The effect of Parliamentary enclosure on the landscape of Caernarvonshire and Merioneth.
       M.Sc., Wales, 1959.

967.   PARKER, L.A.
       Enclosure in Leicestershire, 1485-1607.
       M.A., London, External, 1948.

968. PLUME, G.A.
      The enclosure movement in Caernarvonshire with special reference to the Porth-yr-aur
      papers.
      M.A., Wales, 1935.

969. RODGERS, W.S.
      The distribution of Parliamentary enclosures in the West Riding of Yorkshire, 1729-1850.
      M.Com., Leeds, 1953.

970. SWALES, T.H.
      Parliamentary enclosures in Lindsey: or the enclosures of the eighteenth and nineteenth
      centuries as they affected Lindsey.
      M.A., Leeds, 1936.

971. TATE, W.E.
      Parliamentary enclosure in Oxfordshire, 1696-1882.
      B.Litt., Oxford, 1907.

972. TURNER, M.E.
      Some social and economic considerations of Parliamentary enclosure in Buckinghamshire,
      1783-1865.
      Ph.D., Sheffield, 1973.

973. WALKER, W.H.T.
      The Norfolk rising under Robert Kett, 1549.
      M.A., Wales, 1921.

974. YELLING, J.A.
      Open field, enclosure and farm production in East Worcestershire.
      Ph.D., Birmingham, 1966.

975. YOUD, G.
      Common lands and enclosure in Lancashire.
      M.A., Liverpool, 1958.
            (see also entries nos. 789, 936)

LEISURE AND RECREATION

976. ALLAN, K.
      Recreation and amusements of the industrial working classes in the second quarter
      of the nineteenth century with special reference to Lancashire.
      M.A., Manchester, 1947.

977. BAILEY, P.C.
      "Rational recreation": the social control of leisure and popular culture in Victorian
      England, 1830-1855.
      Ph.D., British Columbia, 1974.
      DA 35 7216A

978. BRANSTON, J.G.
      The development of public open spaces in Leeds during the 19th century.
      M.Phil., Leeds, 1972.

979. DAY, R.
      The motivation of some football club directors: an aspect of the social history
      of Association Football, 1890-1914.
      M.A.*, Warwick, 1975-76.

980. FOSTER, W.R.
      Factors in the development of the public park in the West Midlands.
      M.Soc.Sc., Birmingham, 1973-74.

981. GALLAGHER, A.L.
      The social control of working-class leisure in Preston, c.1850-1875.
      M.A., Lancaster, 1975.

982. HIGLEY, J.J.
      A study of some social, literary and dramatic aspects of the Victorian popular
      theatre as illustrated by the Britannia Theatre, Hoxton, 1843-1870.
      Ph.D., Queen Mary College, London, 1973.

983. JACKSON, W.G.
      A history of the organisation of facilities for recreation in Manchester.
      M.Ed., Manchester, 1940.

984. MALCOMSON, R.W.
      Popular recreations in English Society, 1700-1850.
      Ph.D., Warwick, 1970.

985. MARLOW, L.
      London Working Men's Clubs: some aspects of their history, 1860-1890.
      M.A.*, Warwick, 1972-73.

986. MAYALL, D.
      Leisure and the working class, with special reference to the cinema in Birmingham,
      1908-18.
      M.A.*, Warwick, 1977.

987. MELLER, H.E.
      Organised provisions for cultural improvement and their impact on the community,
      1870-1910 with special reference to Bristol.
      Ph.D., Bristol, 1968.

988. MIDDLETON, T.M.
      An enquiry into the use of leisure amongst the working classes of Liverpool.
      M.A., Liverpool, 1937.

989. MOLYNEUX, D.D.
      The development of physical recreation in Birmingham district, 1871-91.
      M.A., Birmingham, 1958.

990. MONNINGTON, T.
      A socio-historical study of the development and present popularity and viability of
      industrial sports clubs with particular reference to the Birmingham area.
      M.A., Birmingham, 1972.

991. REES, R.
      The development of physical recreation in Liverpool during the 19th century.
      M.A., Liverpool, 1968.

992. RUSHTON, J.I.
      Charles Rowley and the Ancoats recreation movement.
      M.Ed., Manchester, 1959.

993. SMITH, M.B.
      The growth and development of popular entertainment and pastimes in Lancashire
      cotton towns, 1830-70.
      M.Litt., Lancaster, 1970.

994. TISCHLER, S.
      A social history of football in England to 1914.
      Ph.D., Columbia, 1978.
      DA 39 3084A

995. WILD, P.
      Recreation in Rochdale, 1900-1940.
      M.A., Birmingham, 1976.

996. WILKINSON, D.G.
      Association football in Brighton before 1920: a case study in the development
      of popular recreation.
      M.A., Sussex, 1977.

LEVELLERS AND DIGGERS

997. BOYD, A.J.
      The political thought of Gerrard Winstanley.
      M.Sc., Strathclyde, 1967-68.

998. FITZGIBBON, J.
      The Leveller movement.
      M.A., National University of Ireland, 1939.

999. FRANK, J.
      The writings of the Levellers.
      Ph.D., Harvard, 1953.

1000. GOERTZ, R.K.
      To plant the pleasant fruit tree of freedom: consciousness, politics and
      community in Digger and early Quaker thought.
      Ph.D., City University of New York, 1977.
      DA 38 3022A

1001. GREGG, P.E.
      John Lilburne and his relation to the first phase of the Leveller Movement, 1638-49.
      Ph.D., L.S.E., 1939.

1002. JURETIC, G.M.
      The mind of Gerrard Winstanley from millenarian to Socialist.
      Ph.D., Northern Illinois, 1972.
      DA 33 1113A

1003. KNAPTON, S.H.
      The life and works of William Walwyn the Leveller.
      M.A., Queen Mary College, London, 1949.

1004. PETEGORSKY, D.W.
      The Digger Movement in the English Revolution.
      Ph.D., L.S.E., 1940.

1005. POE, L.H.
      The Levellers and the origin of the theory of natural rights.
      D.Phil., Oxford, 1957.

1006. ROBINSON, J.J.
The early life of John Lilburne: a study in Puritan social thought.
Ph.D., California, Los Angeles, 1946.

1007. SEABERG, R.B.
Remembering the past: historical aspects of Leveller political thought.
Ph.D., Syracuse, 1977.
DA 38 4997A

1008. SPEAK, J.E.
The part played by Walwyn and Overton in the Leveller movement.
M.A., Leeds, 1949.

LITERATURE

(A) PERIOD STUDIES

Elizabethan and Stuart

1009. BELTON, E.R.
The figure of the steward: some aspects of master-servant relations in Elizabethan and early Stuart drama.
Ph.D. Columbia, 1971-72.

1010. MACKINLAY, M.M.M.
Dekker and the artizan in the Elizabethan drama.
M.A., Manchester, 1949.

1011. SCHALL, L.M.
The proletarian tradition and Thomas Delaney.
Ph.D., Nevada, 1972.
DA 33 0286A

18th Century

1012. ELLIS, W. de W.
The peasant in English verse, 1660-1750.
Ph.D., Harvard, 1956.

1013. GREBANER, B.D.N.
Revolutionary ideas in the English literary periodicals, 1789-1798.
Ph.D., New York, 1935.

1014. JOHNSTONE, L.
Attitudes towards poverty and crime in the 18th century English novel.
Ph.D., Cambridge, 1962.

1015. NIELSON, E.E.
The lower classes in English literature, 1690-1750.
Ph.D., North Western, 1944.

1016. PUNK, E.G.
The attitude of English literature towards the humble, 1760-1798.
Ph.D., Ohio State, 1931.

18th - 19th Centuries

1017. GRIFFIN, P.R.
Wordsworth, Coleridge, Byron, Shelley and the French Revolution.
M.A., National University of Ireland, 1925.

1018. LOWENSTEIN, A.
Annals of the poor: social fact and artistic response in Gray, Goldsmith, Cowper, Crabbe, Blake, Burns.
Ph.D., City University of New York, 1968.
DA 29 4006A

1019. McCLELLAND, E.M.
The novel in relation to the dissemination of liberal ideas, 1790-1820.
Ph.D., Royal Holloway College, London, 1952-53.

1020. NASH, A.G.
The democratic movement of the 18th and early 19th centuries as expressed in English poetry of that period.
Ph.D., Boston, 1921.

1021. SALES, R.B.
The literature of labour and the 'condition of England question', 1730-1860.
Ph.D., Cambridge, 1976.

19th Century

1022. ADAMS, R.E.
The industrial novel in England, 1832-1851.
Ph.D., Illinois, 1965.
DA 26 362A

1023.   ALPIN, N.S.
        "The condition of England question" in Kingsley and Carlyle and selected mid-Victorian novels.
        M.Phil., Leeds, 1969.

1024.   BRANTLINGER, P.M.
        Chartism and social concern in early Victorian literature.
        Ph.D., Harvard, 1967-68.

1025.   CHRISTENSEN, J.M.
        Utopia and the late Victorians: a study of popular literature, 1870-1900.
        Ph.D., North Western, 1974.
        DA 35 6705A

1026.   CONEY, M.B.
        Reflections of English reform in the literature of the 1870s.
        Ph.D., Washington, 1973.
        DA 34 2552A

1027.   COUGHLIN, J.K.
        Educational opportunity for the poorer classes: some aspects of its evolution as reflected in the English novel.
        M.Ed., Liverpool, 1977.

1028.   DAVIS, P.B.
        Industrial fiction, 1827-1850.
        Ph.D., Wisconsin, 1961.
        DA 22 1995

1029.   EWBANK, D.R.
        The role of women in Victorian society: a controversy explored in six utopias, 1871-1895.
        Ph.D., Illinois, 1968-69.

1030.   FELLMAN, A.C.
        The fearsome necessity: 19th century British and American strike novels.
        Ph.D., North Western, 1969.
        DA 30 4369A

1031.   FOX, M.R.
        The woman question in selected Victorian fiction, 1883-1900.
        Ph.D., City University of New York, 1975.
        DA 36 1495A

1032.   GALLE, B.W.
        Self-sacrifice versus self-help in selected Victorian novels.
        Ph.D., Minnesota, 1976.
        DA 37 7761A

1033.   GRANGER, D.W.
        'The working man' and working men: John Stuart Mill, John Ruskin and the working class.
        Ph.D., Indiana, 1978.
        DA 39 2953A

1034.   GULBENKIAN, V.R.
        The slum movement in English and American fiction, 1880-1900.
        Ph.D., Western Reserve, 1951.

1035.   HARBISON, R.D.
        Industrial diamonds: the English proletarian novel, 1840-1890.
        Ph.D., Cornell, 1969-70.

1036.   HARRIS, J.T.
        The factoryhand in the English novel, 1840-1855.
        Ph.D., Texas, 1967.
        DA 28 4176A

1037.   HESSLER, J.G.
        Victorians and the threat of democracy.
        Ph.D., Stanford, 1977.
        DA 37 7763A
            /Attitude of mid-Victorian literature to the working class.7

1038.   HILTON, E.W.
        The Victorian novel of dissent.
        M.Phil., Leeds, 1972.

1039.   HUDSON, S.
        Victims or parasites? Attitudes about the poor in the early Victorian novel.
        Ph.D., Wayne State University, 1972.
        DA 33 2329A

1040.   HUGHES, B.L.
        The social protests in early Victorian poetry.
        Ph.D., Cornell, 1936.

1041. HYDE, W.J.
The English peasantry in contemporary novels, 1815-1900.
Ph,D., Wisconsin, 1953.

1042. ISAAC, J.
The working class in early Victorian novels.
Ph.D., City University of New York, 1973.
DA 33 6914A

1043. JAMES, W.L.G.
A study of the fiction directed to the urban lower classes in England, 1830-50.
D.Phil., Oxford, 1961.

1044. JOPLING, C.J.
The role of the craftsman in the Victorian novel.
M.A., Wales (Lampeter), 1976.

1044A. LANGMEAD, J.A.
Class and respectability in Victorian England with special reference to selected novels
of Gaskell, Eliot and Hardy.
M.A., Exeter, 1977.

1045. KARMINSKI, A.S.
Writers in Manchester, 1831-1854.
M.Litt., Cambridge, 1954-55.
        (includes a survey of working class writers, the writings of Elizabeth Gaskell
        and other 'sociological' novelists.)

1046. MAYNE, B.H.
The fictional working-class hero and the problem of the industrial poor as seen by
Victorian novelists.
M.A., Hull, 1965.

1047. MERRICK, J.L.
The necessary distinctions of society: an appraisal of the role of class in the
19th century English novel.
Ph.D., Pittsburg, 1976.
DA 37 5287A

1048. MOHAN, R.
The political novel in England in the nineteenth century, 1832-1900.
Ph.D., Leeds, 1954.

1049. NELSON, J.M.
The growth of social criticism in the theatre in England, 1840-1890.
Ph.D., Toronto, 1968.
DA 30 4600A

1050. PENDLETON, P.R.
Towards understanding the image of the working class in nineteenth-century English novels.
Ph.D., City University of New York, 1977.
DA 38 3064A

1051. POUND, A.H.
A critical study of four mid-Victorian political novels: Sybil by Benjamin Disraeli,
Alton Locke by Charles Kingsley, Felix Holt the Radical by George Eliot and Phineas Finn
by Anthony Trollope.
M.A., Manchester, 1970-71.

1052. REITZ, R.H.
Class consciousness in the literature of the Crimean War.
Ph.D., Southern Illinois, 1972.
DA 33 5139A

1053. SHARRATT, B.
Autobiography and class consciousness: an attempt to characterize 19th century working
class autobiography in the light of the writer's class.
Ph.D., Cambridge, 1974-75.

1054. SHUSTERMAN, D.
The Victorian novel of industrial conflict, 1832-1870.
Ph.D., New York, 1953.

1055. SMITH, A.G.M.
The novel of factory life, 1832-55.
Ph.D., Edinburgh, 1971-72.

1056. SMITH, S.M.
The other nation in fact and fiction: the poor in English novels of the 1840s and 1850s
with particular reference to Disraeli's Sybil, Mrs Gaskell's Mary Barton, Charles Kingsley's
Yeast and Alton Locke, Dickens's Hard Times and Charles Reade's It is Never Too Late to Mend.
Ph.D., London, External, 1976.

1057. STEELE, A.
The fictional treatment of industrial relations from 1827 to 1870 with special
reference to the novels of Mrs. Gaskell.
B.Litt., Oxford, 1964.

1058.   TARANTELL, C.B.
        The working class in the "social problem" novel; 1830-1855.
        Ph.D., Brandeis, 1975.
        DA 36 2857A

1059.   TARR, R.L.
        Carlyle's influence on the mid-Victorian social novels of Gaskell, Kingsley and Dickens.
        Ph.D., South Carolina, 1968.
        DA 29 2285A

1060.   TERRY, R.C.
        The working class in some novels and poems of the period, 1825-50.
        M.A., Bristol, 1961.

1061.   THOMSON, M.P.N.
        The changing ideals of womanhood in the novel and its relation to the feminist
        movement, 1837-73.
        Ph.D., Cambridge, 1947.

1062.   VICINUS, M.J.
        The lowly harp: a study of nineteenth century working-class poetry.
        Ph.D., Wisconsin, 1969.
        DA 30 1152A
               (Poetry and songs of Northern England's industrial areas especially in the
               cotton, woollen and coal industries.)

1063.   VINCENT, D.M.
        The growth of working-class consciousness in the first half of the 19th century:
        a study of the autobiographies of working men.
        Ph.D., Cambridge, 1975.

1064.   WEILAND, S.
        Chartism and English literature, 1838-50.
        Ph.D., Chicago, 1970-71.

1065.   WERLIN, R.J.
        The English novel and the industrial revolution: a study in the sociology of literature.
        Ph.D., Harvard, 1967-68.

1066.   WILCOX, J.M.
        East End novelists: the working class in English fiction, 1880-1900.
        Ph.D., Wayne State University, 1968.
        DA 30 1579A

1067.   WILSHER, J.C.
        Popular literary culture in a 19th century cotton town: a social study of the Blackburn
        poets.
        M.A.*, Lancaster, 1970.

19th - 20th Centuries

1068.   DEMARIA, R.
        From Bulwer-Lytton to George Orwell: the utopian novel in England, 1870-1950.
        Ph.D., Columbia, 1959.
        DA 20 0667

1069.   DEVRIES, E.M.S.
        Thomas Carlyle and Bernard Shaw as critics of religion and society.
        Ph.D., Nebraska-Lincoln, 1976.
        DA 37 4365A

1070.   DOMVILLE, E.W.
        The presentation of the London working classes in fiction, 1880-1914.
        PH.D., University College, London, 1965.

1071.   EDDERSHAW, C.R.T.
        The adaptation of the novelist's art to three fictional presentations of the problems
        of an industrial society: Hard Times, Demos and Lady Chatterley's Lover.
        M.A., Manchester, 1966-67.

1072.   GAINES, M.M.S.
        The scholarship boy, 1870-1939: a study of the working class student in the English
        educational system, English society and the English novel.
        Ph.D., Chicago, 1970.

1073.   GIBBONS, T.H.
        Literary criticism and the intellectual milieu: some aspects of the period, 1880-1914,
        with particular reference to the literary and social criticism of Havelock Ellis and
        Alfred Orage.
        Ph.D., Cambridge, 1966.

1074.   MILES, E.C.
        Some aspects of the treatment of the industrial and urban working classes in British
        prose fiction, 1832-1914.
        Ph.D., Keele, 1975.

1075. SAMAAN, A.B.
The novel of Utopianism and prophecy from Lytton, 1871 to Orwell, 1949 with special
reference to its reception.
Ph.D., Birkbeck College, London, 1963.

1076. SCANLON, L.
Essays on the effect of feminism and socialism upon the literature of 1880-1914.
Ph.D., Brandeis, 1973.
DA 34 4218A

1077. STUBBS, P.J.E.
The portrayal of women in English fiction, 1880-1918.
M.A., Sheffield, 1974.

1078. SUFFOLK, J.C.
The novel of industrial town life from Mrs. Gaskell to Arnold Bennett.
M.A., Sheffield, 1939.

20th Century

1079. ANEY, E.T.
British poetry of social protest in the 1930s: the problem of belief in the poetry of
W.H. Auden, C.Day Lewis, 'Hugh McDiarmid', Louis MacNeice and Stephen Spender.
Ph.D., Pennsylvania, 1954.
DA 14 2061

1080. BONE, C.
Literature of political commitment in Britain between the wars: Michael Roberts,
Stephen Spender, W.H. Auden.
Ph.D., Chicago, 1968-69.

1081. CADMAN, M.C.
An analysis of the social criticism implicit in the works of D.H. Lawrence and T.S. Eliot.
M.A., Sheffield, 1951.

1082. DODD, J.T.
The influence of left-wing political theories on English poetry in the 1930s.
M.A., University College, London, 1962.

1083. EADE, D.C.
Contemporary Yorkshire novelist: a study of some themes in the work of Stan Barstow,
John Braine, David Storey and Keith Waterhouse.
M.Phil., Leeds, 1969.

1084. ENDRES, R.B.
Plays and politics: an analysis of various models of 20th century political theatre.
Ph.D., York University (Canada), 1976.
DA 37 7742A
(Includes a study of British working class dramatists of the 1950s and C.N.D.)

1085. GIBSON, S.M.
Love and the vote: fiction of the Suffrage movement in Edwardian England.
Ph.D., Massachusetts, 1975.
DA 36 0900A

1086. HARRISON, J.R.
The social and political ideas of W.B. Yeats, Wyndham Lewis, Ezra Pound,
T.S. Eliot and D.H. Lawrence.
M.A., Sheffield, 1963.

1087. HOSKINS, K.B.
Today the struggle: a study of literature and politics in England during the Spanish
Civil War.
Ph.D., Columbia, 1965.
DA 26 2214

1088. JAGO, D.M.
Tradition and progress in Shaw and Wells, Belloc and Chesterton.
Ph.D., Leicester, 1965.

1089. KINGDON, T.
Social conscience of the English theatre of the 1930s.
M.A., Birmingham, 1973-74.

1090. LOCKWOOD, B.
Four contemporary British working-class novelists: a theoretic and critical approach to
the fiction of Raymond Williams, John Braine, David Storey and Alan Sillitoe.
Ph.D., Wisconsin, 1966.
DA 28 1081A

1091. POVEY, J.F.
The Oxford Group: a study of the poetry of W.H. Auden, Stephen Spender, C.D. Lewis and
Louis MacNeice.
Ph.D., Michigan State, 1965.
DA 25 6633

1092. REPLOGUE, J.M.
       The Auden group: the 1930s poetry of W.H. Auden, C. Day Lewis and Stephen Spender.
       Ph.D., Wisconsin, 1956.
       DA 16 2169

1093. SPOONER, D.E.J.
       The response of some British and American writers to the Spanish Civil War.
       Ph.D., Bristol, 1969.

1094. WILFORD, R.A.
       The political involvements and ideological alignments of left-wing literary
       intellectuals in Britain, 1930-1950.
       Ph.D., Wales (Cardiff), 1974-75.

1095. WILLIAMS, H.M.
       The poetry of Auden, Spender and Day Lewis in relation to the thought of the period,
       1930-1940.
       M.A., Wales, 1953-54.

(B) STUDIES OF INDIVIDUAL WRITERS

W.H. AUDEN

1096. BARDEN, T.E.
       W.H. Auden: the poet's uses of drama.
       Ph.D., Virginia, 1975.
       DA 36 4473A

1097. BUELL, F.H.
       The political voice of W.H. Auden.
       Ph.D., Cornell, 1970.
       DA 31 6592A

1098. FAWCETT, A.M.
       Personal and social themes in W.H. Auden.
       M.Litt., Bristol, 1972-73.

1099. HOOKER, P.J.
       The ideology of W.H. Auden's early poetry.
       M.A., Southampton, 1964-65.
            (Particularly psycho-analysis and Marxism and Auden's concern to define the
            position of the middle class intellectual in the 1930s.)

1100. ROWAN, N.
       Politics in the early poetry of W.H. Auden, 1930-1945.
       Ph.D., Cornell, 1957.
       DA 17 3023

1101. THAIRS, S.M.
       W.H. Auden: the relationship between a writer and his social-cultural environment.
       M.A., Liverpool, 1973-74.

1102. TWINING, E.S.
       Love and politics in the early poetry of W.H. Auden.
       Ph.D., Connecticut, 1966.
       DA 27 4268A

1103. WALSH, A.F.
       The heel of Achilles: dialectic in the long poems of W.H. Auden.
       Ph.D., Columbia, 1967.
       DA 28 5075A

ARNOLD BENNETT

1104. COPEK, P.J.
       The Five Towns novels of Arnold Bennett: a response to industrial society.
       Ph.D., North Western, 1973.
       DA 34 5960A

WILLIAM BLAKE

1105. BLOXHAM, L.J.
       William Blake and visionary poetry in the 20th century.
       Ph.D., Washington State, 1975.
       DA 36 5275A

1106. CURTIS, F.B.
       The vision and the work of William Blake.
       M.Litt., Lancaster, 1970.

1107. FLATTO, E.
       The social and political ideas of William Blake.
       Ph.D., City of New York University, 1966.
       DA 27 2870A

1108. FULBRIGHT, J.S.
       William Blake and the emancipation of women.
       Ph.D., Missouri-Columbia, 1973.
       DA 34 7132A

1109. GALBRAITH, T.W.
       A "fresher morning": Blake labors to awaken man.
       Ph.D., Washington, 1975.
       DA 37 0984A

1110. HILL, M.A.
       Politics and art in the poetry of William Blake.
       Ph.D., Chicago, 1968-69.

1111. ROLLINS, M.E.
       The necessity of art: a study of William Blake.
       Ph.D., Massachusetts, 1974.
       DA 35 6156A
            (Development of Blake's philosophy of social and cultural reform)

1112. SANZO, E.B.
       William Blake: poet of the city in the industrial age.
       Ph.D., City of New York University, 1970.
       DA 33 7640A

1113. SCHORER, M.
       William Blake as Radical.
       Ph.D., Wisconsin, 1936.

1114. TAYLOR, J.A.
       William Blake: the radical context: a study in relationship between Blake's work and
       the popular radical culture in England, 1790-1830.
       Ph.D., Leeds, 1970.

              BYRON

1115. Lord Byron: his classical republicanism, cyclical view of history and their influence
       on his work.
       Ph.D., Vanderbilt, 1963.
       DA 24 0282

1116. GOLDSTEIN, S.L.
       Byron in radical tradition: a study in the intellectual backgrounds and controversiality
       of Cain.
       Ph.D., Columbia, 1970.
       DA 34 2560A

              WILLIAM CARLETON

1117. BRADLEY, W.
       The scope and quality of William Carleton's presentation of Irish peasant life and
       character in his novels and stories.
       M.Phil., London, External, 1974.

1118. IBARRA, E.S.
       Realistic accounts of the Irish peasantry in four novels of William Carleton.
       Ph.D., Florida, 1969.
       DA 34 7193A

              JOYCE CARY

1119. BARNES, R.C.
       The novels of Joyce Cary.
       M.A., Liverpool, 1957-58.

1120. BISHOP, A.G.
       Joyce Cary's Cock Jarvis: an edition and a critical study.
       D.Phil., Oxford, 1969.

1121. ECHERU, M.J.C.
       The dimensions of order: a study of Joyce Cary.
       Ph.D., Cornell, 1965.
       DA 26 5431

1122. KALECHOFSKY, R.D.
       Joyce Cary: his political world and ours.
       Ph.D., City of New York University, 1970.
       DA 31 6614A

1123. KANU, S.H.
       The world in everlasting conflict: Joyce Cary's view of man and society.
       Ph.D., Alberta, 1970-71.

1124. KELLEHER, J.J.
       The theme of freedom in the novels of Joyce Cary.
       Ph.D., Pittsburg, 1964.
       DA 26 0369

1125.   LARSEN, G.L.
Archetype and social change in the novels of Joyce Cary.
Ph.D., Washington, 1963.
DA 24 0299

1126.   NYCE, B.M.
Joyce Cary as a political novelist.
Ph.D., Claremont Graduate School, 1967.
DA 29 0574A

1127.   OBUMSELU, B.E.
The theme of creativity in the novels of Joyce Cary.
D.Phil., Oxford, 1970.

1128.   O'GRADY, W.A.
Political contexts in the novels of Joyce Cary and Graham Greene.
Ph.D., Toronto, 1971.
DA 32 6995A

1129.   THOMPSON, E.J
Innocence, experience and value: a study of Joyce Cary.
Ph.D., Brown, 1974.
DA 35 7331A

CHRISTOPHER CALDWELL

1130.   GIBBONS, R.E.
Christopher Caudwell: Marxist apologist and critic.
Ph.D., Bowling Green State University, 1967.
DA 28 1076A

1131.   MARGOLIES, D.N.
Caudwell's aesthetic: the relation between Marxism and Marxist literary criticism.
B.Litt., Oxford, 1965.

1132.   MOBERG, G.
Christopher Caudwell: an introduction to his life and work.
Ph.D., Columbia, 1968.
DA 29 1903A

1133.   SYPHER, E.B.
Christopher Caudwell: the genesis and function of literary form.
Ph.D., Connecticut, 1976.
DA 37 5819A

SAMUEL COLERIDGE

1134.   COLMER, J.A.
Coleridge as a critic of political and social problems in his prose writings, 1795-1832.
Ph.D., London, 1955.

CHARLES DICKENS

1135.   AUSTEN, Z.
Dickens' ambivalence in the two 'Oliver Twists'.
Ph.D., State University of New York, 1972.
DA 33 2359A

1136.   BRIND, F.W.
"Mind-forged manacles": verbal satire in Bleak House, Little Dorrit and Our Mutual Friend.
Ph.D., Bryn Mawr, 1972.
DA 33 5671A

1137.   BROWN, J.M.
A sociological analysis of the novels of Charles Dickens.
Ph.D., L.S.E., 1977.

1138.   CLARKE, H.
Charles Dickens' contributions to the social novel, 1836-1850.
M.A., Birmingham, 1947.

1139.   COYLE, J.J.
Social studies in Hard Times.
M.A., Queen's University, Belfast, 1960-61.

1140.   DAVIES, H.E.
Social reform in the novels of Charles Dickens.
M.A., Wales, 1935.

1141.   EBBATSON, J.R.
Dickens and early Victorian England.
M.A., Sheffield, 1965.

1142.   METWALLI, A.K.
Charles Dickens as a social critic.
Ph.D., Manchester, 1961.

1143. METWALLI, A.K.
       The treatment of poverty in the works of Charles Dickens.
       M.A., Wales, 1956-57.

1144. METZ, N.A.
       "To understand such wretchedness": Dickens and public health.
       Ph.D., Michigan, 1977.
       DA 38 3486A

1145. MIDDLESBRO', T.G.
       The treatment of industrialism in the later novels of Charles Dickens.
       Ph.D., McGill University, 1972.
       DA 34 0735A

1146. MURANVILLE, D.B.
       The law and the novel: Dickens' Bleak House.
       Ph.D., Kent State University, 1973.
       DA 34 2643A

1147. POWER, M.
       Dickens as city-novelist: a study of London in Dicken's fiction.
       Ph.D., McGill, 1973.
       DA 34 7719A

1148. QUALLS, B.V.
       Carlyle and Dickens: the function of the Victorian prophet.
       Ph.D., North Western, 1973.
       DA 34 3354A

1149. QUINN, M.R.
       Dickens and Shaw: a study of a literary relationship.
       Ph.D., Pennsylvania State University, 1974.
       DA 35 7323A

1150. QUIRK, E.F.
       Dickens' men of law: Dickens' changing vision of English legal practice.
       Ph.D., Illinois, 1972.
       DA 34 0738A

1151. RICE, T.J.
       Charles Dickens as a historical novelist: Barnaby Rudge (1841).
       Ph.D., Princeton, 1971.
       DA 32 6448A

1152. STANBURY, F.E.
       The social ideas of Charles Dickens and their influence upon his art as a novelist.
       M.A., Wales, 1934.

1153. TARTELLA, V.P.
       Charles Dickens' "Oliver Twist": a moral realism and the uses of style.
       Ph.D., Notre Dame, 1961.
       DA 22 1616

1154. WHEELER, B.M.
       Charles Dickens in service of two masters: a study of the novel of social protest.
       Ph.D., Harvard, 1960-61.

GEORGE ELIOT

1155   AZMY, I.
       George Eliot as an analyst of the social life of England in the nineteenth century.
       M.A., Sheffield, 1949.

1156. STEELE, K.B.
       Social change in George Eliot's fiction.
       Ph.D., Brown, 1974.
       DA 35 7329A

EBENEZER ELLIOTT

1157. SEARY, E.R.
       Ebenezer Elliott: a study, including an edition of his work.
       Ph.D., Sheffield, 1932.

1158. SEARY, E.R.
       A reinvestigation into the sources and biographical material of Ebenezer Elliott.
       B.A.*, Sheffield, 1929.

JOHN GALSWORTHY

1159. AMENO, V.
The development of John Galsworthy as a social dramatist.
Ph.D., Michigan, 1953.
DA 13 0385

1160. COLLINS, J.E.
Social background of Galsworthy's novels.
Ph.D., Boston, 1936.

1161. FARRIS, E.C.
John Galsworthy and the drama of social problems.
Ph.D., Columbia, 1974.
DA 35 7301A

1162. KENT, G.E.
Social criticism in the novels, plays and short stories of John Galsworthy.
Ph.D., Boston, 1953.

1163. KILCOYNE, F.P.
The emergence and growth of the social and political extremism in the works of John Galsworthy.
Ph.D., New York, 1945.

1164. YOUNG, I.D.
The social conscience of John Galsworthy.
Ph.D., Texas, 1955.

ELIZABETH GASKELL

1165. BRYANT, A.N.
Ideas and social themes in the work of Mrs. Gaskell: a study of their relationship in the social and literary background.
M.Litt., Strathclyde, 1970-71.

1166. GALLAGHER, C.M.
Elizabeth Gaskell: the social novels.
M.A., Liverpool, 1963-63.

1167. LANCASTER, J.T.
Mrs. Gaskell with special reference to the social reform novel, 1830-50.
M.Litt., Cambridge, 1927.

1168. LOMAS, C.
Mrs. Gaskell's Mary Barton: a critical and historical study.
M.A., Birmingham, 1973-74.

1169. McVEAGH, J.
The novels of Mrs. Gaskell.
Ph.D., Birmingham, 1966-67.

1170. PIKE, A.J.
The Victorian scene in the writings of Mrs. Gaskell.
M.A., Sheffield, 1958.

GEORGE GISSING

1171. COURTNEY, L.F.
George Gissing: Victorian.
Ph.D., Emery, 1975.
DA 36 8076A

1172. FRANCIS, C.J.
Aspects of realism in the novels of George Gissing.
Ph.D., Manchester, 1954-55.

1173. GILMARTIN, R.T.
The social attitudes of George Gissing.
Ph.D., New York, 1953.

1174. HAYDOCK, J.J.
The woman question in the novels of George Gissing.
Ph.D., North Carolina, 1965.
DA 26 3923A

1175. KORG, J.
George Gissing: a study in conflicts.
Ph.D., Columbia, 1953.
DA 13 0389

1176. LELCHUK, A.
George Gissing: the man and the novelist.
Ph.D., Stanford, 1966.
DA 26 6716A

1177. MALBONE, R.G.
George Gissing: novelist.
Ph.D., Minnesota, 1960.
DA 20 4113A

1178. MANLEY, E.F.
A critical biography of the novelist George Gissing.
Ph.D., Nottingham, 1959-60.

1179. MECHERLY, G.J.
Literary influences on the novels of George Gissing.
Ph.D., Temple, 1977.
DA 37 7764A

1180. MOORE, L.D.
A study of George Gissing and social Darwinism with special emphasis on New Grub Street
and The Private Papers of Henry Ryecroft.
Ph.D., The American University, 1974.
DA 35 2233A

1181. NUR SHERIF
The art and thought of George Gissing: a critical study of his development in his
works, 1880-1903.
Ph.D., Bedford College, London, 1952-53.

1182. PECK, J.
The role of the artist in the novels of George Gissing.
M.A., Wales (Cardiff), 1969-70.

1183. POOLE, A.D.B.
George Gissing: a study of his work and its literary context.
Ph.D., Cambridge, 1973-74.

1184. ROGERS, J.A.
The art and challenge of George Gissing.
Ph.D., City of New York University, 1958.
DA 18 4501

1185. ROSENGARTEN, H.J.
The relations between author, publisher and public at the end of the 19th century
with particular reference to the writings of George Gissing.
B.Litt., Oxford, 1965.

1186. RUTLAND, R.B.
The realism of George Gissing: a study of five novels.
M.A., Birkbeck College, London, 1960-61.

1187. SMITH, J.M.M.
An examination of the theme of emancipation in six novels of George Gissing.
M.Phil., Birkbeck College, London, 1969.

1188. THOMAS, D.P.
An enquiry into the nature and importance of the theme of nobility in the writings
of George Gissing.
M.A., Wales (Cardiff), 1962-63.

1189. WALZER, J.B.
Class and character in the work of George Gissing.
Ph.D., Brandeis, 1967.
DA 28 2700A

1190. WOOD, C.F.
The novels of George Gissing: a sociological interpretation.
B.Litt., Oxford, 1957.

WILLIAM GODWIN

1191. McCRACKEN, J.D.
Politics and propaganda in Godwin's novels.
Ph.D., Chicago, 1966-67.

1192. PRESCOT, H.K.
The economic and political theory of William Godwin and his debt to French thinkers.
D.Phil., Oxford, 1931.

1193. ROBINSON, P.
Psychological ethics in William Godwin's Political justice, 1798.
M.A., Kent, 1971-72.

1194. WHITE, M.K.
William Godwin: his life, work and influences.
M.A., Sheffield, 1921.

1195. WILLIAMS, D.A.
William Godwin's struggle for autonomy, 1791-97.
Ph.D., Kentucky, 1974.
DA 35 1582A

THOMAS HARDY

1196. DAWSON, H.D.
The role of the common man in Thomas Hardy's fiction.
Ph.D., Texas, 1976.
DA 37 7759A

1197. HALL, L.M.
Thomas Hardy: use of history in The Mayor of Casterbridge and Tess of the D'Urbervilles.
Ph.D., Illinois at Urbana-Champaine, 1974.
DA 35 0452A

1198. HIGGINS, E.J.
Class consciousness and class conflicts in the novels and tales of Thomas Hardy, O.M.
Ph.D., California, Los Angeles, 1965.
DA 25 5279

WILLIAM HAZLITT

1199. ECKLER, E.A.
Materials for the study of Hazlitt as a social critic.
Ph.D., Pittsburgh, 1937.

1200. FAUTH, L.M.
The invincible democrat: politics in the writing of William Hazlitt.
Ph.D., Indiana, 1975.
DA 36 2842A

1201. HARPER, S.A.
William Hazlitt's 'political essays'.
M.Phil., Reading, 1967-68.

1202. ROBINSON, R.E.
William Hazlitt as social controversialist and propagandist.
Ph.D., California, 1942.

CHRISTOPHER ISHERWOOD

1203. ANANTHAMURTHY, U.R.
Politics and fiction in the 1930s· studies in Christopher Isherwood and Edward Upward.
Ph.D., Birmingham, 1966-67.

D.H. LAWRENCE

1204. DANIEL, J.T.
The influence of the English class-structure on the work of D.H. Lawrence.
Ph.D., Minnesota, 1973.
DA 34 4252A

1205. JAMES, P.A.
Industrialism and class-consciousness in the novels of D.H. Lawrence: a study in realism.
M.A., Durham, 1974.

1206. SOBCHACK, T.J.
Social criticism in the novels of D.H. Lawrence.
Ph.D., City University of New York, 1968.
DA 29 1235A

WILLIAM MORRIS

1207. ALBRECHT, W.T.
William Morris's The Well at the World's End: an explanation and a study.
Ph.D., Pennsylvania, 1970.
DA 31 5347A

1208. ALLEN, P.R.
Patterns in William Morris's narrative poetry and their interpretation.
M.A., University College, London, 1960-61.

1209. BACON, A.K.
William Morris's attitude towards industrialism: a study of the lectures, journalism and letters.
Ph.D., Wales (Bangor), 1977.

1210. BEATON, G.L.J.
William Morris and the good life.
M.A., Leeds, 1955.

1211. CALHOUN, C.B.
The pastoral aesthetic of William Morris: a reading of The Earthly Paradise.
Ph.D., North Carolina, 1972.
DA 33 1137A

1212. CANNING, G.R.
William Morris: man and literary artist.
Ph.D., Wisconsin, 1958.
DA 19 1753

1213. CARMASSI, G.R.
       The expanding vision: changes in emphasis in William Morris' late prose romances.
       Ph.D., Notre Dame, 1975.
       DA 36 5312A

1214. DUNLAP, B.B.
       The search for paradise: a thematic study of the poems of William Morris.
       Ph.D., Harvard, 1966-67.

1215. EKSTROM, W.F.
       The social idealism of William Morris and of William Dean Howells: a study in four
       Utopian novels.
       Ph.D., Illinois, 1947.

1216. ESHLEMAN, L.W.
       William Morris: artist, philosopher and practical Socialist.
       Ph.D., Princeton, 1937.

1217. FROST, S.C.
       A study of William Morris's News from Nowhere.
       M.A., Birmingham, 1966-67.

1218. GENT, M.G.
       Theme and symbol in the poetry of William Morris.
       Ph.D., Leeds, 1970.

1219. GOOCH, V.M.
       William Morris: towards unity in art and life.
       Ph.D., Manchester, 1972-73.

1220. HANNAH, J.
       The new art of William Morris: his contribution to the theory of environmental design
       and its influence.
       B.Litt., Oxford, 1972.

1221. HAWKINS, M.F.
       The late prose romances of William Morris: a biographical interpretation.
       Ph.D., California, Berkeley, 1969.
       DA 30 4451A

1222. HOLZMAN, M.H.
       On attempting to understand the News from Nowhere.
       Ph.D., California, San Diego, 1976.
       DA 37 5805A

1223. JOHN, E.L.
       The social and economic ideas of William Morris and their relation to those of his times.
       M.A., Wales (Swansea), 1944.

1224. LEBOURGEOIS, J.Y.
       The youth of William Morris, 1834-76: an interpretation.
       Ph.D., Tulane University, 1970-71.

1225. LEMIRE, E.D.
       The unpublished lectures of William Morris: a critical edition including an introductory
       survey and a calendar and bibliography of Morris's public speeches.
       Ph.D., Wayne State, 1962.
       DA 24 3325

1226. OBERG, C.H.
       The pagan prophet: unity of vision in the narrative poetry of William Morris.
       Ph.D., Virginia, 1970.
       DA 31 4786A

1227. SILVER, C.G.
       No idle singer: a study on the poems and romances of William Morris.
       Ph.D., Columbia, 1967.
       DA 28 0644A

1228. SOKKARI, S.E.Y.
       The prose romances of William Morris.
       Ph.D., Manchester, 1953-54.

1229. SPATT, H.S.
       William Morris: the languages of history and myth.
       Ph.D., Johns Hopkins, 1975.
       DA 36 4519A

1230. STALLMAN, R.L.
       The quest of William Morris.
       Ph.D., Oregon, 1966.
       DA 27 3064A

1231. STOKES, E.E.
       William Morris and Bernard Shaw: a socialist-artistic relationship.
       Ph.D., Texas, 1951.

1232. TREFMAN, S.
William Morris: the modernisation of myth.
Ph.D., New York, 1967.

1233. TYZACK, C.R.P.
A critical study of William Morris's prose romances with special reference to
their relationship to his social ideals.
B.Litt., Oxford, 1964.

1234. WAHL, J.R.
Two pre-Raphaelite poets: studies in the poetry and poetic theory of William Morris
and D.G. Rossetti.
D.Phil., Oxford, 1953-54.

1235. WEEKS, J.H.
The last romances of William Morris: a critical study.
M.A., Birmingham, 1972-73.

ARTHUR MORRISON

1236. MAPPLETHORPE, B.
Working-class consciousness in the fiction of Arthur Morrison and Robert Tressell.
B.Phil., Hull, 1972.

1237. NWOGA, D.I.
The novels and tales of Arthur Morrison, 1863-1945.
M.A., University College, London, 1962.

1238. RYDER, D.J.G.
Arthur Morrison: working-class novelist.
Ph.D., Reading, 1976.

SEAN O'CASEY

1239. POTRATZ, G.A.
Art and ideology in the plays of Sean O'Casey.
Ph.D., Cornell, 1975.
DA 35 7322A

GEORGE ORWELL

1240. BUCKLEY, D.P.
The novels of George Orwell.
Ph.D., Columbia, 1962.
DA 26 7310A

1241. CALDER, J.R.
Imagination and politics: a study of George Orwell and Arthur Koestler.
M.A., Birkbeck College, London, 1966.

1242. CONCANNON, G.J.
The development of George Orwell's art.
Ph.D., Denver, 1973.
DA 34 3386A

1243. CORBETT, W.R.
A study of the relationship between Conservatism and social conscience in the work
of George Orwell.
Ph.D., Exeter, 1970.

1244. CROMPTON, D.W.
George Orwell's approach to literary criticism with special reference to the personal
factors which influenced it.
M.A., Manchester, 1963-64.

1245. CROMWELL, A.F.
The decline of the British Empire in some British novels of the 20th century.
Ph.D., Minnesota, 1975.
DA 36 5278A
/Includes a study of Orwell.7

1246. EDELHEIT, S.J.
Dark prophecies: essays on Orwell and technology.
Ph.D., Brandeis, 1975.
DA 36 0308A

1247. EDRICH, E.
Literary technique and social temper in the fiction of George Orwell.
Ph.D., Wisconsin, 1960.
DA 21 0620

1248. FINK, H.R.
George Orwell's novels in relation to his social and literary theory.
Ph.D., University College, London, 1968.

1249. GREENFIELD, R.M.
Discursive Orwell.
Ph.D., Columbia, 1967.
DA 28 1818A

1250. HORNUNG, R.
George Orwell: the relationship of his capabilities as a journalist to his achievements as a novelist.
M.A., Exeter, 1973-74.

1251. HUNTER, J.E.
George Orwell and the uses of literature.
Ph.D., Yale, 1973.
DA 34 2629A

1252. JACKSON, A.S.
George Orwell's utopian vision.
Ph.D., South California, 1965.
DA 26 2215A

1253. KEARSE, L.A.
George Orwell: romantic utopian.
Ph.D., Brown, 1973.
DA 34 6593A

1253A. KLITZE, R.
Orwell and his critics: an enquiry into the reception of and critical debate about George Orwell's political works.
Ph.D., Birkbeck College, London, 1977.

1254. KNAPP, J.V.
George Orwell: an evaluation of his early fiction.
Ph.D., Illinois at Urbana-Champaign, 1971.
DA 32 5794A

1255. KUBAL, D.L.
Outside the whole: George Orwell's search for meaning and form.
Ph.D., Notre Dame, 1968.
DA 29 0265A

1256. LEE, R.A.
The Spanish experience: George Orwell and the politics of language.
Ph.D., Oregon, 1967.
DA 27 3053A

1257. MAUND, J.C.
Imperialism: a study of critical attitudes in the writings of E.M. Forster, George Orwell and Joseph Conrad.
M.A., Wales (Aberystwyth), 1971-72.

1258. MELLICHAMP, L.R.
A study of George Orwell: the man, his impact and his outlook.
Ph.D., Emory, 1968.
DA 30 0729A

1259. MORRIS, J.A.
Orwell's picture of collective irrationalism.
Ph.D., Nottingham, 1970-71.

1260. PAWLING, C.
Orwell's political practice to 1945.
M.A., Birmingham, 1973-74.

1261. RANKIN, D.B.
The critical reception of the art and thought of George Orwell.
Ph.D., Birkbeck College, London, 1965.

1262. READER, M.
The political criticism of George Orwell.
Ph.D., Michigan, 1966.
DA 28 0273A

1263. RUPPE, J.P.
In search of common humanity: a critical study of the early novels and essays of George Orwell.
Ph.D., Rutgers, 1972.
DA 32 5244A

1264. SANGER, I.M.
Political allegory in the 20th century: a study of Orwell's Animal Farm and Brecht's Der aufhaltsame Aufstieg des Arturo Ui.
B.Litt., Oxford, 1973-74.

1265. SLATER, I.D.
Orwell and the road to servitude.
Ph.D., British Columbia, 1977.
DA 39 0453A

1266. SMYER, R.I.
Structure and meaning in the works of George Orwell.
Ph.D., Stanford, 1968.
DA 29 0615A

1267. SNYDER, P.J.
Doing the necessary task: the bourgeois humanism of George Orwell.
Ph.D., Western Reserve, 1964.
DA 25 6636A

1268. STEVENSON, M.
George Orwell and the tradition of British socialism.
B.Litt., Oxford, 1973-74.

1269. SUTHERLAND, R.W.
The political ideas of George Orwell: a liberal's odyssey in the 20th century.
Ph.D., Duke, 1968.
DA 29 4536A

1270. VAN DELLEN, R.J.
Politics in Orwell's fiction.
Ph.D., Indiana, 1973.
DA 33 6378A

1271. VORHEES, R.J.
The paradox of George Orwell.
Ph.D., Indiana, 1958.
DA 19 0533A

1272. WARNCKE, W.W.
George Orwell as literary critic.
Ph.D., Michigan, 1965.
DA 27 0488A

J.B. PRIESTLEY

1273. DAY, A.E.
A committed twentieth century man of letters: a study of the social and political writings of J.B. Priestley.
M.Phil., Leeds, 1970.

DOROTHY RICHARDSON

1274. BLAKE, C.R.
A critical study of Dorothy M. Richardson's Pilgrimage.
Ph.D., Michigan, 1958.
DA 19 2087

1275. ROSE, S.
The social and aesthetic views of Dorothy M. Richards: a study of Pilgrimage and her miscellaneous writings in the light of her theoretical and practical views of socialism.
Ph.D., Royal Holloway College, London, 1967.

JOHN RUSKIN

1276. FISHER, J.F.
John Ruskin and the British working man.
Ph.D., Washington, 1977.
DA 38 1407A

GEORGE BERNARD SHAW

1277. ABBOTT, A.S.
Shaw and Christianity.
Ph.D., Harvard, 1961-62.

1278. AL-WAKIL, A.W.A.R.
The themes and methods of Bernard Shaw as a dramatist of ideas with a critical assessment of his achievement.
M.A., Manchester, 1957-58.

1279. BEARD, W.R.
Shaw's John Bull's other island: a critical, historical and theatrical study.
Ph.D., King's College, London, 1974.

1280. BENNETT, K.C.
George Bernard Shaw's philosophy of art.
Ph. D., Indiana, 1961.
DA 22 3197A

1281. BENNETT, T.F.
Shaw's contribution to the theory and practice of modern English drama.
M.A., Wales, 1929.

1282. BERQUIST, G.N.
War and peace in the prose and plays of Bernard Shaw.
Ph.D., Nebraska, 1972.
DA 33 2315A

1283. BEST, B.S.
Development of Bernard Shaw's philosophy of the responsible society.
Ph.D., Wisconsin, 1971.
DA 32 3292A

1284. BHAKRI, A.S.
Shaw's drama in relation to his social and philosophical ideas.
Ph.D., Leeds, 1956.

1285. BHATIA, H.L.
Shaw the dramatist: a class by himself.
M.A., Liverpool, 1967-68.

1286. BHATIA, H.L.
Shaw and the late 19th century theatre: a study on his dramatic criticism.
Ph.D., Keele, 1970-71.

1287. BOND, G.R.
The method of iconoclasm of George Bernard Shaw.
Ed.D., Michigan, 1959.
DA 20 1780A

1288. CLAYTON, R.B.
The salvation myth in the drama of George Bernard Shaw.
Ph.D., California, Berkeley, 1960-61.

1289. COLEMAN, D.C.
Political panaceas in seven plays of Bernard Shaw.
(Heartbreak House, Back to Methuselah, Two True to be Good, The Simpleton of the Unexpected Isles, Geneva, Buoyant Billions, and Far-Fetched Fables.)
B.Litt., Oxford, 1968-69.

1290. COOPER, M.M.
The social background of Shaw's early plays.
M.A., Sheffield, 1947.

1291. CRAWFORD, F.M
Swift and Shaw: satiric attitude and influence.
Ph.D., Pennsylvania State, 1975.
DA 36 4503A

1292. DERVIN, D.A.
George Bernard Shaw and the uses of energy.
Ph.D., Columbia, 1970.
DA 32 0425A

1293. DIETRICH, R.F.
The emerging superman: a study of Shaw's novels.
Ph.D., Florida State, 1965.
DA 26 1644A

1294. ENGLAND, A.W.
Action and argument in the plays of Bernard Shaw's middle period.
M.A., Liverpool, 1966-67.

1295. EL-RASHIDI, G.F.
The moral element in Bernard Shaw's plays.
M.A., Sheffield, 1963.

1296. ER-RAI, A.
The Shavian drama: influence on the technique.
Ph.D., Birmingham, 1954-55.

1297. FORDYCE, W.D.T.
Bernard Shaw and the comedy of medicare: a study of Doctor's Dilemma.
Ph.D., Harvard, 1966-67.

1298. FRAZER, F.M.
An edition of Bernard Shaw's Three Plays for Puritans.
Ph.D., Birkbeck College, London, 1970.

1299. FROMM, H.
Bernard Shaw and the theatre in the nineties.
Ph.D., Wisconsin, 1962.
DA 23 1364A

1300. GEDULD, H.M.
An edition of Bernard Shaw's Back to Methuselah: preface, play and postscript.
Ph.D., Birkbeck College, London, 1961.

1301. HALES, J.
Shaw's comedy.
Ph.D., Texas, 1963.
DA 24 3324A

1302. HARK, I.R.
Bernard Shaw and Victorian satiric inversion.
Ph.D., California, Los Angeles, 1975.
DA 36 4509A

1303. HEXT, V.J.
Shaw as critic and playwright, 1895-1906.
M.A., Birmingham, 1969-70.

1304. HOLDEN, A.M.
A study of George Bernard Shaw's Heartbreak House.
Ph.D., King's College, London, 1970.

1305. HUMMERT, P.A.
Marxist elements in the works of George Bernard Shaw.
Ph.D., North Western, 1953.
DA 13 1183

1306. KEMELMAN, A.F.
The influence of Samuel Butler on George Bernard Shaw.
M.A., Liverpool, 1966-67.

1307. KESTER, D.A.
Shaw and the Victorian "problem" genre: the woman's side.
Ph.D., Wisconsin, 1973.
DA 34 2566A

1308. KNEPPER, B.G.
Back to Methuselah and the utopian tradition.
Ph.D., Nebraska, 1967.
DA 28 0687A

1309. LANE, G.A.
Man's illusory social progress: a quintessential concept in the plays of Bernard Shaw.
M.Litt., Trinity College, Dublin, 1961-62.

1310. LOCKHART, J.H.K.
The relation between Shaw's plays and those of certain late 19th century dramatists.
M.Litt., Trinity College, Dublin, 1962-63.

1311. McFADDEN, K.D.
George Bernard Shaw and the woman question.
Ph.D., Toronto, 1976.
DA 39 2230A

1312. McILWAINE, R.S.
The intellectual force of Bernard Shaw.
Ph.D., Duke, 1971.
DA 32 4761A

1313. MASON, M.A.
The early plays of Bernard Shaw up to 1910 in relation to the social background and ideas of the time.
Ph.D., King's College, London, 1965.

1314. METWALLY, A.A.
The influences of Ibsen on Shaw.
Ph.D., Trinity College, Dublin, 1959-60.

1315. MILLS, C.H.
The intellectual and literary background of George Bernard Shaw's Man and Superman.
Ph.D., Nebraska, 1965.
DA 26 2727

1316. NELSON, R.S.
Religion and the plays of Bernard Shaw.
Ph.D., Nebraska, 1968.
DA 29 0574A

1317. NICKSON, J.R.
The art and politics of the late plays of Bernard Shaw.
Ph.D., Southern California, 1958.

1318. PETTET, E.B.
Shavian socialism and the Shavian life force: an analysis of the relationship between the philosophic and economic systems of George Bernard Shaw.
Ph.D., New York University, 1952.
DA 12 0622

1319. PILECKI, G.A.
Shaw's Geneva: a critical study of the evolution of the text in relation to Shaw's political thought and dramatic practice.
Ph.D., Cornell, 1961.
DA 22 2399

1320. PITT, D.K.
Tragic perspectives with particular reference to plays by Bernard Shaw and Arthur Miller.
M.A., Liverpool, 1966-67.

1321. PLOTINSKY, M.L.
The play of the mind: a study of Bernard Shaw's dramatic apprenticeship.
Ph.D., Harvard, 1962-63.

1322. RADFORD, F.L.
The idealistic iconoclast: aspects of Platonism in the works of Bernard Shaw.
Ph.D., Washington, 1970.
DA 32 0450A

1323. REUBEN, E.
The social dramatist: a study of Shaw's English family play.
Ph.D., Stanford, 1970.
DA 31 1810A

1324. SAMSI, A.R.
The historical plays of George Bernard Shaw in the light of his concept of history.
M.Phil., Birkbeck College, London, 1974.

1325. SHAYER, D.R.G.
The leading political and philosophical ideas in the work of G.B. Shaw.
B.Litt., Oxford, 1961.

1326. SOKKARI, S.E.Y.A.
Some of the early plays of Bernard Shaw in relation to their social background.
M.A., Manchester, 1951.

1327. TURCO, A.
The self and salvation: the intellectual development of Bernard Shaw from immaturity
to Man and Superman.
Ph.D., Harvard, 1968-69.

1328. TYSON, B.F.
The evolution of George Bernard Shaw's Plays unpleasant.
Ph.D., Queen Mary College, London, 1968.

1329. WATSON, B.B.
A Shavian guide to the intelligent woman.
Ph.D., Columbia, 1963.
DA 27 2549A

1330. WEIMER, M.J.
Shaw's conversion plays, 1897-1909.
Ph.D., Yale, 1973.
DA 34 7253A

1331. WISENTHAL, J.L.
The marriage of contraries in Shaw's middle plays: from Man and Superman to Saint Joan.
Ph.D., University College, London, 1970.

PERCY BYSSHE SHELLEY

1332. CAMERON, A.K.N.
Shelley's political, social and economic thought in his prose and poetry.
Ph.D., Wisconsin, 1939.

1333. CAMPBELL, W.R.
Blake and Shelley on man in society.
Ph.D., Oregon, 1967.
DA 28 3632A

1334. CRAMPTON, D.N.
Shelley's political optimism: The mask of anarchy to Hellas.
Ph.D., Wisconsin, 1973.
DA 34 6585A

1335. JACKSON, J.J.
Byron and Shelley considered as types of the revolutionary spirit.
M.A., London, 1912.

1336. KINGSTON, H.P.
The influence of William Godwin on Shelley.
M.A., Birmingham, 1932.

1337. PASHBY, I.T.
The poetry of politics: a study of Shelley's political thoughts.
M.Sc., Bristol, 1972.

1338. ROBERTS, G.O.
The development of the political ideas of Wordsworth and Shelley.
M.A., Wales, 1938.

1339. ROSSER, G.C.
The influence of the French revolutinnary theorists, (Voltaire, Rousseau, D'Holbach etc.)
upon Shelley.
M.A., Wales, 1939.

1340. SHOEMAKER, M.C.
The myth of power: change and imagination in Shelley's poetry.
Ph.D., Syracuse, 1974.
DA 36 6716A

1341. UPHAM, M.R.
Shelley's utopian socialism.
M.Sc., Bristol, 1972.

1342. WHITEHOUSE, F.
The crusade of Shelley against tyranny.
M.A., Birmingham, 1922.

1343. WISENTHAL, J.L.
Shelley and British radicalism, 1810-1900.
B.Litt., Oxford, 1966.

ALAN SILLITOE

1344. BURNS, J.W.
An examination of elements of socialist realism in five novels of Alan Sillitoe.
Ph.D., George Peabody College of Teachers, 1975.
DA 36 2213A

TOBIAS GEORGE SMOLLETT

1345. EASTWOOD, W.
Smollett as critic of social conditions in 18th century England.
M.A., Sheffield, 1949.

1346. FIEBERLING, J.E.
The real substantial chivalry: character and society in Smollett's politics.
Ph.D., Johns Hopkins, 1975.
DA 36 4505A

C.P. SNOW

1347. BOAK, G.S.
Personal and theoretical politics in the writings of C.P. Snow.
M.A., Durham, 1977.

1348. GOODWIN, D.F.
The fiction of C.P. Snow.
Ph.D., Iowa, 1966.
DA 27 3009A

1349. GULLIVER, A.F.
The political novels of Trollope and Snow.
Ph.D., Connecticut, 1969.
DA 30 0684A

H.G. WELLS

1350. SQUIRES, E.L.
The necessity for self-awakening in the scientific romances and early social novels
of H.G. Wells.
Ph.D., California, Davis, 1966.
DA 28 0243A

MARY WOLLSTONECRAFT

1351. PUSTON, C.H.
Mary Wollstonecraft's *A vindication of the rights of woman*: a critical and annotated
edition.
Ph.D., Nebraska, 1973.
DA 34 2575A

WILLIAM WORDSWORTH

1352. CHARD, L.F.
Wordsworth's radical career.
Ph.D., Duke, 1962.
DA 23 4674A

1353. MacGILLIVRAY, J.R.
Wordsworth and his revolutionary acquaintances, 1791-97.
Ph.D., Harvard, 1932.

1354. TODD, F.M.
Wordsworth's political development.
Ph.D., University College, London, 1948.

1355. VENIS, L.D.
The aesthetics and politics of social class in Wordsworth's early poetry, 1789-98.
Ph.D., California, Los Angeles, 1978.
DA 39 6105A

LIVING STANDARDS

1356. BEILBY, O.J.
The productivity of labour and standards of living in British agriculture and a
comparison with selected countries abroad.
B.Litt., Oxford, 1935.

1357. BUTLER, J.M.
The farm worker's standard of living: a study of conditions in Shropshire in 1939.
M.Sc, London, External, 1946.

1358.   FLEISCHMAN, R.K.
Conditions of life among the cotton workers of south eastern Lancashire during the
Industrial Revolution, 1780-1850.
Ph.D., State University of New York, 1973.
DA 34 0699A

1359.   GOLDIE, M.E.
The standard of living of the Scottish farm workers in selected areas at the time
of the first two statistical accounts.
M.Sc., Edinburgh, 1971-72.

1360.   HARGRAVE, J.
Social and economic conditions in the industrial towns of the West Riding of Yorkshire
in the hungry forties.
M.A., Leeds, 1940.

1361.   HAYES, S.
A study of the consumer practice of urban working class families in Cork City.
M.Soc.Sc., National University of Ireland, 1971-72.

1362.   HILL, A.B.
A physiological and economic study of the diets of workers in rural areas as compared
with those of workers resident in urban districts.
Ph.D., London, 1926.

1363.   KEENLEYSIDE, A.M.
A study of the social conditions of the working classes in England, 1815-1820.
M.A., Toronto, 1927.

1364.   LILL-RICHARDSON, T.
The standard of living controversy 1790-1840, with special reference to the agricultural
labourer.
Ph.D., Hull, 1977.

1365.   McCABE, A.T.
The standard of living in Liverpool and Merseyside, 1850-75.
M.Litt., Lancaster, 1974.

1366.   NICHOLSON, J.L.
Variations in working-class family expenditure.
M.Sc., L.S.E., 1949.

1367.   ODDY, D.J.
The working class diet, 1886-1914.
Ph.D., L.S.E., 1971.

1368.   PARSONS, S.
The standard of living of the working class during the Industrial Revolution, with
special reference to Devon.
M.A., Exeter, 1978.

1369.   REES, J.M.
A comparative view of the cost of living and standard of life and comfort, obtaining
in a new and in an old country, as exemplified in the cases of South Africa and England.
M.A., Wales, 1911.

1370.   SCHWARZ, L.D.
Conditions of life and work in London, c.1770-1820 with special reference to East London.
D.Phil., Oxford, 1976.

1371.   SHERGOLD, P.R.
The standard of life of manual workers in the first decade of the 20th century: a
comparative study of Birmingham, U.K. and Pittsburgh, U.S.A.
Ph.D., London, 1976.

LUDDITES

1372.   DARVALL, F.O.
The Luddite disturbances and the machinery of order.
Ph.D., London, External, 1933.

1373.   HALSTEAD, D.
The Luddite disturbances throughout the cotton manufacturing area in 1812.
M.A., Liverpool, 1917.

NATIONALISATION AND NATIONALISED INDUSTRIES

1374.   BHALLA, G.S.
Financial administration of nationalised industries in U.K. and India.
Ph.D., L.S.E., 1963.

1375.   BHALLA, S.M.E.
Investment in the British nationalised fuel industries.
M.Sc., L.S.E., 1963.

1376.   BONAVIA, M.R.
The organisation of British railways, 1948-1964.
Ph.D., L.S.E., 1968.

1377. COLLINS, B.
Public corporations: the problems of accountability and control.
Ph.D., National University of Ireland, 1961-62.

1378. COOMBES, D.L.
The Select Committee on the nationalised industries.
B.Litt., Oxford, 1964-65.

1379. CRAIG, R.
Consumer councils and the nationalised industries.
M.A., Strathclyde, 1969-70.

1380. DALVI, G.R.
Public control of public enterprise in India and Great Britain: a comparative study.
Ph.D., L.S.E., 1957-58.

1381. DAVIES, A.J.
A comparative study of public ownership in Australia and the United Kingdom since
World War II, with special reference to transport and electricity.
M.Sc., L.S.E., 1961.

1382. EL-FEKI, M.Z.
A comparative study of public enterprise in Great Britain, France and Belgium.
Ph.D., Leeds, 1966.

1383. GRAHAM, G.E.
The organisational structure of the National Coal Board.
Ph.D., L.S.E., 1963.

1384. HIGHAM, R.D.S.
Britain and Imperial Airways, 1918-1939: a case study in nationalisation.
Ph.D., Harvard, 1957.

1385. JENCKS, C.E.
The impact of nationalisation on working conditions in British coal mining.
Ph.D., South California, Berkeley, 1964.
DA 25 3873A

1386. JONES, L.R.
Prices and public policy: the nationalised industries.
M.Com., Birmingham, 1970-71.

1387. JONES, W.F.
Nationalisation and accountability: a study of the problems arising from the
control of the public corporation.
M.A., Nottingham, 1954-55.

1388. KELLY, D.W.
Administrative problems of operational management in nationalised industries.
Ph.D., Wales, 1954-55.

1389. KELLY, D.W.
The study of the administration of the coal industry in Great Britain since 1946
with special reference to the problem of decentralisation.
M.A., Wales, 1952-53.

1390. LEE, N.
Factors responsible for the financial results of British railways, 1948-58.
Ph.D., L.S.E., 1963.

1391. LONG, M.F.
The price of coal: a study of the policies of the National Coal Board.
Ph.D., Chicago, 1960-61.

1392. MACDONALD, A.W.H.
The schemes for compensation in the nationalisation acts.
M.Sc., London, External, 1962.

1393. MUI, H.-C.
The emergence of the nationalisation issue in the coal-mining industry of
Great Britain, 1893-1919.
Ph.D., Columbia, 1950.
DA 11 0324

1394. OSTERGAARD, G.N.
Public ownership in Great Britain: a study on the origin and development of socialist
ideas concerning the control and administration of publicly owned industries and services.
D.Phil., Oxford, 1953.

1395. OVENDEN, K.W.
The renationalisation of the iron and steel industry, 1964-67: a study in the
legislative politics.
D.Phil., Oxford, 1971-72.

1396. PLOWMAN, R.J.
The Miners' Federation of Great Britain and nationalisation: a study of the Sankey
Commission, 1919.
Ph.D., Catholic University of America, 1971.
DA 32 3932A

1397. RACHID, A.R.H.
British nationalised transport: a study of the administration of a public concern.
B.Litt., Glasgow, 1962-63.

1398. ROSS, G.W.
The Labour Party and the iron and steel industry, 1945-51.
M.Sc., L.S.E., 1964.

1399. SABINE, J.A.
Ministerial control of nationalised industries.
M.A.(Econ.), Manchester, 1961-62.

1400. SHARMA, A.K.
Management training and development in some nationalised industries in the United Kingdom.
Ph.D., Birmingham, 1973-74.

1401. SHEPHERD, W.G.
Prices and investment in public firms: the British fuel industries.
Ph.D., Yale, 1962-63.

1402. SIMONS, R.B.
The path to nationalisation: the British coal industry, 1919-1946.
Ph.D., Chicago, 1952.

1403. STEWART, F.G.
Consultative councils in the nationalised gas and electricity industries.
M.A., Liverpool, 1959-60.

1404. VIGREN, N.H.
The effect of nationalisation on the exercise of public control over industry.
B.Litt., Oxford, 1952-53.

1405. WEINER, H.E.
British trade unionism and nationalisation, 1868-1945: the evolution of the nationalisation policies of the British Trades Union Congress.
Ph.D., Columbia, 1957.
DA <u>17</u> 1490

1406. WITHANA, R.
Grants policy to nationalised industries, with reference to London transport.
M.Com., Birmingham, 1971-72.

NEWSPAPERS AND PERIODICALS

1407. BERRIDGE, Mrs. V.S. (née Cook)
Popular journalism and working-class attitudes, 1854-86: a study of <u>Reynold's Newspaper</u>, <u>Lloyd's Weekly Newspaper</u> and the <u>Weekly Times</u>.
Ph.D., London, 1976.

1408. CALHOUN, D.F.
Radicalism and socialism in the English reviews, 1883-1900.
Ph.D., Chicago, 1959.

1409. COLBURN, A.M.B.
<u>The Economist</u>, 1860-1877: mid-Victorian moderate liberalism, a study in paradox.
Ph.D., Radcliffe, 1957.

1410. COLTHAM, S.W.
George Potter and the <u>Bee-Hive</u> newspaper.
D.Phil., Oxford, 1956.

1411. COOLSON, J.G.
The evolution of selected major English socialist periodicals, 1883-1889.
(Justice, Commonweal, Our Corner, Today.)
Ph.D., The American University, 1973.
DA <u>34</u> 3291A

1412. DAWN, A.F.
The history of the freedom of speech and of the press in England since 1900.
M.Sc., L.S.E., 1933.

1413. DOWNING, J.D.H.
Some aspects of the presentation of industrial relations and race relations in some major British news media.
Ph.D., London, External, 1974.

1414. FRASER, D.
Newspapers and opinion in three Midland cities, 1800-1850.
(Leicester, Birmingham, Nottingham.)
M.A., Leeds, 1962.

1415. HAPPS, M.E.
The Sheffield newspaper press and parliamentary reform, 1787-1832.
B.Litt., Oxford, 1974.

1416. HOLLIS, P.L.
The unstamped press in London and the taxes on knowledge, 1830-6.
D.Phil., Oxford, 1968.

1417. JONES, D.M.
The Liberal press and the rise of Labour: a study with particular reference to Leeds
and Bradford, 1850-1895.
Ph.D., Leeds, 1973.

1418. LUKE, H.J.
Drums for the vulgar: a study of some Radical publishers and publications of
early 19th century London.
Ph.D., Texas, 1963.
DA 24 2893A

1419. McCUE, D.L.
Daniel Isaac Eaton and Politics for the People.
Ph.D., Columbia, 1974.
DA 35 6148A

1420. McKEOWAN, M.D.
The principles and politics of the Manchester Guardian under C.P. Scott to 1914.
Ph.D., Case Western Reserve, 1972.

1421. MENNELL, J.E.
William T. Stead: social politics and the new journalism.
Ph.D., Iowa, 1967.
DA 28 2179A

1422. MILNE, J.M.
The press in Northumberland and Durham, 1868 to 1906.
M.Litt., Newcastle, 1969.

1423. MONCURE, J.A.
James Wilson and the Economist, 1805-1860.
Ph.D., Columbia, 1960.
DA 20 4642

1424. MOORE, M.C.
The history of the agitation against the stamp duty on newspapers, 1830-1855.
M.A., King's College, London, 1935.

1425. MOUNTJOY, P.A.
The working-class religious periodical press, 1850-75.
M.Litt., Cambridge, 1976.

1426. NORLING, B.
Mirror of illusions: political opinions of the English Liberal press, 1919-1939.
Ph.D., Notre Dame, 1955.
DA 15 0401

1427. OSBURN, J.D.
Lloyd Jones, Labour journalist, 1871-1878: a study in British working class thought.
Ph.D., Oklahoma, 1969.
DA 30 2947A
/Working-class journalist; support for co-operation and trade unionism;
secretary of the Labour Representation League./

1428. PYENSON, S.S.
Low scientific culture in London and Paris, 1820-1875.
Ph.D., Pennsylvania, 1976.
DA 37 7277A
/Includes a study of "mechanics'" magazines/

1429. READ, D.
Press and people, 1790-1850: opinion in three English cities.
(Leeds, Manchester, Sheffield.)
Ph.D., Sheffield, 1961.

1430. RYGH, A.R.
English periodicals and the democratic movement, 1865-85.
Ph.D., South Carolina, 1960.
DA 21 1547A

1431. SAMA, A.
The Times and the women's suffrage movement, 1900-1918.
M.Litt., St. Andrews, 1974-75.

1432. SPANN, G.R.
The British periodical press and political opinion, 1860-1880.
Ph.D., Pennsylvania, 1974.
DA 35 2196A

1433. STREICHER, L.H.
The political imagery in the caricatures of David Low.
Ph.D., Wisconsin, 1965.
DA 26 0531A

1434. WICKWAR, W.H.
The struggle for the freedom of the press, 1819-1832.
M.A., London, 1926.

1435. WIENER, J.H.
The movement to repeal the "taxes in knowledge", 1825-1840: a study in British working-class radicalism.
Ph.D., Cornell, 1965.
DA 26 6012

ROBERT OWEN AND OWENITES

1436. ALLEY, S.
Robert Owen and New Lanark.
M.Sc., Strathclyde, 1974.

1437. BAPTISTE, R.E.
Education and the search for Utopia: the educational theories and experiments of Robert Owen and Charles Fourier.
Ph.D., Boston, 1968-69.

1438. BLACK, A.M.
The educational work of Robert Owen.
Ph. D., St. Andrews, 1949.

1439. BROWNING, M.M.
Robert Owen and the New Lanark institution, 1800-25.
M.Ed., Glasgow, 1970.

1440. DALTON, G.
Robert Owen and Karl Polanyi as socio-economic critics and reformers of industrial capitalism.
Ph.D., Oregon, 1959.
DA 20 1635A

1441. EISEL, W.C.
The social views of Robert Owen: their source and their influence on the social reform movement since his time.
M.Litt., Durham, 1934.

1442. FRASER, F.
Robert Owen and Christian Socialism.
Ph.D., Edinburgh, 1927.

1443. GARNETT, R.G.
Co-operation and the Owenite-Socialist communities in Britain, 1825-45.
Ph.D., London, External, 1970.

1444. KALIM, M.S.
The use of Shelley in the writings of the Owenites during the 1830s and 1840s.
M.A., Birkbeck College, London, 1960.

1445. KNIGHT, F.L.P.
Owenite socialism in the period 1817-1840.
M.A., Manchester, 1967.

1446. LIGHTFOOT, A.
The educational philosophy and practices of Robert Owen: an educational iconoclast of the 19th century.
Ph.D., Marquette, 1969.
DA 29 2973A

1447. LLOYD, E.
Robert Owen and social legislation.
M.A., Wales (Aberystwyth), 1932.

1448. RAWSON, M.E.
Robert Owen and the Soviet kolkhozy.
M.A., British Columbia, 1952.

1449. SILVER, H.
Robert Owen and the concept of popular education.
M.Ed., Hull, 1964.

1450. TURNER, D.A.
The educational influence of Robert Owen in England with particular reference to the development of infant schools in England, 1819-39.
M.Phil., London, 1969.

POLITICAL PARTIES AND MOVEMENTS

A.   LABOUR POLITICAL PARTIES AND MOVEMENTS

Independent Labour Party

1451.   COOPER, S.
John Wheatley: a study in Labour history.
M.Litt., Glasgow, 1974.

1452.   DENOMME, M.C.
The Independent Labour Party and the problem of unemployment, 1921-29.
Ph. D., Catholic University of America, 1971.
DA 33 6920A

1453.   DOWSE, R.E.
The Independent Labour Party, 1918-1932 with special reference to its relationship
with the Labour Party.
Ph.D., London, External, 1962.

1454.   DRAKE, H.J.O.
A biography of John Lister of Shibden Hall, first treasurer of the Independent
Labour Party.
Ph.D., Bradford, 1973.

1455.   HORNBY, S.
Left-wing pressure groups in the British Labour movement, 1930-1940: some aspects of
the relations between the Labour left and the official leadership with special
reference to the experience of the I.L.P. and the Socialist League.
M.A., Liverpool, 1965-66.

1456.   MARWICK, A.J.B.
The Independent Labour Party, 1918-32.
B.Litt., Oxford, 1960.

1457.   PELLING, H.M.
Origins and early history of the Independent Labour Party, 1880-1900.
Ph.D., Cambridge, 1951.

1458.   REID, F.
The early life and political development of James Keir Hardie, 1856-92.
D.Phil., Oxford, 1969.

1459.   SACKS, B.
The Independent Labour Party during the World War.
Ph.D., Stanford, 1934.

1460.   SMITH, C.
A comparison of the philosophy and tactics of the I.L.P. with those of the Labour
Party in England, 1924-31.
Ph.D., Chicago, 1936.

1461.   SOLBERG, C.T.
Independent Labour Party, 1893-1918.
B.Litt., Oxford, 1939.

1462.   THWAITES, P.J.
The Independent Labour Party, 1938-50.
Ph.D., London, 1976.

1463.   WOOLVEN, G.B.
Publications of the Independent Labour Party, 1893-1932.
Dip.Lib.+ University College, London, 1967.

Labour Party

-   General studies

1464.   ALDERMAN, R.K.
Discipline in the Parliamentary Labour Party from the formation of the Labour
Representation Committee in 1900 to 1964.
Ph.D., London, External, 1971.

1465.   BJÖRN, L.
Labor parties and the redistribution of income in capitalist democracies.
Ph.D., University of North Carolina at Chapel Hill, 1976.
DA 38 1055A
/Sweden, Denmark, United Kingdom, U.S.A. and Australia; 1920-1970.7

1466.   BONNER, J.
The British Labour Party.
M.A., Liverpool, 1954.

1467.   STUBBS, B.
The attitude of the British Labour Party to the Irish question, 1906-1951.
M.Phil., L.S.E., 1974.

- Origins and early history

1468. BROWN, G.
Some problems related to the rise of the Labour Party: a study of North Lanarkshire, 1885-1914.
M.A., Edinburgh, 1972.

1469. GOOD, D.
Economic and political origins of the Labour Party, 1854-1906.
Ph.D., L.S.E., 1936.

1470. HASSAM, S.E.
The Parliamentary Labour Party and its relations with the Liberals, 1910-14.
M.Litt., Aberdeen, 1967.

1471. HILL, J.
Working-class politics in Lancashire, 1885-1906: a regional study in the origins of the Labour Party.
Ph.D., Keele, 1971.

1472. McKIBBIN, R.I.
Evolution of a National Party: Labour's political organisation, 1910-24.
D.Phil., Oxford, 1970.

1473. MILLER, J.
The rise of Labour representation in Parliament.
Ph.D., Iowa, 1942.

1474. POIRIER, P.P.
The advent of the British Labour Party.
Ph.D., Harvard, 1954.

1475. PURDUE, A.W.
Parliamentary elections in North East England, 1900-1906: the advent of Labour.
M.Litt., Newcastle, 1974.

1476. SPOONER, R.T.
An examination of the Labour Party during its formative years, 1900-20.
M.A., Birmingham, 1946.

1477. TICHELAR, M.
The Labour Party and agricultural policy, 1912-14.
M.A.*, Warwick, 1975-76.

- Inter-war period

1478. BARKER, B.
The politics of propaganda: a study in the theory of educational socialism.
M.Phil., York, 1972.

1479. BROOKSHIRE, J.H.
British Labour recovery: Labour between the General Elections of 1931 and 1935.
Ph.D., Vanderbilt, 1970.
DA 31 2834A

1480. CLINE, C.A.
Recruits to the Labour Party, 1914-1931.
Ph.D., Bryn Mawr, 1957.
DA 19 0308

1481. DUGDALE, K.
Conservatives, Liberals and Labour in Yorkshire, 1918-1929.
M.A., Sheffield, 1968.

1482. GOLANT, W.
The political development of C.R. Attlee to 1935.
B.Litt., Oxford, 1968.

1483. HOWARD, C.J.
Henderson, MacDonald and the leadership in the Labour Party 1914-22.
Ph.D., Cambridge, 1978.

1484. MALAMENT, B.C.
British politics and the crisis of 1931.
Ph.D., Yale, 1969.

1485. PALMIERI, F.L.
Alienation and the persistence of the left-wing in the British Labour Party, 1918-39: a case study of the Miners' Federation of Great Britain.
M.Phil., Sussex, 1973.

1486. ROBERTS, D.M.
Hugh Dalton and the Labour Party in the 1930s.
Ph.D., Council for National Academic Awards, 1978.

- 1939 - 1945

1487. ROTH, I.M.
The Labour Party in the Second World War.
Ph.D., Stanford, 1957.
DA 17 2588

1488. TAYLOR, I.H.
War and the development of Labour's domestic programme 1937-47.
Ph.D., London, 1978.

- 1945 - and contemporary

1489. CASE, L.A.
The Parliamentary Left Wing of the British Labour Party, 1964-68.
Ph.D., Columbia, 1970.
DA 33 5788A

1490. FREEMAN, J.S.
A study of the reasons for membership of a constituency Labour Party.
M.Sc., L.S.E., 1951.

1491. GODFREY, R.J.
Labour and capital: the development of social democratic revisionist theory and
policy within the British Labour Party.
M.A., Sussex, 1976.

1492. GOODMAN, E.J.
Hugh Gaitskill and the 'modernisation' of the Labour Party.
Ph.D., Nebraska, 1965.
DA 26 5526

1493. GORE, J.V.
The miners' groups in the Parliamentary Labour Party.
M.A*, Sheffield, 1970.

1494. HALE, T.F.
The British Labour Party and the Monarchy.
Ph.D., Kentucky, 1972.
DA 33 5087A

1495. HASELER, S.M.A.
Revisionism in the Labour Party, 1951-1964.
Ph.D., L.S.E., 1967.

1496. HOWELL, D.
The restatement of socialism in the Labour Party, 1947-1961.
Ph.D., Manchester, 1970-71.

1497. KRUG, M.M.
Aneurin Bevan: the cautious rebel.
Ph.D., Chicago, 1960.

1498. LOEWENBERG, G.
The effect of governing on the British Labour Party.
Ph.D., Cornell, 1954.
DA 15 1103,

1499. McKENZIE, R.T.
British political parties: the distribution of power within the Conservative
and Labour Parties.
Ph.D., L.S.E., 1954-55.

1500. McNEVIN, M.T.
The Left Wing in the British Labour Party: 1951 to 1955.
B.Litt., Oxford, 1964-65.

1501. MARTIN, A.
The revision of gradualist socialism: C.A.R. Crosland and the ideology of the
British Labour Party.
Ph.D., Columbia, 1967.
DA 28 5119A

1502. MASON, W.L.
Cognitive foundations of stability in the electoral support of the British
Labour Party.
Ph.D., Minnesota, 1967.
DA 28 1108A

1503. MUSHOLLAND, E.J.
An economic analysis of the political behaviour of the British Labour Party.
Ph.D., Boston College, 1974.
DA 35 3241A

1504. MUSSEN, W.A.
Socialism and the British Parliamentary Labour Party, 1945-1975.
Ph.D., University of Connecticut, 1977.
DA 38 5025A

1505. PIPER, J.R.
The unofficial opposition: Labour Party backbenchers in the British House of
Commons, 1966-1970.
Ph.D., Cornell, 1972.
DA 33 5797A

1506. POPHAM, G.T.
Some revisions of Socialist thought on the Labour Party, 1951-1961.
Ph.D., Leicester, 1963-64.

1507. RUSH, M.D.
The selection of parliamentary candidates in the Conservative and Labour Parties.
Ph.D., Sheffield, 1965.

1508. SEYD, C.P.
Factionalism within the Labour Party: a case study of the Campaign for Democratic
Socialism.
M.Phil., Southampton, 1967-68.

1509. SILVERMAN, L.
The political sociology of the contemporary Labour Party in Britain.
Ph.D., L.S.E., 1966.

1510. STECK, H.J.
Factionalism, leadership and ideology in the British Labour Party, 1951-59.
Ph,D., Cornell, 1967.
DA 28 4682A

1511. WARDE, A.
Ideology, strategy and intra-party division in the British Labour Party, 1956-1974.
Ph.D., Leeds, 1976.

        - Local constituency parties

1512. BAXTER, R.J.
The Liverpool Labour Party, 1918-63.
D.Phil., Oxford, 1969.

1513. BERRY, D.R.
The significance of party membership: rank and file members in a Liverpool constituency.
M.A., Liverpool, 1966-67.

1514. BOCHEL, J.M.
Activists in the Conservative and Labour Parties: a study of ward secretaries in
Manchester.
M.A., Manchester, 1965-66.

1515. COX, D.
The rise of the Labour Party in Leicester.
M.A., Leicester, 1959.

1516. DEAN, K.J.
Parliamentary elections and party organisations in Walsall, 1906-45.
M.A., Birmingham, 1969.

1517. FAIRLIE, L.D.
Secretary/agents in the British Conservative and Labour Parties.
Ph.D., Indiana, 1973.
DA 34 4343A

1518. HINDESS, B.
Politics and urban structure: the case of the Liverpool Labour Party.
M.A., Liverpool, 1966-67.

1519. THOMPSON, P.R.
London working-class politics and the formation of the London Labour Party, 1885-1914.
D.Phil., Oxford, 1963.

1520. WAUGH, A.
The Sheffield City Labour Party in the post-war period.
M.A.*, Sheffield, 1974.

1521. WOOD, J.
The Labour left in the constituency Labour Parties, 1945-51.
M.A., Warwick, 1977.

1522. WOOD, S.M.
Political participation: a comparative study of the Labour parties and Conservative
associations of two Scottish constituencies.
Ph.D., Edinburgh, 1970-71.

Labour Governments

- 1924

1523. ELEY, S.R.
Britain, France and the German problem, 1924: Ramsay MacDonald at the Foreign Office.
M.A., Kent, 1971-72.

1524. HARRISON, S.J.
The British General Election of 1924.
Ph.D., Catholic University of America, 1971.
DA 32 5149A

1525. LYMAN, R.W.
The Labour Government of 1924 in Great Britain.
Ph.D., Harvard, 1954.

1526. POLLARD, S.M.
The first minority Labour Government and Labour Party policy, 1918-1924.
M.A., London, 1977.

1527. SCHNEIDER, F.D.
The first British Labour Government.
Ph.D., Stanford, 1950.

- 1929-1931

1528. CARLTON, D.
The foreign policy of the second Labour administration, 1929-31, with special
reference to disarmament, foreign trade and the German situation.
Ph. D., L.S.E., 1966.

1529. JANEWAY, W.H.
The economic policy of the Second Labour Government, 1929-31.
Ph.D., Cambridge, 1971.

1530. ROBERTS, J.A.
Economic aspects of the unemployment policy of the government 1929-31.
Ph.D., L.S.E., 1978.

1531. ROWE, E.A.
The British General Election of 1929.
B.Litt., Oxford, 1960.

1532. SKIDELSKY, R.J.A.
The Labour Government and the unemployment question, 1929-1931.
D.Phil., Oxford, 1968.

1533. SNYDER, R.K.
The second British Labour Government and the General Election of 1931.
M.A., Stanford, 1934.

- 1945-1951

1534. DAY, A.J.
Location of industry and population: post-war policy in the West Midlands.
M.Com., Birmingham, 1954-55.

1535. FISS, J.
The theory and non-practice of British socialism.
Ph.D., New York, 1968.
DA 30 4509A

1536. GRAVES, H.D.
British atomic weapons development and the Labour Government, 1945-51.
B.Litt., Oxford, 1970-71.

1537. HAQQI, S.A.H.
The colonial policy of the Labour Government, 1945-51.
Ph.D., L.S.E., 1958.

1538. JACQUES, D.
The state control of the location of industry in Great Britain - mainly from 1945 to 1950.
M.Sc., Cambridge, 1954-55.

1539. ROGOW, A.A.
The Labour Government and British industry, 1945-51.
Ph.D., Princeton, 1953.
DA 14 0386.

- 1964-1970

1540. JOHN, R.A.
Economic concentration and Labour Government policy, 1964-70.
M.A., Sussex, 1970-71.

1541. MORGAN, J.P.
The House of Lords and the Labour Government, 1964-70.
D.Phil., Oxford, 1972-73.

1542. SCHMIDMAN, J.T.
British unions and economic planning.
Ph.D., Wisconsin, 1968.
DA 29 2821A
(Economic policies of Wilson administration, 1964-68.)

1543. WILKINSON, N.L.
British energy policy under the Wilson administration (1964-70).
Ph.D., North Carolina, 1973.
DA 34 5892A

Northern Ireland Labour Party

1544. GRAHAM, J.A.V.
The consensus-forming strategy of the Northern Ireland Labour Party, 1949-68.
M.Soc.Sc., Queen's University, Belfast, 1972-73.

1545. HARBINSON, J.F.
A history of the Northern Ireland Labour Party.
M.Sc.(Econ.), Queen's University, Belfast, 1966.

Co-operative Party

1546. ARDITTI, C.I.
The history of the Co-operative Party in Manchester and Salford.
M.A.(Econ.), Manchester, 1953.

1547. CARBERY, T.F.
An examination and evaluation of the Co-operative Party of the Co-operative Union Ltd.
Ph.D., London, External, 1966.

1548. FLICKINGER, R.S.
The Co-operative Party of Great Britain.
Ph.D., Syracuse, 1972.
DA 33 0370A

Common Wealth Party

1549. CALDER, A.L.R.
The Common Wealth Party, 1942-5.
D.Phil., Sussex, 1968.

Communist Party and Organisations

1550. COLLINS, H.J.
England and the First International, 1864-1872.
D.Phil., Oxford, 1959.

1551. DENVER, D.T.
The Communist Party in Dundee: a study of activists.
B.Phil., Dundee, 1971-72.

1552. DONOGHUE, A.P.
History of the Communist Party of Great Britain, 1939-46.
Ph.D., Stanford, 1953.
DA 13 0907

1553. GOLDSTEIN, R.
The Comintern and British Communism, 1921-1926.
Ph.D., Columbia, 1972.
DA 37 0531A

1554. GREENWALD, N.D.
Communism and British Labour: a study of British Labour Party politics, 1933-1939.
Ph.D., Columbia, 1958.
DA 19 0309

1555. JONES, D.I.L.
The 'United Front' in the Communist International: the debate on the affiliation of
the British Communist Party to the Labour Party, 1920-1925.
M.Phil., Ulster, 1977.

1556. KENDALL, W.F.H.
The formation of the Communist Party of Great Britain, 1918-21.
B.Litt., Oxford, 1966.

1557. MacFARLANE, L.J.
The origins of the Communist Party of Great Britain and its early history, 1920-1927.
Ph.D., London, External, 1962.

1558. MacINTYRE, S.F.
Marxism in Britain, 1917-33.
Ph.D., Cambridge, 1976.

1558A. MILOTTE, M.H.
     Communist politics in Ireland, 1916-1945.
     Ph.D., Queen's University, Belfast, 1977.

1559. NEWTON, K.
     British Communism: the sociology of a radical political party.
     Ph.D., Cambridge, 1966.

1560. RICHARDS, N.A.C.
     The 1929 debates in the Society of Marxist Historians.
     M.Sc., Salford, 1972-73.

Socialist Labour Party

1561. CHEWTER, D.M.
     The history of the Socialist Labour Party of Great Britain from 1902 until 1921 with
     special reference to the development of its ideas.
     B.Litt., Oxford, 1965.

1562. VERNON, H.R.
     The Socialist Labour Party and the working class movement on the Clyde, 1903-21.
     M.Phil., Leeds, 1967.

"Popular Front" Movement

1563. CALTON, J.N.
     The party that never was: a study of the campaign for political integration among
     left-wing and radical groups in Britain, 1929-1939.
     Ph.D., Washington, 1970.
     DA 31 1720A

1564. EATWELL, R.
     The Labour Party and the Popular Front Movement in Britain in the 1930s.
     D.Phil., Oxford, 1976.

B.   RADICALISM AND PARLIAMENTARY REFORM MOVEMENTS (see also CHARTISM and LIBERALISM)

1565. ALDSTADT, D. .
     The radical movement in England, 1806-1814.
     Ph.D., Case Western Reserve, 1968.
     DA 29 4410A

1566. ALLAN, M.B.G.
     The Reform movement on Tyneside and Wearside, 1812-1832.
     M.A., Liverpool, 1919.

1567. ASPINWALL, B.
     William Smith, M.P., 1756-1835 and his importance in the movements for parliamentary
     reform, religious toleration, and the abolition of the slave trade.
     M.A., Manchester, 1962.

1568. BARTLE, G.F.
     The political career of Sir John Bowring, 1792-1872, between 1820 and 1849.
     M.A., London, 1959.

1569. BELCHEM, J C.
     Radicalism as a "platform" agitation in the periods, 1816-1821 and 1848-1851; with
     special reference to the leadership of Henry Hunt and Feargus O'Connor.
     D.Phil., Sussex, 1975.

1570. BELL, A.D.
     The Reform League from its origin to the passing into law of the Reform Act of 1867.
     D.Phil., Oxford, 1961.

1571. BENNETT, J.A.
     A study in London radicalism: the Democratic Association, 1837-1841.
     M.A., Sussex, 1968.

1572. BETKA, J.A.
     The ideology and rhetoric of Thomas Paine: political justification through metaphor.
     Ph.D., Rutgers, 1975.
     DA 36 3078A

1573. BILLINGTON, L.
     Some connections between British and American reform movements with special
     reference to the anti-slavery movement.
     M.Litt., Bristol, 1966.

1574. BLACK, E.C.
     The Association: the growth and development of extra-parliamentary political
     organisations from 1779-1793.
     Ph.D., Harvard, 1958.

1575. BONWICK, M.H.R.
     The radicalism of Sir Francis Burdett (1770-1844) and early nineteenth century "radicalisms".
     Ph.D., Cornell, 1967.
     DA 28 3103A

1576. BOYER, B.L.
Reform and revolution: the Parliamentary debates on the Reform Bill of 1832.
Ph.D., Claremont Graduate School, 1977.
DA 37 7283A

1577. BRAND, C.F.
The movement for parliamentary reform in England from 1832 to 1867.
Ph.D., Harvard, 1923.

1578. BROADBENT, A.
The new radicals and the making of programme politics, 1870-1880.
Ph.D., London, 1977.

1579. BRUNSDON, P.J.
The Association of the Friends of the People, 1792-1795.
M.A., Manchester, 1961-62.

1580. BUCKLEY, J.K.
Joseph Parkes of Birmingham and the part he played in the reform movements to 1845.
M.A., London, 1924.

1581. BURNELL, P.J.
The political and social thought of Thomas Paine, 1737-1809.
Ph.D., Warwick, 1971-72.

1582. CHURGIN, N.H.
Major John Cartwright: a study in radical parliamentary reform, 1774-1824.
Ph.D., Columbia, 1963.
DA 27 1749A

1583. COMBER, W.H.
Parliamentary reform and the Cornish boroughs, 1800-1870.
M.A., Exeter, 1977.

1584. COTTON, J.N.
Popular movements in Ashton-under-Lyne and district before 1832.
M.Litt., Birmingham, 1977.

1585. COX, N.G.
Aspects of English radicalism: the suppression and re-emergence of the constitutional democratic tradition, 1795-1809.
Ph.D., Cambridge, 1971.

1586. CRAWSHAW, H.N.
Movements for political and social reform in Sheffield, 1792-1832.
M.A., Sheffield, 1954.

1587. CULCHETH, B.
Some aspects of Sheffield radicalism, 1830-70.
M.A., Durham, 1960.

1588. DARNTON, R.C.
Trends in radical propaganda on the eve of the French Revolution, 1782-8.
D.Phil., Oxford, 1965.

1589. DAVIES, M.W.
The debate on democracy at the time of the Second Reform Act, 1867.
M.A., Wales (Cardiff), 1969.

1590. DAVIS, R.W.
William Smith and the politics of dissent, 1791-1828.
M.Litt., Cambridge, 1962.

1591. DENHOLM, A.F.
Some aspects of the radical and democratic career of the first Marquise of Ripon, 1827-1909.
M.A., Wales (Swansea), 1966.

1592. DINWIDDY, J.R.
Parliamentary reform as an issue in English politics, 1800-1860.
Ph.D., London (Makerere University College), 1971.

1593. DITCHFIELD, G.M.
Some aspects of Unitarianism and Radicalism, 1760-1810.
Ph.D., Cambridge, 1968.

1594. DRINKWATER-LUNN, D.
John Cartwright, political education and English radicalism, 1774-94.
D.Phil., Oxford, 1972.

1595. DUFF, G.A.
William Cobbett's agrarian vision of national reform.
Ph.D., Illinois, 1966.
DA 27 3837A

1596. DUNCAN, R.S
British parliamentary Radicalism, 1886-1895: the origins and impact of the Newcastle Program.
Ph.D., Ohio State, 1974.
DA 35 5295A

1597. DUNSMORE, M.R.
The working classes, the Reform League and the reform movement in Lancashire and Yorkshire.
M.A., Sheffield, 1961.

1598. EAGLESTONE, A.A.
Major John Cartwright: his place in contemporary radical movements.
B.Litt., Oxford, 1930.

1599. EATON, J.W.
Archibald Prentice: a case study in Radicalism.
Ph.D., Kent State, 1973.
DA 34 4149A

1600. ELVINS, W.B.
The reform movement and county politics in Cornwall, 1809-1852.
M.A., Birmingham, 1959.

1601. FEARN, E.
Radical movements in Derby and Derbyshire, 1790-1832.
M.A., Manchester, 1964.

1602. FERGUSON, H.
The Birmingham Political Union, 1830-1832.
Ph.D., Harvard, 1958.

1603. GADIAN, D.S.
A comparative study of popular movements in the North West industrial towns, 1830-50.
Ph.D., Lancaster, 1976.

1604. GADIAN, D.S.
The social history of Oldham radicalism in the 1830s.
M.A.*, Lancaster, 1970.

1605. HONE, J.A.
The ways and means of London radicalism, 179L-1821.
D.Phil., Oxford, 1975.

1606. HOOPER, A.F.
Mid-Victorian radicalism: community and class in Birmingham 1850-80.
Ph.D., London, 1978.

1607. HUCH, R.K.
The radical Lord Radnor: a political biography of William Pleydell-Bouverie,
Viscount Folkestone, third Earl of Radnor, 1799-1869.
Ph.D., Michigan, 1971.
DA 32 6342A

1608. HUNT, W.K.
Effects of the Reform Bill of 1832 on Liverpool.
M.A., Manchester, 1924.

1609. IDDON, F.M.
The reform movement in Northumberland.
M.A., Liverpool, 1923.

1610. JARRETT, J.D.
The Bowood Circle, 1780-1793.
B.Litt., Oxford, 1955.

1611. JONES, I.
David Rees y Cynhyrfwr: astudiaeth o waith y radical ymneilltuol Cymreig, 1801-1869.
(David Rees the Agitator: a study of the work of the Welsh non-conformist radical,
1801-1869.)
M.A., Wales (Bangor), 1971-72.

1612. JOWETT, S.K
Political language and theory of English radicalism, 1778-85.
Ph.D., Manchester, 1976.

1613. KENT, C.A.
Aspects of academic radicalism in mid-Victorian England: a study on the politics of
thought and action, with special relation to Frederic Harrison and John Morley.
D.Phil., Sussex, 1969.

1614. KING, S.T.
James Silk Buckingham, 1786-1858: social and political reformer.
M.A., King's College, London, 1937.

1615. KINSEY, W.W.
Some aspects of Lancashire radicalism, 1816-1821.
M.A., Manchester, 1927.

1616. KINZER, B.L.
The ballot question in English politics, 1830-1832.
Ph.D., Toronto, 1975.
DA 38 3651A

1617. KNOX, E.
The political influence of William Cobbett, 1794-1815.
M.A., Liverpool, 1907.

1618. LEVENTHAL, F.M.
George Howell, 1833-1910: a career in radical politics.
Ph.D., Harvard, 1968.

1619. LEWIS, B.H.
The political ideas of the English Radicals particularly in nonconformist
circles from John Lilburne to John Wilkes.
M.A., Wales, 1925.

1620. LINCOLN, W.E.
Popular radicalism and the beginnings of the new socialist movement in Britain, 1870-85.
Ph.D., University College, London, 1977.

1621. LIVELEY, J.F.
Ideas of parliamentary representation in England, 1815-1832.
M.Litt., Cambridge, 1958.

1622. MACCOBY, S.
English radicalism, 1832-52.
Ph.D., L.S.E., 1934.

1623. MAIN, J.M.
The movement for parliamentary reform in Manchester, 1825-32.
B.Litt., Oxford, 1951.

1624. MASON, F.M.
Charles F.G. Masterman, an Edwardian Radical.
Ph.D., Connecticut, 1974.
DA 35 2181A

1625. MASON, G.C.H.
The radical bequest: continuity in English popular politics, 1799-1832.
M.Phil., York, 1977.

1626. METZGAR, J.V.
Thomas Paine: a study in social and intellectual history.
Ph.D., New Mexico, 1965.
DA 26 6001A

1627. MITCHELL, A.V.
Radicalism and political repression in the north of England, 1791-1797.
M.A., Manchester, 1958.

1628. MONTGOMERY, F.A.
Glasgow radicalism, 1830-48.
Ph.D., Glasgow, 1974.

1629. MOSS, D.J.
Thomas Attwood: the biography of a radical.
D.Phil., Oxford, 1973.

1630. MURIS, C.
The Northern Reform Union, 1858-62.
M.A., Durham, 1953.

1631. MYERS, C.J.
The Victorian critics and the Second Reform Bill.
Ph.D., Toronto, 1967.
DA 29 2221A

1632. NASSOUR, A.J.
The political thought of Thomas Paine.
D.Phil., Oxford, 1947.

1633. NEWMAN, W.J.
Henry Hunt and English working class radicalism, 1812-1832.
Ph.D., Princeton, 1950.
DA 15 0570

1634. NOTT, J.W.
The artisan as agitator: Richard Carlile, 1816-1843.
Ph.D., Wisconsin, 1970.
DA 31 4686A

1635. NURSEY-GRAY, P.F.
Thomas Paine's concept of natural law in eighteenth-century English radicalism.
M.A., Bristol, 1965-66.

1636. OSBORNE, J.W.
William Cobbett and his England: a study in social and political ideas.
Ph.D., Rutgers, 1961.
DA 22 1604

1637. PARKER, D.O.
Social and political agitation in the West Riding of Yorkshire, 1817-19: the
political movement in the West Riding, 1815-32.
M.A., Manchester, 1923.

1638. PLATT, F.D.
The English parliamentary radicals: their collective character, their failure to become
a party and their failure to find a leader; a study in the psycho-sociological sources
of radical behaviour, 1833-1841.
Ph.D., Washington, 1969.
DA 30 2950A

1639. PROCHASKA, A.M.S.
Westminster radicalism, 1807-32.
D.Phil., Oxford, 1975.

1640. RAPP, D.R
Samuel Whitbread, 1764-1815: a social and political study.
Ph.D., Johns Hopkins, 1971.
DA 32 0894A

1641. READ, D.
Peterloo: a study in Manchester political history.
B.Litt., Oxford, 1955.

1642. RIDD-SMITH, J.V.
The influence of the French Revolution on the British radical movement 1789-95.
M.A., Wales (Swansea), 1978.

1643. ROACH, W.M.
Radical reform movements in Scotland, 1815-1822.
Ph.D., Glasgow, 1970.

1644. ROBINSON, K.
Karl Marx, the International Working Men's Association and London radicalism, 1864-1872.
Ph.D., Manchester, 1976.

1645. ROWE, D.J.
London radicalism, 1829-1841 with special reference to the relationship of its middle
and working class components.
M.A., Southampton, 1965.
    (includes a discussion of the development and failure of Chartist movement in London.)

1646. SEAMAN, W.A.L.
British democratic societies in the period of the French Revolution.
Ph.D., University College, London, 1954.

1647. SEYMOUR, C.
The development of democracy in England since 1832 as shown in the reform of
the representative system.
Ph.D., Yale, 1911.

1648. SHARP, B.
Rural radicalism in England.
Ph.D., California, Berkeley, 1971-72.

1649. SHEPS, A.N.
English radicalism and revolutionary America.
Ph.D., Toronto, 1973.
DA 35 1030A

1650. SMITH, C.G.
Joseph Hume, M.P.: political activities, 1818-25.
M.A., Liverpool, 1921.

1651. SMITH, F.B.
The making of the Second Reform Bill.
Ph.D., Cambridge, 1962.

1652. SMITH, H.G.
The reform movement in Birmingham, 1830-1848.
Ph.D., London, External, 1930.

1653. STEINBERG, A.G.R.
The City of Westminster and the British radical movement of the late 18th century.
Ph.D., St. John's, 1976.
DA 37 5290A

1654. STURGIS, J.L.
British parliamentary radicalism, 1846-52.
Ph.D., Toronto, 1972.
DA 34 6578A

1655. TAYLOR, G.C.
Some American reformers and their influence on reform movements in Great Britain, 1830-60.
Ph.D., Edinburgh, 1960.

1656. THOMIS, M.I.
       Nottingham Radicalism, 1785-1835.
       Ph.D., Nottingham, 1966.

1657. URBANSKI, S.W.
       Parliamentary politics, 1796-1832 in an industrializing borough; Preston, Lancashire.
       Ph.D., Emory, 1976.
       DA 37 7914A

1658. WAGER, D.A.
       Welsh politics and parliamentary reform, 1780-1835.
       Ph.D., Wales, 1972.

1659. WALIGORSKI, C.P.
       Radical traditionalism: William Cobbett on the Industrial Revolution.
       Ph.D., Wisconsin, 1973.
       DA 34 3502A

1660. WALKER, E.
       Struggle for the reform of Parliament, 1853-1867.
       Ph.D., Western Reserve, 1964.

1661. WALLACE, R.D.
       Political reform societies in Wales 1832-84.
       Ph. D., Wales, 1978.

1662. WALVIN, J.
       English democratic societies and popular radicalism, 1791-1810.
       D.Phil., York, 1969.

1663. WHALE, G.B.M.
       The causes of the movement for radical parliamentary reform in England between 1763 and
       1789 with special reference to the influence of the so-called Rational Protestants.
       B.Litt., Oxford, 1930.

1664. WILCOCK, C.M.
       The Yorkshire County Association and the reform movement, 1779-80.
       M.A., Manchester, 1953.

1665. WOLFE, S.F.
       The political rhetoric of English radicalism, 1760-1830.
       Ph.D., York University (Canada), 1976.
       DA 37 7770A

1666. ZAGORIN, P. de S.
       A history of English democratic and radical political thought from the Levellers to
       the Restoration.
       Ph.D., Harvard, 1952.

1667. ZEGGER, R.E.
       John Cam Hobhouse at Westminster, 1818-1833.
       Ph.D., Columbia, 1965.
       DA 26 2153

1668. ZIEGLER, P.R.
       Joseph Hume and the Whigs, 1830-41: a study of inter-party co-operation.
       Ph.D., Fordham, 1975.
       DA 36 1749A

1669. ZIMMER, L.B.
       The politics of John Stuart Mill and the Second Reform Bill of 1867 evaluated against
       the background of his political and moral philosophy.
       Ph.D., New York, 1970.
       DA 31 6498A

Anti-Corn Law League

1670. CAMERON, K.J.
       Anti-Corn Law agitations in Scotland with particular reference to the Anti-Corn Law League.
       Ph.D., Edinburgh, 1971.

1671. HINYTZKE, S.E.
       An analysis of the ideas and arguments in the parliamentary corn law speeches of
       Richard Cobden, 1841-1846.
       Ph.D., Pennsylvania State, 1972.
       DA 33 0436A

1672. McCORD, N.
       The activities and organisation of the Anti-Corn Law League, 1838-46.
       Ph.D., Cambridge, 1956.

1673. WILLIAMS, T.H.
       Wales and the corn laws, 1815-46.
       M.A., Wales (Swansea), 1952.

C.   LIBERALISM (especially related to Labour movement)

1674. ADAMS, R.J.
Arms and the wizard: David Lloyd George and the Ministry of Munitions.
Ph.D., California, Santa Barbara, 1972.
DA 34 1199A

1675. ANDERTON, P.
The Liberal Party of Stoke-on-Trent and parliamentary elections, 1862-80: a case
study in Liberal-Labour relations.
M.A., Keele, 1974.

1676. BARKER, M.K.
The formation of Liberal Party policy, 1885-92.
Ph.D., Wales (Swansea), 1972.

1677. BAXENDALE, J.D.
The development of the Liberal Party in England, with special reference to the North-
West, 1886-1900.
D.Phil., Oxford, 1971.

1678. BENTLEY, M.J.
The Liberal mind, 1914-29.
Ph.D., Cambridge, 1974.

1679. BERNSTEIN, G.L.
Liberalism and the Liberal Party in Britain 1899-1908.
Ph.D., Chicago, 1978.
DA 39 2452A

1680. BRADEN, J.A.
The Liberals as a third party in British politics, 1926-1931: a study in political
communication.
Ph.D., Ohio State, 1971.
DA 32 3908A

1681. CAMPBELL, J.M
Lloyd George in British politics, 1922-31.
Ph.D., Edinburgh, 1975.

1682. CLARK, L.A.
The Liberal Party and collectivism, 1886-1906.
M.Litt., Cambridge, 1957.

1683. CLARKE, P.F.
Elections and the electorate in north-west England: an inquiry into the course of
political change, 1910-1914.
Ph.D., Cambridge, 1966.

1684. COLLINI, S.A.
Liberalism and sociology: L.T. Hobhouse and political argument in England, 1880-1914.
Ph.D., Cambridge, 1977.

1685. COOK, C.P.
The Liberal Party in decline.
D.Phil., Oxford, 1974.

1686. CYR, A.I.
The British Liberal Party: a political critique in the collectivist age.
Ph.D., Harvard, 1970-71.

1687. DAVID, E.I.
The Liberal Party during the First World War, with special reference to the split of 1916.
M.Litt., Cambridge, 1968.

1688. DUNCAN, W.G.K.
Liberalism in England, 1880-1914.
Ph.D., L.S.E., 1931.

1689. EBERDT, M.L. Sister
Evolution of Liberalism in England from laissez-faire individualism of the Victorian
compromise to the new Liberalism, 1914: causes for the change of thought and policy.
Ph.D., St. Louis, 1952.

1690. EDSALL, N.C.
The Liberal Party division and decline, 1916-1929.
M.A., L.S.E., 1960.

1691. ELLIOT, D.C.
The Liberal Party in Scotland from the Midlothian Election to the First World War.
Ph.D., Harvard, 1951.

1692. ELLSWORTH, J.W.
Humanistic ethics and Liberal politics: a study of John Stuart Mill's political thought.
Ph.D., Claremont Graduate School, 1963.
DA 26 2300

1693. EMY, H.V.
The Liberal Party and the social problem, 1892-1914.
Ph.D., L.S.E., 1969.

1694. ERNST, D.J.
The social policies of David Lloyd George.
Ph.D., Wisconsin, 1943.

1695. FLETCHER, D.E.
Aspects of Sheffield Liberalism, 1849-1886.
Ph.D., Sheffield, 1972.

1696. GARNIE, D.F.
Bradford: radical city in the Liberal age.
M.Sc., Bradford, 1977.

1697. GRIFFITH, G.E.H.
The Liberal Party and nationalism: 1850-1914.
M.A., Wales (Bangor), 1957.

1698. HAMER, D.A.
John Morley: a political study, with special emphasis on the relationship between
his political thought and practice.
D.Phil., Oxford, 1965.

1699. HARGRAVE, E.C.
The tragic hero in politics: Theodore Roosevelt, David Lloyd George, Firello La Guardia.
Ph.D., Yale, 1963.
DA 25 1313

1700. HEALY, V.J.
John Morley: interpreter of the French enlightenment.
Ph.D., St. Louis, 1961.

1701. HENNESSY, P.J.
The establishment of the Liberal-Labour alliance, 1848-1885.
M.Sc.(Econ.), Wales (Swansea), 1973.

1702. HEPBURN, A.C.
Liberal policies and nationalist politics in Ireland, 1905-1910.
Ph.D., Kent, 1968.

1703. HIGGINBOTHAM, M.
The career of A.J. Mundella with special reference to his Sheffield connections.
M.A., Sheffield, 1941.

1704. HOSKIN, D.G.
The genesis and significance of the 1886 'Home Rule' split in the Liberal Party.
Ph.D., Cambridge, 1964.

1705. HOWARD, T.C.
The Liberal Party in British politics, 1922-1924: a study in the three party system.
Ph.D., Florida State, 1965.
DA 26 1612

1706. INGLE, S.J.
The policy, leadership and organisation of the Liberal Party since 1945.
M.A.(Econ.), Sheffield, 1964-65.

1707. INMAN, W.G.
The British Liberal Party, 1892-1939.
Ph.D., Clark, 1939.

1708. JONES, K.T.
The political philosophy of L.T. Hobhouse.
M.A., Wales (Swansea), 1973.

1709. KELLAS, J.G.
The Liberal Party in Scotland, 1885-1895.
Ph.D., University College, London, 1962.

1710. KEZIRIAN, R.P.
David Lloyd George and the origins of the British welfare state, 1909-1914.
Ph.D., University of California, Santa Barbara, 1976.
DA 38 0959A

1711. KING, A.S.
Some aspects of the history of the Liberal Party in Britain between 1906 and 1914.
D.Phil., Oxford, 1962.

1712. LAWLESS, M.A.
Liberty and class conflict in the 19th-century British liberal state: T.H. Green's
concept of freedom in relation to the development of liberal theory in Britain.
Ph.D., London, 1976.

1713. LIPCHITZ, J.W.
The little loaf and free trade reaction, 1895-1906.
Ph.D., Case Western Reserve, 1970.
DA 31 3476A

1714.   LOWERSON, J.R.
The political career of Sir Edward Baines, 1800-1890.
M.A., Leeds, 1965.

1715.   McCARTHY, J.P.
Hilaire Belloc: critic of the New Liberalism.
Ph.D., Columbia, 1969.
DA 33 2863A

1716.   McEWEN, J.M.
The decline of the Liberal Party in the United Kingdom, 1914-1926.
M.A., Manchester, 1952-53.

1717.   McLEAN, J.J.
Campbell-Bannerman: the New Imperialism and the struggle for leadership within the
Liberal Party, 1892-1906.
Ph.D., Connecticut, 1974.
DA 35 7229A

1718.   MARIZ, G.E.
The life and work of L.T. Hobhouse: a study in the history of ideas.
Ph.D., Missouri-Columbia, 1970.
DA 31 4092A

1719.   MAYER, J.L.
Liberalism and democracy: the significance of L.T. Hobhouse.
Ph.D., Columbia, 1973.
DA 34 3492A

1720.   MURRAY, B.K.
The People's Budget.
Ph.D., Kansas, 1967.
DA 28 4997A

1721.   O'DEA, P.V.
Gladstone and the leadership of the Liberal Party, 1886-1892.
Ph.D., Notre Dame, 1973.
DA 34 4164A

1722.   PETTER, M.E.
Liberals and the Labour Party, 1906-1914.
D.Phil., Oxford, 1974.

1723.   PRICE, R.E.
Lloyd George's pre-parliamentary political career.
M.A., Wales, 1974.

1724.   REES, T.D.M.
The political thought of John Stuart Mill.
M.Litt., Cambridge, 1951.

1725.   ROBERTS, A.W.
The Liberal Party in West Yorkshire, 1885-1906.
Ph.D., Leeds, 1969.

1726.   ROSSI, J.P.
The transformation of the British Liberal Party: decline and revival, 1873-76.
Ph.D., Pennsylvania, 1965.
DA 26 3914

1727.   RUBINSTEIN, B.D.
The decline of the Liberal Party, 1880-1900.
Ph.D., L.S.E., 1956.

1728.   RUSSELL, A.K.
The General Election of 1906.
D.Phil., Oxford, 1962.

1729.   SEAMAN, J.W.
L.T. Hobhouse and the development of Liberal-Democratic theory.
Ph.D., Toronto, 1976.
DA 39 5704A

1730.   SMITH, H.L.
The new Liberal movement in Great Britain, 1888-1914.
Ph.D., Iowa, 1971.
DA 32 2621A

1731.   SNYDER, T.S.
Matthew Arnold and Victorian Liberalism.
Ph.D., Miami, 1972.
DA 33 2310A

1732.   SOFFER, R.
Liberalism and the Liberal attitude to early twentieth century England.
Ph.D., Ratcliffe College, 1962.

1733. STANSKY, P.D.L.
       The leadership of the Liberal Party, 1894-1899.
       Ph.D., Harvard, 1961.

1734. THOMPSON, H.J.
       The new Liberalism in Great Britain: the Liberal mind and party politics in a time
       of crisis and reconstruction, 1890-1914.
       Ph.D., Harvard, 1954.

1735. THORN, J.M.
       An unexplored chapter in recent English history: distributism and the Distributist League.
       Ph.D., University of Wisconsin-Madison, 1976.
       DA 38 0431A

1736. THORNTON, N.S.
       The problems of Liberalism in the thought of John Stuart Mill.
       Ph. D., London, 1969.

1737. VINCENT, J.R.
       The formation of the Liberal Party, 1857-68.
       Ph.D., Cambridge, 1962.

1738. WAITT, E.I.
       The divisions of Liberalism: Newcastle politics, 1870-1902.
       Ph.D., Manchester, 1972.

1739. WALKER, F.F.
       British Liberalism: some philosophic origins - the contributions of Adam Smith,
       Thomas Robert Malthus, Jeremy Bentham and Herbert Spencer.
       Ph.D., Stanford, 1957.
       DA 17 2996

1740. WATKINSON, C.D.
       The Liberal Party on Merseyside in the nineteenth century.
       Ph.D., Liverpool, 1968.

1741. WEBB, H.
       The domestic policies of the Liberal Party of Great Britain, 1906-1914:
       their effect upon the future of the party.
       Ph.D., Brown, 1957.
       DA 18 0641

1742. WEILER, P.H.
       Liberal social theory in Great Britain, 1896-1914.
       Ph.D., Harvard, 1968-69.

1743. WERNER, S.E.
       Reason and reform: the social thought of L.T. Hobhouse.
       Ph.D., Wisconsin, 1973.
       DA 34 5892A

1744. WHITAKER, D.
       The growth of Liberal organisation in Manchester from the 1860s to 1903.
       Ph.D., Manchester, 1956.

1745. WHITE, C.W.
       The historiography of the Edwardian era.
       Ph.D., Duke, 1975.
       DA 35 7240A

1746. WHITE, W.W.
       Acton and Gladstone: their friendship and mutual influence.
       Ph.D., Catholic University of America, 1973.
       DA 34 1229A

1747. WILSON, M.R.
       The new Liberalism in Great Britain and the United States: a study in reform
       thought with special reference to the problem of industrial concentration.
       M.A., Manchester, 1967.

1748. WILSON, T.G.
       The Parliamentary Liberal Party in Britain, 1918-1924.
       D.Phil., Oxford, 1959.

1749. WINTER, H.H.
       The Liberal Party and parliamentary reform, 1832-1867.
       Ph.D., Harvard, 1961.

1750. WRIGHT, R.A.
       Liberal party organization and politics in Birmingham, Coventry and Wolverhampton,
       1886-1914, with particular reference to the development of independent Labour representation.
       Ph.D., Birmingham, 1978.

1751. WRIGLEY, C.J.
       Lloyd George and the labour movement with particular reference to the years 1914-22.
       Ph.D., London, 1974.

1752. ZIMMERMAN, K.C.
       The political thought of John Morley.
       Ph.D., Minnesota, 1967.
       DA 28 3242A

D.   CONSERVATISM

1753. BREISETH, C.N.
British Conservatism and French revolutions: John Wilson Croker's attitudes to
reform and revolution in Britain and France.
Ph.D., Cornell, 1964.
DA 25 1869

1754. DEMPSEY, M.
The political career of Lord Randolph Churchill.
M.A., Liverpool, 1949.

1755. DWYER, F.J.
The rise of Richard Assheton Cross and his work at the Home Office, 1868-80.
B.Litt., Oxford, 1954.

1756. HALL, E.P.
Localism in Joseph Chamberlain's social politics, 1869-1895.
Ph.D., University of Massachusetts, 1977.
DA 38 0428A

1757. HILL, R.L.
The attitude of the Tory Party to labour questions, 1832-46.
B.Litt., Oxford, 1928.

1758. HUGHES, T.O.
The political significance of R.A. Cross.
M.A., Wales (Bangor), 1954.

1759. JACOB, E.D.
Disraeli's social reforms, 1874-1880.
Ph.D., Western Reserve, 1961.

1760. JOYCE, P.J.
Popular Toryism in Lancashire, 1860-90.
D.Phil., Oxford, 1975.

1761. KOHAN, R.A.
The British Conservative Party leadership and social reform 1886-1905.
Ph.D., Ohio State, 1978.
DA 39 3096A

1762. KOPSCH, H.
The approach of the Conservative Party to social policy during World War II.
Ph.D., L.S.E., 1970.

1763. LEES, S.G.
The economic and social policy of the Conservative Party during the period 1919-1939.
M.A., Manchester, 1953.

1764. LEWIS, C.J.
Disraeli's Conservatism.
Ph.D., Kentucky, 1956.
DA 21 2692

1765. LYNCH, M.A.
Winston Churchill and the post-war social reconstruction plans of his wartime
administration, 1940-1945.
Ph.D., University of Notre Dame, 1977.
DA 38 0960A

1766. MANLEY, J.F.
Disraeli's Tory democracy: a parliamentary study.
Ph.D., St. Louis, 1968.
DA 29 2646A

1767. MASON, J.
Anti-Socialist thought in Britain, 1880-1914.
Ph.D., Birmingham, 1975.

1768. MITCHELL, D.J.
Richard Assheton Cross: a political biography.
Ph.D., Mississippi, 1976.
DA 37 5287A

1769. NORDLINGER, E.A.
The working-class Tories: a study in English political culture.
Ph.D., Princeton, 1966.
DA 27 1087A

1770. SCALLY, R.J.
The sources of the National Coalition of 1916: a political history of British
Social-Imperialism.
Ph.D., Princeton, 1966.
DA 28 2187A

1771. SCHAFER, D.F.
      Young England and Conservative social policy.
      Ph.D., Oklahoma, 1972.
      DA 33 6851A

1772. SMITH, P.
      The Young England movement.
      Ph.D., Columbia, 1951.
      DA 12 0430

1773. SMITH, P.
      The Conservative Party and some social problems primarily affecting the condition
      of the working classes, 1866-80.
      D.Phil., Oxford, 1965.

1774. STONE, G.L.
      Derby, Disraeli and the Reform Bill of 1859.
      Ph.D., Illinois, 1975.
      DA 36 0495A

1775. VAN HALL, R.W.
      The Unionist Party, Balfour and social reform, 1900-1905.
      Ph.D., South Carolina, 1975.
      DA 36 7578A

E.   PARTIES OF THE RIGHT: FASCISM

1776. BENEWICK, R.J.
      The British Fascist movement, 1932-40: its development and significance.
      Ph.D., Manchester, 1963.

1777. BREWER, J.D.
      The B.U.F., Sir Oswald Mosley and Birmingham: an analysis of the content and context
      of an ideology.
      M.Soc.Sc., Birmingham, 1975-76.

1778. FIELDING, N.G.
      The National Front: a sociological study of political organization and ideology.
      Ph.D., L.S.E., 1977.

1779. MORRELL, J.E.
      Arnold Leese: his life and work, his ideas and his place in British Fascism.
      M.A., Sheffield, 1975.

POSITIVISM

1780. ADELMAN, P.
      The social and political ideas of Frederic Harrison in relation to English thought
      and politics, 1855-1886.
      Ph.D., L.S.E., 1968.

1781. EISEN, S.
      Frederic Harrison: the life and thought of an English positivist.
      Ph.D., Johns Hopkins, 1957.

1782. HARRISON, R.J.
      The activity and influence of the English positivists in labour movements, 1859-85.
      D.Phil., Oxford, 1955.

1783. McCREADY, H.W.
      Frederic Harrison and the British working-class movement, 1860-1875.
      Ph.D., Harvard, 1952.

1784. McGEE, J.E.
      A crusade for humanity: the history of organised positivism in England.
      Ph.D., Columbia, 1931.

1785. MURPHY, J.M.
      Positivism in England: the reception of Comte's doctrines, 1840-1870.
      Ph.D., Columbia, 1968.
      DA 30 1601A

1786. NYLAND, T.
      The English Positivists.
      M.A., L.S.E., 1937.

1787. PRESSWOOD, W.L.
      The influence of Auguste Comte and the rise of positivism in England up to the
      formation of the English Positivist Society in 1867.
      Ph.D., Sheffield, 1935.

1788. SALMON, M.
      Frederic Harrison: the evolution of an English Positivist, 1831-1881.
      Ph.D., Columbia, 1969.
      DA 20 1356A

POVERTY AND THE POOR LAW

1789. ADAMS, B.K.
Charity, voluntary work and professionalisation in late Victorian and Edwardian
England with special reference to the C.O.S. and Guilds of Help.
M.A., Sussex, 1976.

1790. ALLIN, W.E.
Poor law administration in Glamorganshire before the Poor Law Amendment Act of 1834.
M.A., Wales, 1936.

1791. ANDERSON, K.
The treatment of vagrancy and the relief of the poor and destitute in the Tudor period
based upon the local records of London to 1552 and Hull to 1576.
Ph.D., Royal Holloway College, London, 1933.

1792. ANDERSON, P.
The Leeds workhouse under the Old Poor Law, 1726-1844.
M.Phil., Leeds, 1978.

1793. BAKER, K.H.
Records of Boards of Guardians and joint Poor Law Committees in the custody of Surrey
County Council in the Surrey Record Office, County Hall, Kingston-upon-Thames.
Dip.Arch.Admin.+ University of London, 1963.

1794. BARKER, R.G.
The Houghton-le-Spring Poor Law Union, 1834-1934.
M.Litt., Newcastle, 1974.

1795. BEIER, A.L.
Studies in poverty and poor relief in Warwickshire, 1540-1680.
Ph.D., Princeton, 1969.
DA 31 2831A

1796. BELL, L.H.
The respective spheres of the State and of voluntary organisations in the
prevention and relief of poverty in London at the present.
M.A., L.S.E., 1935.

1797. BODY, G.A.
The administration of the Poor Laws in Dorset, 1760-1834 with special
reference to agrarian distress.
Ph.D., Southampton, 1965.

1798. BOONE, G.
The Poor Law of 1601 with some consideration of modern developments of the Poor Law problem.
M.A., Birmingham, 1917.

1799. BOYSON, R.
The history of Poor Law administration in North East Lancashire, 1834-1871.
M.A., Manchester, 1960.

1800. BRIMELOW, F.A.
The Royal Poor Law Commission, 1905-1909.
Ph.D., South Carolina, 1971.
DA 32 5703A

1801. BRUNDAGE, A.L.
The landed interest and the establishment of the New Poor Law in Northamptonshire.
Ph.D., California, Los Angeles, 1970.
DA 31 3462A

1802. BUCHANAN, C.A.
The introduction of the New Poor Law of 1834 into the parishes of Bridgewater, Taunton,
Wells and Williton in the county of Somerset.
M.Sc., Bristol, 1974.

1803. BUTCHER, E.E.
The Bristol Corporation of the Poor, 1696-1834.
M.A., Bristol, 1930.

1804. CADMAN, G.
The administration of the Poor Law Amendment Act in Hexham, 1836-40 and 1862-69.
B.A.*, Newcastle, 1965.

1805. CADMAN, G.
The Hexham Poor Law Union, 1834-1930.
M.Litt., Newcastle, 1976.

1806. CAGE, R.A.
The Scottish Poor Law, 1745-1845.
Ph.D., Glasgow, 1974.

1807. CAPLAN, M.
The administration of the Poor Law in the Unions of Southwell and Basford, 1836-71.
Ph.D., Nottingham, 1967.

1808.   CHRISTMAS, E.A.
        The administration of the Poor Law in some Gloucestershire Unions, 1815-47.
        M.Litt., Bristol, 1974.

1809.   CONWAY, E.
        Public assistance in Manchester and Salford, 1930-42.
        M.A., Manchester, 1973.

1810.   CONWAY, T.G
        The extension of the Poor Law to Ireland.
        Ph.D., Loyola University, Chicago, 1969.

1811.   DAVIES, A.M.E.
        Poverty and its treatment in Cardiganshire, 1750-1850.
        M.A., Wales (Aberystwyth), 1968.

1812.   DIGBY, A.
        The operation of the Poor Law in the social and economic life of nineteenth century
        Norfolk.
        Ph.D., East Anglia, 1971.

1813.   DITTBRENNER, C.H.
        The Poor Law and the problem of poverty in Norwich and Norfolk, 1660-1760.
        Ph.D., Wisconsin, 1973.
        DA 34 4147A

1814.   DOYLE, E.M.M.
        Distress in Ireland, 1879-84.
        M.A., National University of Ireland, 1971.

1815.   DUNKLEY, P.J.
        Deference, order and the coming of the New Poor Law, 1795-1834.
        Ph.D., Stanford, 1976.
        DA 36 8243A

1816.   DUNKLEY, P.J.
        The New Poor Law and County Durham.
        M.A., Durham, 1971.

1817.   EDSALL, N.C.
        The New Poor Law and its opponents, 1833-1844.
        Ph.D., Harvard, 1966.

1818.   EDWARDSON, J.
        The conditions and needs of the cottage homes child (poor law) together with a short
        history of the rise and development of the cottage homes system.
        M.A., Liverpool, 1923.

1819.   EVANS, N.
        Philanthropy in Cardiff, 1850-1914.
        M.A., Wales (Swansea), 1973.

1820.   FARNIE, D.A.
        The establishment of the New Poor Law in Salford, 1838-50.
        B.A.*, Manchester, 1951.

1821.   FIDELER, P.A.
        Discussion of poverty in sixteenth century England.
        Ph.D., Brandeis, 1971.
        DA 32 2578A

1822.   FROSHAUG, A.J.
        Poor Law administration in selected London parishes between 1750 and 1850.
        M.A., Nottingham, 1969.

1823.   GITSHAM, E.
        The Irish poor in Great Britain: causes, extent and effects of their coming.
        B.A.*, Leeds, 1923.

1824.   GLADSTONE, D.E.
        The administration and reform of poor relief in Scotland, 1790-1850 with special
        reference to Stirlingshire.
        M.Litt., Stirling, 1973.

1825.   GREGSON, K.
        The Hartlepool Poor Law Union.
        M.Litt., Newcastle, 1977.

1826.   GREY, P.
        The operation of the Poor Law in Bedfordshire, 1820-1834.
        M.Phil., Leicester, 1976.

1827.   GRIFFITHS, A.R.G.
        The Irish Board of Works, 1831-1878 with particular reference to the famine years.
        Ph.D., Cambridge, 1968.

1828. HALE, R.W.
       The establishment of the permanent Poor Law Commission, 1830-1836.
       Ph.D., Harvard, 1937.

1829. HAMPSON, E.M.
       Pauperism and vagrancy in Cambridgeshire to 1834.
       Ph.D., Cambridge, 1931.

1830. HANDLEY, M.D.
       Local administration of the Poor Law in the Great Broughton and Wirral Unions and
       the Chester Local Act Incorporation, 1834-71.
       M.A., Wales (Bangor), 1969.

1831. HASTINGS, R.P.
       Poverty and its treatment in the North Riding of Yorkshire, c.1780-1947.
       D.Phil., York, 1978.

1832. HERLAN, R.W.
       Poor relief during the great Civil War and the Interregnum, 1642-60.
       Ph.D., State University of New York, 1973.
       DA 34 0701A

1833. HILL, J.
       A study of poverty and poor relief in Shropshire, 1550-1685.
       M.A., Liverpool, 1973.

1834. HINDLE, G.B.
       Provision for the relief of the poor in Manchester, 1754-1826.
       M.A., Manchester, 1972.

1835. HODGKINSON, G.R.
       The medical services of the New Poor Law, 1834-71.
       Ph.D., L.S.E., 1951.

1836. HOPKIN, N.D.
       The old and the new Poor Law in east Yorkshire, c.1760-1850.
       M.Phil., Leeds, 1968.

1837. HOWARD, J.H.
       Phases of poor law policy and administration, 1760-1834.
       M.A., Liverpool, 1921.

1838. HOWE, B.J.
       Clubs, culture and charity: Anglo-American upper-class activities in the late
       nineteenth-century city.
       Ph.D., Temple, 1976.
       DA 37 2358A

1839. HUGHES, C.F.
       The development of the Poor Laws in Caernarvonshire and Anglesey between 1815 and 1914.
       M.A., Wales (Bangor), 1945.

1840. HUMPHREYS, A.
       Henry Mayhew and the London poor.
       Ph.D., Columbia, 1968.
       DA 29 2675A

1841. HUZEL, J.
       Poverty and rural distress in late 18th-century and early 19th-century Kent.
       Ph.D., Kent, 1975.

1842. JONES, T.M.
       Poor Law and Public Health administration in the area of Merthyr Tydfil Union, 1834-1894.
       M.A., Wales (Cardiff), 1961.

1843. KAMINSKI, D.C.
       The radicalization of a ministering angel: a biography of Emily Hobhouse 1860-1926.
       Ph.D., Connecticut, 1977.
       DA 38 6885A

1844. KELLY, S.
       Select vestry of Liverpool and the administration of the Poor Law, 1821-1871.
       M.A., Liverpool, 1972.

1845. LANE, J.
       Poor Law administration in Butlers Marston, Warwickshire, 1713-1822.
       M.A., Wales (Cardiff), 1969.

1846. LEVY, I.H
       The working of the new Poor Law, 1834-42.
       M.A., Manchester, 1923.

1847. LINDSAY, J.
       The operation of the Poor Laws in the north-east of Scotland, 1745-1845.
       Ph.D., Aberdeen, 1961.

1848. McGRATH, B.
       Introduction of the Poor Law to Ireland, 1831-8.
       M.A., National University of Ireland, 1915.

1849. MACKEY, H.
       Humanitarian opposition to the economists on the Poor Law and Factory legislation,
       1802-1847.
       Ph.D., Lehigh, 1955.
       DA 15 1606

1850. MACKINNON, J.M.
       The English Poor Law of 1834 with special reference to its working between 1834 and 1847:
       a study in social pathology.
       M.A., University College, London, 1930.

1851. McNAULTY, M.
       Some aspects of the history of the administration of the Poor Laws in Birmingham
       between 1730 and 1834.
       M.A., Birmingham, 1942.

1852. McSWEENEY, M.
       Poverty and the wage-earning class.
       M.A., National University of Ireland, 1914.

1853. MALTBY, A.
       The Poor Law Commission, 1905-1909: an investigation of its task and achievement.
       M.A., Liverpool, 1969.

1854. MARSHALL, D.
       The English Poor Laws and social conditions.
       Ph.D., Cambridge, 1926.

1855. MAWSON, P.
       Poor Law administration in South Shields, 1830-1930.
       M.A., Newcastle, 1972.

1856. MIDWINTER, E.C.
       Social administration in Lancashire, 1830-60: Poor Law, public health and police.
       D.Phil., York, 1966.

1857. MILLER, H.
       The administration of the Poor Laws in Ireland till 30th November 1921 and in
       Northern Ireland from the 1st December 1921 till present date.
       M.Com.Sc., Queen's University, Belfast, 1942.

1858. MISHRA, R.C.
       A history of the relieving officer in England and Wales from 1834 to 1948.
       Ph.D., L.S.E., 1969.

1859. MOORE, M.J.
       Casework and community organisation in Great Britain: the emergence of guilds of
       help and councils of social welfare, 1900-1919.
       Ph.D., Washington, 1971.
       DA 32 1450A

1860. MORGAN, S.M.
       Local government and poor relief in Oldham, 1826-50.
       B.A.*, Manchester, 1959.

1861. MOSLEY, J.V.
       Poor Law administration in England and Wales, 1830-50 with special reference to
       the problem of the able-bodied labourer.
       Ph.D., London, External, 1976.

1862. NELSON, C.A.
       Vagrancy in the West Midlands, 1840-80.
       M.A., Wales (Swansea), 1977.

1863. NEUMAN, M.D.
       Aspects of poverty and poor law administration in Berkshire, 1782-1834.
       Ph.D., California, Berkeley, 1967.
       DA 28 4099A

1864. O'DRISCOLL, E.
       The poor in English literature.
       M.A., National University of Ireland, 1917.

1865. O'NEILL, Thomas P.
       The organisation and administration of relief during the great famine.
       M.A., National University of Ireland, 1946.

1866. O'NEILL, Timothy P.
       The Irish famine of 1822.
       M.A., National University of Ireland, 1965.

1867.   O'NEILL, Timothy P.
        The State, poverty and distress in Ireland, 1815-45.
        Ph.D., National University of Ireland, 1971.

1868.   O'SULLIVAN, D.M.
        The causes, development and relief of distress in Mayo in 1831.
        M.A., National University of Ireland, 1968.

1869.   OXLEY, G.W.
        Administration of the old "poor law" in the West Derby hundred of Lancashire, 1607-1837.
        M.A., Liverpool, 1966.

1870.   PACK, L.F.C.
        A study of the evolution of the methods of poor relief in the Winchester area, 1720-1845.
        M.A., Southampton, 1967.

1871.   PARKER, D.R.
        The Poor Law in the area of the Eastbourne and Steyning Poor Law Union, 1790-1840.
        M.A., Sussex, 1972-73.

1872.   PARKER, W.A.
        The Bishops and the poor law, 1782-1834.
        M.A., Manchester, 1939.

1873.   PATERSON, A.
        A study of poor relief administration in Edinburgh city parish between 1845 and 1894.
        Ph.D., Edinburgh, 1974.

1874.   PETTY, R.N.
        The disintegration of the Poor Law.
        M.Sc., Bradford, 1974.

1875.   PIERCE, E.M.
        Town-county relations in England and Wales in the pre-railway age as revealed in the
        Poor Law Unions.
        M.A., London, 1957.

1876.   PIKE, W.
        The administration of the Poor Law in the rural areas of Surrey, 1830-1850.
        M.A., Birkbeck College, London, 1950.

1877.   PRITCHARD, M.F.L.
        The treatment of poverty in Norfolk from 1700 to 1850.
        Ph.D., Cambridge, 1950.

1878.   RAUP, R.M.
        The change in Britain from local to national assistance, 1930-1950.
        B.Litt., Oxford, 1952.

1879.   RILLING, J.R.
        The administration of poor relief in the counties of Essex and Somerset
        during the personal rule of Charles I, 1629-1640.
        Ph.D., Harvard, 1959.

1880.   ROBINS, J.A.
        The charity child in Ireland, 1700-1900.
        Ph.D., Trinity College, Dublin, 1968.

1881.   ROSE, M.E.
        The administration of the Poor Law in the West Riding of Yorkshire, 1820-55.
        D.Phil., Oxford, 1965.

1882.   ROSS, E.M
        Women and Poor Law administration, 1857-1909.
        M.A., L.S.E., 1956.

1883.   RUSSELL, V.J.
        Poor Law administration, 1840-1843 with particular reference to the Cardiff Union.
        M.A., Wales (Cardiff), 1966.

1884.   SATRE, M.C.
        Poverty in Berkshire: a descriptive synthesis of the effects of the 1834 Poor Law
        Amendment.
        Ph.D., State University of New York at Buffalo, 1978.
        DA 39 0411A

1885.   SHAWKY, K. El Ed.
        Studies in poverty and health during the nineteenth century in Britain and Egypt.
        Ph.D., London School of Hygiene and Tropical Medicine, 1953-54.

1886.   SKINNER, K.E.M.
        Poor Law administration in Glamorgan, 1750-1850.
        M.A., Wales (Swansea), 1936.

1887.   STEWART, P.
        Poor Law administration at Abingdon, Berkshire, before 1834.
        M.Sc., London, External, 1978.

1888. TAYLOR, J.S.
       Poverty in rural Devon, 1780-1840.
       Ph.D., Stanford, 1966.
       DA 27 2125A

1889. THOMAS, E.G.
       The parish overseer in Essex, 1597-1834.
       M.A., Exeter, 1956.

1890. THOMAS, E.G.
       The treatment of poverty in Berkshire, Essex and Oxfordshire, 1723-1834.
       Ph.D., London, External, 1971.

1891. THOMAS, J.E.
       Poor Law administration in West Glamorgan, 1834-1930.
       M.A., Wales (Swansea), 1951.

1892. THOMPSON, R.N.
       The new Poor Law in Cumberland and Westmorland, 1834-71.
       Ph.D., Newcastle, 1976.

1893. THURBER, J.N.
       The poor of London, 1688-1702.
       Ph.D., California, 1943.

1894. TOFT, J.
       The New Poor Law in Leeds.
       B.A.*, Manchester, 1964.

1895. TRANT, M.A.
       Government policy and Irish distress.
       M.A., National University of Ireland, 1965.

1896. VORSPAN, R.
       The battle over the workhouse: English society and the New Poor Laws.
       Ph.D., Columbia, 1975.
       DA 36 1747A

1897. WALSH, Y.J.
       The administration of the Poor Laws in Shropshire: 1820-1855.
       Ph.D., Pennsylvania, 1970.
       DA 31 2860A

1898. WARD, D.
       The deformation of the gift: the Charity Organisation Society in Leamington Spa.
       M.A.*, Warwick, 1974-75.

1899. WHICHER, D.S.
       The administration of poor relief (with special reference to Watford, 1601-1836).
       Dip.Pub.Admin.+, London, 1970.

1900. WOOD, J.R.
       The transition from the Old to the New Poor Law in Manchester.
       B.A.*, Manchester, 1938.

1901. WOOD, P.A.
       The activities of the Sunderland Poor Law Union, 1834-1930.
       M.Litt., Newcastle, 1976.

1902. ZUCKER, E.M.M.
       A history of the workhouse system to the end of the eighteenth century and with
       special reference to the period from 1722 to 1732 and the industrial aspects.
       M.A., Manchester, 1925.

PUBLIC HEALTH AND THE NATIONAL HEALTH SERVICE

1903. ABEL-SMITH, B.
       The cost of the National Health Service: an application of social accounting.
       Ph.D., Cambridge, 1955.

1904. ALKER, A.
       The social pathology of Wigan, 1800-1850: some aspects of the town's growth.
       M.A.*, Lancaster, 1971.

1905. ARCHER, A.J.
       A study of local sanitary administration, 1830-75, in certain selected areas
       (Burton, Lichfield, Tamworth).
       M.A., Wales (Bangor), 1968.

1906. AYERS, G.M.
       The origins and development of England's first state hospital with special reference
       to the services provided by the Metropolitan Asylums Board for Patients with Infectious
       Diseases.
       Ph.D., London, 1967.

1907. BATE, W.
Sanitary administration of Liverpool, 1847-1900.
M.A., Liverpool, 1955.

1908. BECK, A.F.
The beginning of public health control in England, 1870-1890.
Ph.D., Illinois, 1948.

1909. BLACKDEN, S.M.B.
The development of public health administration in Glasgow, 1842-72.
Ph.D., Edinburgh, 1976.

1910. BLACKETT, J.F.
Fifty years of public health and social welfare in Bath, 1896-1945.
M.A., Bristol, 1949.

1911. BRAND, J.E.
The British medical profession and state intervention in public health, 1870-1911.
Ph.D., London, 1953.

1912. BURNETT, J.
The history of food adulteration in Great Britain in the nineteenth century
with special reference to bread, tea and beer.
Ph.D., London, 1958.

1913. DALTRY, R.W.
A history of the public health of the borough of Reading up to 1872.
M.A., Reading, 1933.

1914. DOWLING, W.C.
The Ladies' Sanitary Association and the origins of the health visiting service.
M.A., London, 1963.

1915. DUREY, M.J.
Social history of cholera in 19th-century Britain.
D.Phil., York, 1976.

1916. ELLIOTT, M.J.
The Leicester Board of Health.
M.Phil., Nottingham, 1971.

1917. FIEDLER, G.D.
Public health and hospital administration in Swansea and West Glamorgan since the
end of the eighteenth century to 1914.
M.A., Wales (Swansea), 1962.

1918. FRAMPTON, B.A.
The role of Dr Dyke in the public health movement of Merthyr Tydfil, 1865-1900.
M.A., Wales (Swansea), 1969.

1919. FRANKLIN, R.
Medical education and the rise of the general practitioner, 1760-1860.
Ph.D., Birmingham, 1951.

1920. GATHERER, A.
A socio-medical study of the first cholera epidemic in Great Britain, 1831-1832.
M.A., Aberdeen, 1959.

1921. GIBSON, E.H.
The public health agitation in England, 1838-1848: a newspaper and parliamentary history.
Ph.D., North Carolina (Chapel Hill), 1956.

1922. GILBERT, B.B.
The British Government and the nation's health, 1890-1952.
Ph.D., Wisconsin, 1954.

1923. GRIFFITH, J.R.
Regionalism in hospital management under the National Health Service Act (England and
Wales), 1946. B.Litt., Oxford, 1960.

1924. HADFIELD, J.
Health provision in the industrial North East, 1919-1939.
Ph.D., Sheffield, 1977.

1925. HALLETT, M.E.J.
Economic and social aspects of the piped water supply in Portsmouth, 1800-1860.
M.Phil., C.N.A.A., 1971.

1926. JAMES, D.C.
Public health in nineteenth century Cardiff.
M.A., Wales (Swansea), 1974.

1927. JOHNSON, M.
The health of Sheffield citizens in the nineteenth century.
M.A., Sheffield, 1977.

1928.   JONES, D.D.
        Edwin Chadwick and the early public health movement in England.
        Ph.D., Iowa, 1929.

1929.   JONES, M.S.S.
        Observations of the evolution of public health law and administration with
        special reference to its bearing on mother and child.
        M.D., Liverpool, 1925.

1930.   KNOX, G.S.
        Cholera and society in Glasgow in the 19th century.
        M.Litt., Strathclyde, 1976.

1931.   LAMBERT, R.J.
        Some aspects of state activity in public health, 1858-1871, with special reference to
        the Medical Department of the Privy Council and the Local Government Act Office.
        Ph.D., Cambridge, 1959.

1932.   LEWIS, R.A.
        Edwin Chadwick and the public health movement, 1832-1854.
        Ph.D., Birmingham, 1949.

1933.   MACDONALD, H.
        Public health legislation and problems in Victorian Edinburgh, with special
        reference to the work of Dr. Littlejohn, Medical Officer of Health.
        Ph.D., Edinburgh, 1972.

1934.   MORRIS, R.W.
        Geographical and historical aspects of the public water supply of London, 1852-1902.
        Ph.D., London, 1947.

1935.   MUKHOPADHYAY, A.K.
        The politics of London water supply, 1871-1971.
        Ph.D., London, 1972.

1936.   NEWBERY, J.A.
        Public health in Grimsby, 1800-c.1872.
        M.A., Hull, 1976.

1937.   O'KELLY, Sister P.
        From workhouse to hospital: medical relief in Ireland, 1838-1929.
        M.A., National University of Ireland (Galway), 1972.

1938.   O'NEILL, J.
        Health and the state in Great Britain, 1865-1900: a study in the origins of
        the Welfare State.
        Ph.D., Chicago, 1961.

1939.   PELLING, M.H.
        Some approaches to nineteenth century epidemiology, with particular reference
        to John Shaw and William Budd.
        B.Litt., Oxford, 1972.

1940.   PENNINGTON, C.I.
        Mortality, public health and medical improvements in Glasgow, 1855-1914.
        Ph.D., Stirling, 1977.

1941.   PEPPER, R.S.
        The growth and development of Leeds waterworks undertakings.
        M.Phil., Leeds, 1973.

1942.   PINKER, R.A.
        The utilisation of hospital in-patient services for the physically ill in England
        and Wales, 1861-1938.
        M.Sc., London, 1965.

1943.   RIDDELL, J.
        A study of the history and development of the School medical service in Liverpool
        from 1908 to 1939.
        M.A., Liverpool, 1946.

1944.   ROSS, D.L.
        The British anti-vaccination movement in the nineteenth century.
        M.Sc., Leicester, 1967.

1945.   SELDON, M.E.
        The National Health Service Act, 1946.
        Ph.D., Indiana, 1959.
        DA 20 4091

1946.   SILLETT, R.E.W.
        A historical biography of Edwin Lankester M.D., F.R.S., 1814-1874, Coroner and
        Medical Officer of Health (St. James, Westminster).
        M.D., Birmingham, 1957.

1947.   TOFT, J.
        Public health in Leeds in the nineteenth century: a study in the growth of local
        government responsibility, 1850-1880.
        M.A, Manchester, 1966.

1948. TOWNLEY, W.E.
Urban administration and health: a case study of Hanley in the mid-nineteenth century.
M.A., Keele, 1969.

1949. WALTERS, A.V.
The paradox of the British National Health Service: an analysis of its sources.
Ph.D., McGill University, 1976.
DA 38 0494A

1950. WILLCOCKS, A.J.
Interest groups and the National Health Service Act, 1946.
Ph.D., Birmingham, 1953-54.

1951. WILLIAMS, D.B.
The health conditions in a mining community and how they were tackled: Aberdare c.1845-80.
M.A., Swansea, 1978.

1952. WOLLAND, C.
Social and political influences on public health in Birmingham and Wolverhampton:
a comparative study, 1845-58.
M.A., Warwick, 1974.

1953. WOODWARD, J.H.
The development of the voluntary hospital system to 1875, with special reference to
the incidence of mortality.
D.Phil., York, 1970.

1954. WOOLLMAN, D.C.
Public health in Leeds, 1836-48.
M.A., Leeds, 1949.

1955. YOUNG, R.K.J.F.
Sanitary administration under the Local Government Board, 1871-1888.
B.Litt., Oxford, 1964.

RELIGION /see also CHRISTIAN SOCIALISM/

1956. ABEL, E.K.
Canon Barnett and the first thirty years of Toynbee Hall.
Ph.D., Queen Mary College, London, 1969.

1957. BAXTER, J.L.
The Methodist experience in Sheffield, 1780-1820: a study of popular religion and
social change.
M.A.*, Sheffield, 1970.

1958. BRACKWELL, C.
The Church of England and social reform, 1830-1850.
M.A., Birmingham, 1949.

1959. BRAND, M.V. Sister
The Social Catholic movement in England, 1920-1955.
Ph.D., St. Louis, 1963.
DA 25 0424A

1960. BREADY, J.W.
The influence of Christianity on social progress as illustrated by the career
of Lord Shaftesbury.
Ph.D., London, 1927.

1961. COMAN, P.W.
An analysis of the social teaching of the English Roman Catholic Church in relation
to the British Welfare State, 1940-68.
Ph.D., Leeds, 1975.

1962. CRAIG, R.
The theoretical basis of William Temple's social teaching.
Ph.D., St. Andrews, 1950.

1963. DUNCAN, A.
The London City Mission: a study of lay evangelicalism 1835-70.
M.A.*, Warwick, 1977.

1964. EVANS, H.A.
Religion and the working classes in mid-19th century England.
M.Phil., Bedford College, London, 1970.

1965. FOSTER, J.H.
Henry Scott Holland, 1847-1918.
Ph.D., Wales (Swansea), 1970.

1966. GWYTHER, C.E.
Methodist social and political theory and practice, 1848 to 1914, with particular
reference to the Forward movement.
M.A., Liverpool, 1961.

1967. GWYTHER, C.E.
Methodism and syndicalism in the Rhondda Valley, 1906-26.
Ph.D., Sheffield, 1967.

1968. HEASMAN, K.J.
       The influence of Evangelicals upon the development of voluntary charitable
       institutions in the second half of the 19th century.
       Ph.D., London, 1960.

1969. HEATON, R.L.
       The interrelation of sacramental and ethical conceptions in the thought of
       Frederick D. Maurice, Henry S. Holland, Charles Gore and William Temple.
       Ph.D., Edinburgh, 1968-69.

1970. HOLT, J.H.
       The Quakers in the great Irish famine.
       M.Litt., Trinity College, Dublin, 1967.

1971. HORNER, J.P.
       The influence of Methodism on the social structure and culture of rural
       Northumberland from 1820-1914.
       M.A., Newcastle, 1970.

1972. HUTSON, H.M.
       Methodist concern with social problems in England, 1848-1873.
       Ph.D., Iowa, 1952.

1973. INGLIS, K.S.
       English churches and the working classes, 1880-1900, with an introductory
       survey of tendencies earlier in the century.
       D.Phil., Oxford, 1956.

1974. JONES, F.W.
       Social concern in the Church of England as revealed in the pronouncements on
       social and economic matters especially during the years, 1880-1940.
       Ph.D., London, 1968.

1975. KENT, J.H.S.
       The clash between radicalism and conservatism in Methodism, 1815-48.
       Ph.D., Cambridge, 1951.

1976. KNOTT, J.P.
       Evangelicalism and its influence on English social reform during part of the
       18th and 19th centuries.
       Ph.D., Southern California, 1939.

1977. LEESE, R.
       The impact of Methodism on Black Country society, 1760-1860.
       Ph.D., Manchester, 1972.

1978. LLOYD, E.C.
       The influence of the Methodist movement on social life in Wales.
       B.Litt., Wales, 1921.

1979. MACCAGNO, D.B.M.
       Some aspects of the foundation of the young Christian worker movement in
       Belgium and England.
       M.Phil., Institute of Education, London, 1970.

1980. MACCONOMY, E.N.
       The political thought of William Temple.
       Ph.D., Michigan, 1962.
       DA 23 3955A

1981. McENTEE, G.P.
       Social Catholic movement in Great Britain.
       Ph.D., Columbia, 1927.

1982. McGEE, E.W.
       The Anglican Church and social reform, 1830-50.
       Ph.D., Kentucky, 1952.
       DA 20 3710

1983. McILHINEY, D.B.
       A gentleman in every slum: Church of England missions in East London, 1837-1914.
       Ph.D., Princeton, 1977.
       DA 38 0334A

1984. MACLAREN, A.A.
       Religion and social class in mid-19th century Aberdeen.
       Ph.D., Aberdeen, 1971.

1985. MARKWELL, B.K.
       The Anglican Left: radical social reformers in the Church of England and the
       Protestant Episcopal Church 1846-1954.
       Ph.D., Chicago, 1977.
       DA 38 7490A

1986. MAYOR, S.H.
       Organised religion and English working-class movement, 1850-1914.
       Ph.D., Manchester, 1960.

1987.   MOORE, R.S.
        The influence of Methodism in inhibiting the development of class consciousness and
        reducing class conflict with particular reference to four west Durham mining villages
        in the period, 1870-1926.
        Ph.D., Durham, 1972.

1988.   NEWMAN, E.V.
        The relation of theology to social theory and action in the Christian Social
        movement in England, 1877-1914.
        B.Litt., Oxford, 1936.

1989.   ORENS, J.R.
        The mass, the masses and the music hall: a study of Stewart Headlam's radical
        Anglicanism.
        Ph.D., Columbia, 1976.
        DA 39 5668A

1990.   PARRY, R.I.
        The attitude of the Welsh Independents towards working-class movements
        (including public education) from 1815 to 1870.
        M.A., Wales (Bangor), 1931.

1991.   PIERSON, S.A.
        Socialism and religion: a study of their interaction in Great Britain, 1889-1911.
        Ph.D., Harvard, 1957.

1992.   RICHARDS, N.J.
        The political and social impact of British nonconformity in the late 19th century,
        1870-1902.
        Ph.D., Wisconsin, 1968.
        DA 29 1851A

1993.   SAINT, J.G.
        The influence of the nonconformist religions in the character of the British
        Labour movement.
        M.A., McGill, 1962.

1994.   SCOTLAND, N.A.
        The role of Methodism in the growth and development of the "Revolt of the Field"
        in Lincolnshire, Norfolk and Suffolk, 1872-95.
        Ph.D., Aberdeen, 1975.

1995.   SMITH, H.L.
        The structure of Christian ethics in the thought of William Temple.
        Ph.D., Duke, 1972.
        DA 23 4764A

1996.   STIGANT, E.P.
        Methodism and the working class, 1760-1821.
        M.A., Keele, 1968.

1997.   SUMMERS, D.F.
        The Labour Church and allied movements of the late nineteenth and early
        twentieth centuries.
        Ph.D., Edinburgh, 1958.

1998.   TUCKER, L.R.
        The English Quakers and World War I, 1914-1920.
        Ph.D., North Carolina, 1972.
        DA 33 1666A
              (Movement of the Society of Friends towards Socialist ideas.)

1999.   WAGNER, D.O.
        The Church of England and social reform since 1854.
        Ph.D., Columbia, 1930.

2000.   WARNER, W.J.
        The humanitarian movement in England in the eighteenth century with special reference to
        the relation between the revival in religious life and industrial change: a study in the
        sociology of religion.
        Ph.D., London, 1929.

2001.   WEARMOUTH, R.F.
        Methodism and the working classes in England, 1800-1850.
        Ph.D., L.S.E., 1935.

2002.   WELLER, T.
        The influence of nonconformity on the wage earning population of Nottingham in the
        nineteenth century.
        M.A., Nottingham, 1957.

2003.   WHYATT, C.B.
        The Baptists and political and social conditions in Lancashire during the Industrial
        Revolution.
        M.A., Manchester, 1948.

2004. WOLFENDEN, J.W.
English non-conformity and the social conscience.
Ph.D., Yale, 1954.

2005. WRIGHT, E.R.
The social and political thought of William Temple.
Ph.D., Duke, 1961.
DA 23 0290

SECULARISM AND HUMANISM

2006. ARNSTEIN, W.L.
The Bradlaugh case: a study in late Victorian opinion and politics.
Ph.D., North Western, 1961.
DA 22 2769

2007. BUDD, S.
The British Humanist movement, 1860-1966.
D.Phil., Oxford, 1969.

2008. HARTZELL, K.D.
The origins of the English secularist movement, 1817-46.
Ph.D., Harvard, 1934.

2009. KACZKOWSKI, C.J.
John MacKinnon Robertson: freethinker and radical.
Ph.D., St. Louis, 1964.
DA 26 2163

2010. KRANTZ, C.K.
The British secularist movement: a study in militant dissent.
Ph.D., Rochester, 1964.
DA 25 2946A

2011. NELSON, W.D.
British rational secularism: unbelief from Bradlaugh to the mid-twentieth century.
Ph.D., Washington, 1963.
DA 24 4659A

2012. ROSS, J.S.
English free thought 1875-93: secularism and connected movements in late-Victorian England.
M.A., Exeter, 1978.

2013. ROYLE, E.
George Jacob Holyoake and the Secularist movement in Britain, 1841-1861.
Ph.D., Cambridge, 1968.

2014. STEELE, M.R.
Secularist literature of Victorian England, 1870-1880.
Ph.D., Michigan State, 1975.
DA 36 6121A

SOCIAL CONTROL

2014A. EVANS, G.
Social leadership and social control: Bolton, 1870-98.
M.A.*, Lancaster, 1974.

2015. HALL, A.A.
Social control and the working-class challenge in Ashton-under-Lyne, 1886-1914.
M.A.*, Lancaster, 1975.

2016. HEARN, F.J.
Domination and legitimation in industrial capitalism: the incorporation of the English working class and the historical roots of one-dimensionality.
Ph.D., Connecticut, 1975.
DA 36 6974A
/Transformation of working class social protest activities in England, 1780-1860./

2017. REID, C.
Middle class values and working class culture in 19th century Sheffield.
Ph.D., Sheffield, 1976.

2018. TRODD, G.N.
The local elite of Blackburn and the response of the working class to social control, 1880-1900.
M.A.*, Lancaster, 1974.

2018A. WARD, C.E.
Education as social control: Sunday schools in Oldham, c.1780-1850.
M.A.*, Lancaster, 1975.

SOCIAL REFORM AND SOCIAL POLICIES

2019. BOWEN, E.M.
Aspects of taxation and expenditure in the United Kingdom, 1890-1914 with special
reference to the growth of the social services.
M.A., Wales, 1934.

2020. BROWN, J.
Ideas concerning social policy and their influence on legislation in Britain, 1902-1911.
Ph.D., King's College, London, 1964.

2021. BYRNE, B.C.
Social services in the Irish Free State.
M.A., National University of Ireland, 1937.

2022. CHRISTIAN, W.E.
Society and social reform in English political thought, 1789-1797.
Ph.D., L.S.E., 1970.

2023. FORSTER, M.J.
Some physical planning proposals of the early 19th and early 20th centuries in Britain
and their effectiveness in dealing with social distress in urban areas.
M.Phil., University College, London, 1973.

2024. FREEDEN, M.S.
English Liberal thought: problems of social reform, 1886-1914.
D.Phil., Oxford, 1972.

2025. GORSKY, J.N.
Middle class attitudes and social reform in Manchester, 1826-47.
M.A., Manchester, 1976.

2026. HOPE, R.B.
Dr.Thomas Percival: a medical pioneer and social reformer, 1740-1804.
M.A., Manchester, 1947.

2027. LEVERING, D.L.
James Burgh: moralist and reformer.
Ph.D., Claremont Graduate School, 1974.
DA 35 7842A

2028. McGLASHAN, J.J.
German influences on aspects of English educational and social reform, 1867-1908.
Ph.D., Hull, 1973.

2029. MIRICK, H.D.
The voluntary welfare movement in Leeds and Philadelphia during the late 19th and
early 20th centuries.
Ph.D., Cambridge, 1972-73.

2030. MORITZ, E.
Winston S. Churchill and social reform, 1908-1912.
Ph.D., Wisconsin, 1953.

2031. NICHOLLS, D.
Sir Charles Dilke and social reforms.
Ph.D., Kent, 1971-72.

2032. PRICE, T.W.
Social legislation and theory in Great Britain from 1906 to 1914.
B.Litt., Oxford, 1930.

2033. RICHARDS, P.
The State and the working class: private M.P.s and social policy, 1833-1841.
Ph.D., Birmingham, 1975.

2034. RITT, L.
The Victorian conscience in action: the National Association for the Promotion of
Social Science, 1857-1886.
Ph.D., Columbia, 1959.
DA 20 3713

2035. WALLING, R.P.
The emerging Victorian social conscience.
Ph.D., Ohio State, 1972.
DA 33 1699A
     (Social conditions discussed in periodicals, 1833-48.)

2036. WIGHTMAN, E.M.
The 7th Earl of Shaftesbury as a social reformer.
M.A., Birmingham, 1920.

2037. WILLIAMS, L.
Movements towards social reform in South Wales during the period, 1832-50.
M.A., Wales, 1933.

SOCIAL SECURITY AND THE WELFARE STATE

2038.   AULD, R.E.
        Compensation for industrial accidents.
        Ph.D., King's College, London, 1963.

2039.   BERRY, Sister M.F.
        Exposition of British Welfare Liberalism, 1815-1914.
        Ph.D., St. Louis, 1966.
        DA 27 3391A

2040.   BULL, S.L.
        An history and critical analysis of British health insurance.
        M.Sc., L.S.E., 1938.

2041.   CHANDLER, D.
        Pressure groups and the reform of social security in England and Wales, 1919-1925.
        M.Phil., Nottingham, 1971-72.

2042.   CLANCY, T.J.
        Social security in Ireland.
        M.Econ.Sc., National University of Ireland, 1951.

2043.   CUDMORE, J.S.
        Comparative study of health insurance and public medical care schemes in Germany,
        Great Britain, the U.S.A. and Canada.
        Ph.D., Toronto, 1971.

2044.   EDGAR, W.S.
        Old age pensions: a study opinion on the subject of state aid to necessitous old age
        in Great Britain.
        M.A., McGill, 1932.

2045.   FERRILL, E.W.
        The background of old age pension legislation in England, 1886-1914.
        D.Phil., Oxford, 1972.

2046.   FULBROOK, J.G.H.
        Relief for the unemployed: some aspects of the development and present administration
        of the law relating to unemployment insurance and supplementary benefits.
        Ph.D., Cambridge, 1974.

2047.   GIBBON, J.G.
        Unemployment insurance: a study of schemes of assisted insurance.
        D.Sc., London, 1911.

2048.   JENKINS, E.
        The constitution, workings and practice of administrative tribunals under the
        National Insurance and Industrial Injuries Act, 1946.
        Ph.D., University College, London, 1953-54.

2049.   McGLYNN, E.M.
        Unemployment insurance in England.
        Ph.D., Boston College, 1934.

2050.   MacNICOL, J.S.
        The movement for family allowances in Great Britain, 1918-45.
        Ph.D., Edinburgh, 1978.

2051.   MACPHERSON, S.
        Poverty and low wages: means tested benefits and the working poor.
        M.Phil., York, 1972.

2052.   MANN, S.
        Trade Unionism, the Labour Party and the issue of Family Allowances 1925-30.
        M.A.*, Warwick, 1977.

2053.   RAPHAEL, M.
        The origins of public superannuation schemes in England, 1684-1859.
        Ph.D., L.S.E., 1957.

2054.   SCLARE, M.
        Social insurance: a study of the destitution caused by the early death of the wage earner.
        M.A., Leeds, 1923.

2055.   SMITH, N.
        Social reform in Edwardian Liberalism: the genesis of the policies of National Insurance
        and old age pensions, 1902-11.

2056.   SPENCE, A.C.
        Linguistic changes in official non-statutory documents with special reference to those
        relating to unemployment and sickness benefit published between 1948 and 1958.
        Ph.D., University College, London, 1962.

2057.   WILLIAMS, P.M.
        The development of old age pensions policy in Great Britain, 1878-1925.
        Ph.D., L.S.E., 1970.

2058.   WOODARD, C.
        The Charity Organisation Society and the rise of the Welfare State.
        Ph.D., Cambridge, 1961.

SOCIALIST ORGANISATIONS, SOCIETIES AND MOVEMENTS

2059. AUGUSTIN, G.
The political thought of the Social Democratic Federation 1881-1901.
M.A.*, Sheffield (Department of Medieval and Modern History), 1978.

2060. BARROW, L.J.W.
The socialism of Robert Blatchford and the Clarion, 1889-1918.
Ph.D., London, 1975.

2061. BOR, M.H.
The Socialist League and its connection with the Labour movement, 1932-37.
M.A., Wales, 1973.

2062. DARE, R.G.
The Socialist League, 1932-7.
D.Phil., Oxford, 1973.

2063. FILNER, R.E.
Science and politics in England, 1930-1945: the Social Relations of Science
movement (Marxist organisation).
Ph.D., Cornell, 1973.
DA 34 6563A

2064. HALL, R.
The politics of dissent in the fifties: the New Left.
M.A., Manchester, 1962-63.

2065. HUGHES, G.
The New Left in Britain, 1956-64.
M.A., Keele, 1973-74.

2066. JONES, C.M.
Crisis of Parliamentary Liberalism: extremism in Britain in the 1930s.
Ph.D., Duke, 1974.
DA 35 5305A
        (Case studies of Cripps and the Socialist League: Mosley and the B.U.F.,
        I.L.P. and the Left Book Club.)

2067. JONES, L.
Sylvia Pankhurst and the Workers' Socialist Federation: the red twilight, 1918-24.
M.A.*, Warwick, 1971-72.

2068. JUPP, J.
The Left in Britain, 1931-1941.
M.Sc.(Econ.), L.S.E., 1955-56.

2069. LAIRD, J.A.
The Clarion movement: a study of a Socialist attempt to implement the co-operative
commonwealth in England, 1891-1914.
M.A., Manchester, 1972.

2070. MACDONALD, C.S.
The Art-Worker Guild and schools of arts and crafts, 1884-1914.
Ph.D., Manchester, 1970-71.

2071. PARRY, C.
Socialism in Gwynedd, 1900-1920.
Ph.D., Wales (Bangor), 1966.

2072. PRYNN, D.L.
The Socialist Sunday Schools, the Woodcraft Folk and allied movements: their moral
influence on the British Labour movement since the 1890s.
M.A., Sheffield, 1971.

2073. RANSOM, B.C.
James Connolly and the Scottish Left, 1890-1916.
Ph.D., Edinburgh, 1975.

2074. SCHERR, A.
Robert Blatchford and Clarion Socialism.
Ph.D., Iowa, 1974.
DA 35 5317A

SOCIALIST THOUGHT AND THINKERS

2075. BELL, M.
Social Darwinism and Labour.
M.A.*, Warwick, 1973-74.
        /Examines five thinkers thought to have been influenced by Social Darwinism and
        what impact their ideas had on the British and American Labour movements, 1880-1914.7

2076. BROWN, R.C.
Guild socialism and the idea of function.
M.A., Wales (Swansea), 1977.

2077. BUSH, R.D.
       Individualism and the role of the individual in British and French Socialism·
       the early years, 1800-1848.
       Ph.D., Kansas, 1969.
       DA 30 2935A

2078. CHENG, C.C.
       The transition from individualist to socialist political thinking in England.
       B.Litt., Oxford, 1948.

2079. EGGER, N.T.C.E.F.
       Nationalist currents in nineteenth century Socialist doctrines.
       Ph.D., L.S.E., 1949.

2080. ELKINS, C.L.
       The development of British Marxist literary theory· toward a genetic-functional
       approach to literary criticism.
       Ph.D., Southern Illinois, 1972.
       DA 33 5119A

2081. GERBER, L.E.
       Political pluralism and recent Christian political thought: a tradition of discourse.
       Ph.D., Emory, 1975.
       DA 36 8270A
            ⎾Thinkers considered include G.D.H. Cole, Harold Laski and William Temple.⏌

2082. GLASS, S.T.
       The political theory of the British Guild Socialists.
       B.Litt., Oxford, 1963.

2083. JOHN, M.
       The development of English socialism from 1848 to 1884.
       M.A., London, 1934.

2084. JONES, P.d'A.
       Henry George and British socialism, 1879-1924.
       M.A., Manchester, 1953.

2085. LOWENTHAL, E.
       The Ricardian Socialists, 1820-40.
       Ph.D., Columbia, 1910.

2086. MEAGHER, N.
       Socialism and socialist ideas.
       M.A., Dalhousie, 1962.
            ⎾Includes British socialism - Robert Owen, Fabians, etc.⏌

2087. MORGANS, H.
       The teachings of Karl Marx and their influence on English labour organisations, 1850-1900.
       M.A., Wales (Swansea), 1936.

2088. PAREKH, B.C.
       The idea of equality in English political thought.
       Ph.D., L.S.E., 1966.

2089. RYAN, Mary T. Sister
       An analysis of modern Socialism by Catholic journalists, 1848-1914 (including England).
       Ph.D., St. Louis, 1952.
       DA 20 4749

2090. SAMUELS, S.R.
       Marx, Freud and English intellectuals: a study of the dissemination and
       reconciliation of ideas.
       Ph.D., Stanford, 1971.
       DA 32 5721A

2091. SKEHAN, J.
       Mid-twentieth crisis in British Socialism and its roots.
       Ph.D., Georgetown, 1963-64.

2092. STEVENSON, J.A.
       Daniel De Leon: the relationship of the Socialist Labour Party and European
       Marxism 1890-1914.
       Ph.D., Wisconsin-Madison, 1977.
       DA 39 6267A
            (English, Irish, French and German influences.)

2093. WALSH, J.J.
       Socialist theory in Ireland in the nineteenth and early twentieth centuries.
       M.A., National University of Ireland (Cork), 1973.

2094. WHELAN, J.
       The working class in British socialist thought, 1880-1914.
       M.Phil., Leeds, 1974.

2095. WILKINS, M.S.
The influence of Socialist ideas on English prose writing and political thinking, 1880-95.
Ph.D., Cambridge, 1957.

2096. WINTER, J.M.
The development of British socialist thought, 1912-1918.
Ph.D., Cambridge, 1970.

2097. WOLFE, W.W.
From radicalism to socialism: men and ideas in the formation of English socialist theories, 1881-1889.
Ph.D., Yale, 1967.
DA 28 0184A

STUDIES OF INDIVIDUAL SOCIALIST THINKERS

ANNIE BESANT

2098. MODY, C.M.S.
The political thought of Mrs. Annie Besant: the English years, 1847-1893.
Ph.D., Kansas, 1973.
DA 34 3493A

JOHN FRANCIS BRAY

2099. WADE, H.E.
John Francis Bray: an evaluation of his place in the history of Socialist thought.
Ph.D., St. Louis, 1967.
DA 28 3129A

EDWARD CARPENTER

2100. BARUA, D.K.
The life and work of Edward Carpenter in the light of intellectual, religious, political and literary movements of the later half of the nineteenth century.
Ph.D., Sheffield, 1966.

2101. EAGLETON, T.F.
Nature and spirit: a study of Edward Carpenter - his intellectual context.
Ph.D., Cambridge, 1969.

2102. SQUIRES, J.C.
Aspects of the life and writing of Edward Carpenter.
M.A., Birmingham, 1966-67.

E.H. CARR

2103. EVANS, G.
E.H. Carr and the study of international relations.
M.A., Wales (Swansea), 1972.

2104. LOGUE, J.J.
The political philosophy of Edward Hallett Carr.
Ph.D., Chicago, 1966-67.

G.D.H. COLE

2105. CARPENTER, L.P.
G.D.H. Cole: an intellectual biography.
Ph.D., Harvard, 1966-67.

2106. HAGGAR, G.S.
The political and social thought of G.D.H. Cole.
Ph.D., Columbia, 1966.
DA 28 0740A

2107. KRAMER, D.C.
C.D.H. Cole, guild socialism and workers' control of industry.
Ph.D., Pennsylvania, 1964.
DA 25 2596A

2108. WILLGROS, R.G.
George Douglas Howard Cole: his guild socialist period.
Ph.D., Catholic University of America, 1970.
DA 31 1922A

ISAAC DEUTSCHER

2109. NELSON, B.R.
Isaac Deutscher and contemporary Marxism.
Ph.D., California, Riverside, 1972.
DA 33 2993A

PATRICK GEDDES

2110. REILLY, J.P.
The early social thought of Patrick Geddes.
Ph.D., Columbia, 1972.
DA 35 7847A

JOHN ATKINSON HOBSON

2111. HARRISON, D.E.
The economics of John Atkinson Hobson.
Ph.D., Southern Illinois, 1974.
DA 35 7484A

2112. LEE, A.J.F.
A study of the social and economic thought of J.A. Hobson.
Ph.D., L.S.E., 1970.

2113. SCHNEIDER, M.P.
Underconsumption and imperialism: a study in the work of J.A. Hobson.
M.Sc., Cambridge, 1959-60.

2114. TOWNSHEND, J.
J.A. Hobson and the crisis of liberalism.
Ph.D., Southampton, 1972-73.

THOMAS HODGSKIN

2115. LEVIN, M.B.
Thomas Hodgskin: a study in the development of Ricardian Socialism.
Ph.D., Columbia, 1954.
DA 15 1246

GEORGE JACOB HOLYOAKE

2116. BLASZAK, B.J.
George Jacob Holyoake: an attitudinal study.
Ph.D., State University of New York at Buffalo, 1978.
DA 39 5672A

2117. GRUGEL, L.E.
George Jacob Holyoake: a study in the progress of labour and the British reform
tradition in the nineteenth century.
Ph.D., Chicago, 1970-71.

H.M. HYNDMAN

2118. TSUZUKI, C.
H.M. Hyndman and British socialism, 1881-1921.
D.Phil., Oxford, 1959.

ERNEST CHARLES JONES

2119. PORTER, T.W.
The political thought of Ernest Charles Jones.
Ph.D., Northern Illinois, 1972.
DA 33 5102A

HAROLD J. LASKI

2120. CHESTER, E.W.
Trends in recent European thought on America.
Ph.D., Pitt., 1961.
(includes study of Laski.)

2121. DEANE, H.A.
The political ideas of Harold J. Laski.
Ph.D., Columbia, 1953.
DA 14 0168

2122. RICE, M.C.
Holmes and Laski: on natural law.
Ph.D., Boston, 1962.
DA 23 1676

2123. ROBERTS, E.M.
The attitude of the intellectual left in Britain to the New Deal in America with special
reference to the works of Harold J. Laski and Samuel Kirkham Ratcliffe.
M.A., Kent, 1969-70.

2124. SHARMA, S.K.
The origins and nature of Laski's opinions on international politics.
Ph.D., L.S.E., 1972.

2125. YEE, R.
Harold J. Laski from pluralism to Marxism.
Ph.D., Washington, 1956.
DA 17 1373

TOM MANN

2126. SICHEL, J.R.
The political thought of Tom Mann, 1856-1941.
M.Sc., Bristol, 1968-69.

JOHN STUART MILL

2127. DAVIS, E.G.
Three essays on unsettled questions in the economics of John Stuart Mill.
(1. Mill, Socialism and the English romantics; 2. Mill and public goods;
3. Mill and property rights analysis: land tenure and the 'Irish question'.)
Ph.D., Texas, 1978. DA 39 6266A

2128. SARVASY, W.J.
From democrat to socialist: John Stuart Mill's political theory and class analysis.
Ph.D., University of California, Los Angeles, 1978.
DA 39 3809A

SYDNEY OLIVIER

2129. EL AMIN, M.N.
The socialism of Sydney Olivier.
M.A., Wales (Swansea), 1972.

BERTRAND RUSSELL

2130. GREENSPAN, L.I.
Russell, the Whig Socialist.
Ph.D., Brandeis, 1973.
DA 34 4153A

2131. RADLO, G.
Bertrand Russell's political thought and its relevance to philosophic Radicalism.
Ph.D., Tufts, 1975.
DA 36 1778A

R.H. TAWNEY

2132. SANSOM, T.R.
Political elements in the writings of Matthew Arnold, P.H. Wicksteed and R.H. Tawney.
Ph.D., L.S.E., 1960.

2133. TERRILL, R.G.
Tawney's Socialism.
Ph.D., Harvard, 1969-70.

2134. ZWIEBACH, B.M.
The political thought of R.H. Tawney.
Ph.D., Columbia, 1964.
DA 25 3089A

GRAHAM WALLAS

2135. HOPCUTT, G.S.
The political and social thought of Graham Wallas: a critical survey.
B.Litt., Oxford, 1958-59.

2136. KANG, S.
Graham Wallas, political thinker: an intellectual portrait.
Ph.D., Columbia, 1972.
DA 36 0511A

2137. WALTER, E.J.
Moral basis of the great society: a study of Graham Wallas.
Ph.D., Chicago, 1967-68.

2138. WIENER, M.J.
New and untried circumstances: the intellectual career of Graham Wallas.
Ph.D., Harvard, 1967.

SIDNEY & BEATRICE WEBB

2139. NOLAN, B.E.
The political theory of Beatrice Webb.
Ph.D., Bryn Mawr, 1978.
DA 39 5701A

2140. O'HAGAN, D.J.
Liberalism and socialism: some aspects of the social thought of Sidney and Beatrice Webb.
Ph.D., Toronto, 1976.
DA 39 1810A

2141. WARNER, M.
The Webbs: a study of the influence of intellectuals in politics, largely between 1889 and 1918.
Ph.D., Cambridge, 1966.

H.G. WELLS

2142. THOMAS, S.J.
The political thought of H.G. Wells.
Ph.D., Southampton, 1967-68.

THE SOVIET UNION AND BRITISH LABOUR

2143.   COWDEN, M.H.
Soviet and Comintern policies towards British labour, 1917-21.
Ph.D., Columbia, 1963.
DA 28 4238A

2144.   CULLEN, R.G.
The British Labour Party and Russia, March-November, 1917.
Ph.D., Georgetown, 1971.
DA 32 5143A

2145.   GORODETSKY, G.
Anglo-Soviet relations, 1924-7.
D.Phil., Oxford, 1974.

2146.   GRAUBARD, S.R.
The Russian Revolution in British Labour history, 1917-1924.
Ph.D., Harvard, 1952.

2147.   HANEBRINK, W.T.
Labour intellectuals and the Soviet Union: a study in intellectual contact and understanding.
Ph.D., Washington, 1973.
DA 34 1823A

2148.   JONES, D.A.
The British Labour Party and the Soviet Union, 1939-1949.
Ph.D., Wales (Aberystwyth), 1976.

2149.   LAMMERS, D.N.
British foreign policy, 1929-1934: the problem of Soviet Russia.
Ph.D., Stanford, 1960.
DA 21 00179

2150.   RITTER, G.A.
The British Labour movement and its policy towards Russia from the first Russian
revolution until the Treaty of Locarno.
B.Litt., Oxford, 1959.

2151.   SHANE, T.K.
British reaction to the Soviet Union, 1924-1929: a study of policy and public opinion.
Ph.D., Indiana, 1953.
DA 13 0787

2152.   STARR, E.
The British Labour Party and the Soviet Union: leadership and dissent, 1939-1949.
Ph.D., Chicago, 1962-63.

STATE AND ECONOMIC AFFAIRS; ECONOMIC PLANNING

2153.   BARR, J.E.
British economic planning, 1962-70.
Ph.D., Boston College, 1976.
DA 36 6201A

2154.   BLAND, D.E.
The proper role of the State as seen by British economists in the period 1603-1870.
Ph.D., Sheffield, 1967.

2155.   BLAND, D.E.
The role of the State in British economics, 1870-1914.
M.Litt., Durham, 1968.

2156.   BLANK, S.
Industry and the state: the changing relationship of government and industry in Britain.
Ph.D., Harvard, 1967-68.

2157.   BRANTON, N.
Some effects of state interference in the British coal industry with special reference to
the period 1930-39.
Ph.D., London, External, 1944.

2158.   HURWITZ, S.J.
State intervention in Great Britain: a study of economic control and social response,
1914-1919.
Ph.D., Columbia, 1946.

2159.   LUBENOW, W.C.
The politics of government growth: early Victorian attitudes towards state intervention,
1833-1848.
Ph.D., Iowa, 1968.
DA 29 1849A

2160.   McDONALD, G.W.
Aspects of industrial politics, 1924-1929.
M.Litt., Cambridge, 1973.
/Relationship between government, industry and labour in relation to industrial
relations and industrial organisation and in particularly the contribution made
by the second Baldwin Government./

2161. MACLEOD, R.M.
Specialist policy in government growth: aspects of state activity, 1860-1900.
Ph.D., Cambridge, 1967.

2162. MILLIGAN, F.S.
Politics and industry in the state.
M.A., Birmingham, 1921.

2163. OLDFIELD, R.A.T.
The growth of the concept of economic planning in the doctrine of the British
Labour Party, 1914-1935.
Ph.D., Sheffield, 1973.

2164. PRICHARD, W.J.
A study of State co-operation with "private industry".
M.Comm., Leeds, 1949.

2165. RACICH, D.E.
Planning and politics: British reactions to the economic depression of the inter-war years.
Ph.D., University of Illinois at Chicago Circle, 1977.
DA 39 0421A

2166. SHARP, C.H.
The public and private ownership of industrial enterprise.
Ph.D., Birmingham, 1954-55.

2167. SHIPLEY, V.A.
The public corporation in Great Britain as a device of democratic government.
Ph.D., L.S.E., 1950.

STRIKES, LABOUR DISPUTES AND LABOUR UNREST

2168. BARRETT, J.
Busmen's punch: rank and file organisation and unofficial industrial action among
London busmen, 1913-37.
M.A.*, Warwick, 1972-73.

2169. BRADSHAW, R.P.
The Preston lock-out: a case-study of a mid nineteenth century cotton strike, and its
role in the development of trade union organisation amongst the textile workers.
M.A.*, Lancaster, 1972.

2170. BRUNDAGE, D.
The glass-bottle makers of Yorkshire and the lock-out of 1893.
M.A.*, Warwick, 1975-76.

2171. CLARK, N.
Unofficial strikes on the South Yorkshire coalfield in the Second World War.
M.A.*, Warwick, 1975-76.

2172. CRONIN, J.E.
Strikes in Britain, 1888-1974: a structural and historical analysis.
Ph.D., Brandeis, 1977.
DA 37 7909A

2173. DAVIES, R.D.
The anthracite coal strike of 1925.
M.A.*, Warwick, 1971-72.

2174. DESMARAIS, R.H.
The Supply and Transport Committee, 1919-1926: a study of the British government's
method of handling emergencies stemming from industrial disputes.
Ph.D., Wisconsin, 1970.
DA 31 2300A

2175. DOBSON, C.R.
Labour disturbances in the eighteenth century: a study in the pre-history of British
industrial relations 1717-1800.
D.Phil., Sussex, 1978.

2176. DOXEY, J.M.
The seamen's strike of 1960.
M.A.(Econ.), Manchester, 1962-63.

2177. EVANS, B.
A history of the trades disputes and the formation and operation of the several sliding
scale agreements in the South Wales coal trade, 1870-1903, with special reference to
the work of Sir William Thomas Lewis, first Baron Merthyr of Genghenydd.
M.A., Wales (Cardiff), 1944.

2178. FOSTER, K.
Effect of strikes on the contract of employment and on the rights arising from that
contract.
LL.M., Manchester, 1969-70.

2178A. FURNISS, C.
Industrial unrest in Manchester and Salford, 1910-14.
M.A., Manchester, 1971.

2179.   GENNARD, J.
        Major post-war disputes in the printing industry.
        M.A.(Econ.), Manchester, 1967-68.

2180.   GIBLIN, P.J.
        The strike weapon in Irish Unionism.
        M.A., National University of Ireland, 1952-53.

2181.   HEBERT, R.G.
        Syndicalism and industrial strife, 1910-1912: the significance of the Cambrian Combine
        strike, Liverpool general transport strike and London dock strikes as barometers for a
        better understanding of the 'labour unrest, 1910-1912' in the British Isles.
        Ph,D., Maryland, 1975.
        DA 36 6879A

2182.   HERON, W.C.
        The Commission of Enquiry into Industrial Unrest, 1917.
        M.A.*, Warwick, 1975-76.

2183.   JACKSON, M.P.
        A critical assessment of the Ministry of Labour's method of analysing the causes of
        stoppages, with special reference to major stoppages in the port, transport and coal
        mining industries between 1963 and 1966 (inclusive).
        M.A., Hull, 1971-72.

2184.   JAMES, B.
        The right to strike: a concept to legitimise the disruption of industrial relationships
        by the concerted withdrawal of labour.
        Ph.D., L.S.E., 1972.

2185.   LLOYD, P.
        The influence of syndicalism in the dock strikes of 1911 in Hull and Manchester (and
        Salford).
        M.A.*, Warwick, 1971-72.

2186.   NARAYANASWAMY, B.V.
        Trade disputes in Great Britain: a brief enquiry into causes of and an examination of
        methods of dealing with these and probably the experience and possibilities of conciliation
        and arbitration and with a reference to Indian labour.
        Ph.D., Edinburgh, 1929.

2187.   PRATTEN, J.D.
        The reaction to working class unrest, 1911-1914.
        Ph,D., Sheffield, 1975.

2188.   SAPSFORD, D.R.
        The United Kingdom's industrial disputes, 1893-1971: a study in the economics of
        industrial unrest.
        M.Phil., Leicester, 1974.

2189.   SCOTT, H.
        The history of the miners' bond in Northumberland and Durham with special reference
        to its influence on industrial disputes.
        M.A., Manchester, 1946.

2190.   SHEA, R.A.
        A general analysis and case study of unofficial strikes in the manual-worker section
        of the British engineering industry.
        M.Sc.(Econ.), L.S.E., 1960-61.

2191.   SHOREY, J.C.
        A quantitative analysis of strike activity in the United Kingdom with reference to the
        time pattern and to inter-industry differences.
        Ph.D. (Econ.), L.S.E., 1974.

GENERAL STRIKES

2192.   COPLEY, J.
        The General Strike in South Yorkshire.
        M.A.*, Sheffield, 1972.

2193.   DALGLEISH, J.
        The Limerick General Strike, 1919.
        M.A.*, Warwick, 1975-76.

2194.   MASON, A.
        The miners' unions of Northumberland and Durham, 1918-1931 with special reference to
        the General Strike of 1926.
        Ph.D., Hull, 1967.

2195.   MORRIS, R.L.
        The Labour Party and the General Strike of 1926.
        Ph.D., South California, 1969.
        DA 30 1962A

2196.   PLUMMER, A.
        The general strike during one hundred years.
        M.Sc., London, 1927.

2197. POELS, J.A.
Law and history of the general strike.
B.Litt., Oxford, 1952.

2198. QUINE, W.G.
A.J. Cook: miners' leader in the General Strike.
M.A., Manchester, 1964.

2199. SCHEPS, A.E.
Trade unions and government, 1925-7 with particular reference to the General Strike.
D.Phil., Oxford, 1972.

2200. SHEFFTZ, M.C.
British labour, the General Strike and the Constitution, 1910-1927.
Ph.D., Harvard, 1961-62.

2201. THOMSON, L.D.
The relations between government and the trade unions in the General Strike of May 1926.
Ph.D., L.S.E., 1951-52.

STUDENT MOVEMENTS AND YOUTH ORGANISATIONS

2202. FERRIS, J.
The Labour League of Youth, 1924-40.
M.A.*, Warwick, 1975-76.

2203. JOSEPHSON, E.
Political youth organisations in Europe, 1900-1950: a comparative study of six radical
parties and their youth auxilaries.
Ph.D., Columbia, 1959.
DA 20 3385
        (Comparisons of Social Democratic parties in Germany and Austria; Italian and
        German Fascist movements; Soviet Communist Party; British Labour Party.)

2204. KLEIN, R.D.
A comparative study of student political activism: the free University of Berlin, the
London School of Economics, the University of Paris at Nanterre.
Ph.D., Columbia University Teachers' College, 1969.
DA 31 3622A

2205. LAYTON-HENRY, Z.A.T.
Political youth organisations in Britain: a comparative study of the Young
Conservatives and the Labour Party Young Socialists.
Ph.D., Birmingham, 1972-73.

2206. O'CONNOR, R.E.
The activist examined: political and apolitical students at the Universities of Essex,
St. Andrews and Montpelier.
Ph.D., North Carolina, 1971.
DA 32 7060A

TECHNOLOGICAL CHANGE /see also LUDDITES/

2207. BERG, M.L.
The machinery question: conception of technical change in the political economy during
the Industrial Revolution.
D.Phil., Oxford, 1976.

2208. BURGESS, K.R.
The influence of technological change in the social attitudes and trade union
policies of workers in the engineering industry, 1780-1860.
Ph.D., London, 1970.

2209. CHADWICK-JONES, J.K.
The social and psychological effects of change in the tinplate industry of
South-West Wales: a study of the handmill worker.
Ph.D., Wales (Cardiff), 1960-61.

2210. COLLINS, E.J.T.
Harvest technology and labour supply in Britain, 1790-1870.
Ph.D., Nottingham, 1970.
2211 (No entry)
2212. GARDNER, C.W.
The attitude of the English people towards the introduction of labour-saving machinery
during the Industrial Revolution.
M.A., McGill, 1933.

2213. GINTZ, H.
Effects of technological change on labour in selected sections of the iron and steel
industries of Great Britain, the United States and Germany, 1901-1939.
Ph.D., L.S.E., 1954.

2214. HEAD, P.
Industrial organisation in Leicester, 1844-1914: a study in changing technology,
innovation and conditions of employment.
Ph.D., Leicester, 1960.

2215.   JONES, T.K.
         The effect of large scale technological development and industrial expansion
         upon the local organisation of a trade union.
         M.A., Wales (Cardiff), 1959-60.

2216.   LEVINE, A.L.
         Industrial change and its effects upon labour, 1900-1914.
         Ph.D., L.S.E., 1954.

2217.   LINDQUIST, C.N.
         Iron ships and the new Unionism: technological change and the British seamen, 1850-1910.
         Ph.D., Michigan, 1973.
         DA 35 0373A
              /National Amalgamated Sailors and Firemen's Union._7

2218.   LYONS, J.S.
         The Lancashire cotton industry and the introduction of the power loom, 1815-1850.
         Ph.D., University of California, Berkeley, 1977.
         DA 38 4962A
              (includes sections on the effects on labour.)

2219.   MUSGRAVE, P.W.
         Technical change, the labour force and education in the British and German iron and
         steel industries from 1860.
         Ph.D., London, 1964.

2220.   RANDALL, A.J.
         The Shearmen's campaign: a study of the woollen industry in the industrial revolution,
         1800-1809.
         M.A.*, Sheffield, 1972.
              /Campaign against excessive mechanisation in woollen industry._7

2221.   SALTER, W.E.G.
         A consideration of the nature of technological change with particular reference to
         labour productivity.
         Ph.D., Cambridge, 1955-56.
              (U.K. industries, 1924-50.)

2222.   SARKAR, K.K.
         Scottish experience on the impact of farm mechanisation in the employment and use of
         man labour, with observations on possible Indian problems in this field.
         Ph.D., Edinburgh, 1961-62.

TEMPERANCE QUESTION

2223.   BRETHERTON, G.C.
         The Irish Temperance Movement 1829-47.
         Ph.D., Columbia, 1978.
         DA 39 2472A

2224.   BURROWS, H.R.
         Studies in social sciences: /2/
         Some social and economic effects of alcohol consumption.
         M.Com., Leeds, 1932.

2225.   HARRISON, B.H.
         The temperance question in England, 1828-69.
         D.Phil., Oxford, 1966.

2226.   LAMBERT, W.R.
         Drink and sobriety in Wales, 1835-1895.
         Ph.D., Wales (Swansea), 1970.

2227.   MARTIN, C.C.
         The British Liquor Licensinc Act of 1904 and its historical background.
         Ph.D., North Carolina, Chapel Hill, 1953.

2228.   PATON, D.C.
         Drink and the temperance movement in nineteenth-century Scotland.
         Ph.D., Edinburgh, 1977.

2229.   SHIMAN, L.L.
         Crusade against drink in Victorian England.
         Ph.D., Wisconsin, 1970.
         DA 31 5303A

2230.   WRIGHT, D.E.
         The British Liberal Party and the liquor licensing question, 1895-1905.
         Ph.D., McMaster, 1971-72.

TRADE UNIONS

GENERAL STUDIES

2231. ALLEN, V.L.
A study of power in trade unions in Great Britain.
Ph.D., London, External, 1953-54.

2232. COOK, F.G.
The concept of ideology and its application to the study of trade unions.
M.A., Liverpool, 1971-72.

2233. GOLDSTEIN, J.
Apathy and the democratic process in the government of a British trade union.
Ph.D., L.S.E., 1950.

2234. HEAD, P.J.
The status, functions and policy of the trade union official, 1870-1930.
M.Litt., Cambridge, 1956.

2235. McCARTHY, W.E.J.
The closed shop in British trade unions.
D.Phil., Oxford, 1962.

2236. MACPHERSON, C.B.
Voluntary associations within the State, 1900-1934, with special reference to the place of trade unions in relation to the State in Great Britain.
M.Sc., L.S.E., 1935.

2237. McPHERSON, E.
The trade union as a local pressure group.
M.A., Liverpool, 1972-73.

2238. MILNE-BAILEY, W.
Trade unions and the state.
Ph.D., L.S.E., 1934.

2239. OSAHON, N.
Trade union militancy in retailing (a study of members' attitude to their trade union).
M.Sc., Salford, 1968-69.

2240. PETRIDIS, A.
The economic analysis of trade unions by British economists, 1870-1930.
Ph.D., Duke, 1974.
DA 35 4842A

2241. RABINOVITCH, Y.
British Marxist socialism and trade unionism.
D.Phil., Sussex, 1978.

PERIOD STUDIES

Early 19th century

2242. KIRBY, R.G.
John Doherty, trade unionist and factory reformer, 1798-1854.
Ph.D., Manchester, 1972-73.

2243. OLIVER, W.H.
Organisations and ideas behind the efforts to achieve a general union of the working classes in England in the early 1830s.
D.Phil., Oxford, 1954.

Mid-19th century and legal recognition struggle

2244. BUCHANAN, R.A.
Trade unions and public opinion, 1850-75.
Ph.D., Cambridge, 1957.

2245. HANSON, C.G.
The development of trade unionism and trade union law with special reference to the Royal Commission of 1867.
Ph.D., Newcastle, 1972.

2246. HARRIS, J.R.
The Trade Union charter: a struggle for legal status, 1867-1876.
Ph.D., Oklahoma, 1971.
DA 32 6340A

2247. SMITH, E.G.
The establishment of the British Royal Commission of 1867-69 to investigate trade unionism.
Ph.D., Pennsylvania, 1932.

2248. STAINTON, D.C.
Aspects of trade union interest in judicial reform, 1867-82.
M.Phil., Southampton, 1969.

Late 19th century and early 20th century

2249. BURDICK, E.L.
Syndicalism and industrial unionism in England until 1918.
D.Phil., Oxford, 1950.

2250. CARLTON, B.F.
'A substantial and sterling friend of the labouring men': the Kent and Sussex
Labourers' Union, 1872-95.
D.Phil., Sussex, 1978.

2251. DUFFY, A.E.P.
The growth of trade unionism in England from 1867-1906 in its political aspects.
Ph.D., London, External, 1956.

2252. HAMMOND, T.T.
Revolutionarism and vanguardism: Lenin on trade unions under Capitalism, 1893-1917.
Ph.D., Columbia, 1954.
DA 14 1374

2253. LEVINE, S.H.
St. Loe Strachey and the ideology of free trade unionism.
Ph.D., City University of New York, 1975.
DA 35 7227A

2254. NORTON, S.P.
Trade union growth in the late nineteenth century.
M.Phil., Kent, 1976.

2255. TAPLIN, E.L.
The origins and development of new unionism, 1870-1910.
M.A., Liverpool, 1966-67.

2256. WILSON, B.
The surge of industrial unionism.
M.A., Western Ontario, 1937.

Inter-war period

2257. DRISLANE, R.M.
British trade unions and class conflict, 1910-1921: a study in political mobilisation.
Ph.D., L.S.E., 1974-75.

2258. HYMAN, R.
The Workers' Union, 1898-1929.
D.Phil., Oxford, 1968.

2259. MARTIN, R.
The National Minority Movement: a study of the organisation of trade union militancy
in the inter-war period.
D.Phil., Oxford, 1965.

Post 1945 period

2260. DERBYSHIRE, J.D.
The Royal Commission on Trade Unions and Employers' Association, 1965-1968: an analysis
of a Royal Commission as an instrument of public policy making.
Ph.D., London, External, 1976.

2261. HARRISON, M
The political activities of British trade unions, 1945-1954.
D.Phil., Oxford, 1957-58.

2262. MULLER, W.D.
The parliamentary activity of trade union M.P.s, 1959-64.
Ph.D., Florida, 1966.
DA 27 3094A

2263. WARNER, A.W.
British trade unionism under a Labour Government, 1945-51.
Ph.D., Columbia, 1954.
DA 14 1576

TRADES UNION CONGRESS

2264. ACKROYD, D.E.
The economic policy of trade unions in Great Britain in the post-war period as
illustrated by the proceedings of the Trades Union Congress.
B.Litt., Oxford, 1936.

2265. CRAIGEN, J.M.
The Scottish Trades Union Congress, 1897-1973: a study of a pressure group.
M.Litt., Heriot-Watt, 1974.

2266. JACQUES, M.
The emergence of 'responsible' trade unionism: a study of the 'new direction' in
T.U.C. policy, 1926-1935.
Ph.D., Cambridge, 1977.

2267. THOMSON, A.W.J.
       The reaction of the American Federation of Labour and the Trades Union Congress to
       labour law, 1900-1935.
       Ph.D., Cornell, 1969.
       DA 29 3754A
             See also entry nos.: 1405, 2443, 2490.

OCCUPATIONAL STUDIES

Agricultural Workers

2268. HORN, P.L.R.
       Agricultural labourers' trade unionism in four midland counties, 1860-1900.
       Ph.D., Leicester, 1968.

2269. MADDEN, M.
       The National Union of Agricultural Workers.
       B.Litt., Oxford, 1957.

2270. MILLS, F.D.
       The National Union of Agricultural Workers.
       Ph.D., Reading, 1964-65.

Boot and Shoe Industry

2271. JONES, R.L.
       The social context of trade union activity in the East-Midlands boot and shoe
       industry in the late 19th century.
       M.Sc., Loughborough, 1971.

2272. THORN, G.
       Statement aristocrats and sweated militants.
       M.A.*, Warwick, 1973-74.
             /London boot makers, 1884-1890; including Jewish boot makers' unions from 1886
       and their relations to the other unions; account of 1890 strike.7

Cabinet Makers

2273. BLANKENHORN, D.
       Cabinet makers in Victorian Britain: a study of two trade unions.
       M.A., Warwick, 1978.
             /A study of the Friendly Society of Operative Cabinet Makers and the
       Alliance Association of Cabinet Makers.7

Engineering

2274. HINTON, J S.
       Rank and file militancy in the British engineering industry, 1914-1918.
       Ph.D., Birkbeck College, London, 1969.

2275. LEWIS, D.R.
       The Electrical Trades Union and the growth of the electrical industry in 1926.
       D.Phil., Oxford, 1970.

2276. McLAINE, W.
       The Engineers' Union, Book 1: The millwrights and 'old mechanics'.
       Ph.D., London, External, 1939.

2277. NEWELL, P.M.
       The political activity of a trade union (the E.T.U., 1944-1956).
       M.A., Manchester, 1958-59.

2278. OAKLEY, P.A.
       Demarcation and amalgamation: a study of union antagonism between the shipwrights
       and boilermakers in the Cammell Laird shipyard, Birkenhead, 1953-64.
       M.A.(Econ.), Manchester, 1967-68.

2279. ROBINSON, T.H.
       The antecedents and beginnings of the Amalgamated Society of Engineers.
       B.Litt., Oxford, 1928.

General Workers' Union

2280. WILD, A.
       The origins of the National Union of General and Municipal Workers at Pilkingtons'
       Brothers, St. Helens: a study of the years 1900-1923.
       M A.*, Warwick, 1973-74.

Iron and Steel Workers

2281. PARSONS, C.J.
       Workplace and union: a study of the relation between workplace and union-member
       involvement in two trade union branches of a large steel works.
       M.A., Liverpool, 1959-60.

Mining and Allied Industries

2282. ALLEN, G.C.
       The history of an 18th century combination in the copper-mining industry.
       M.Com., Birmingham, 1922.

2283. CADE, J.
       The Miners' Federation of Great Britain and the Politics of the Coal Industry
       Commission 1919.
       M.A., Warwick, 1977.

2284. CAMPBELL, A.B.
       Honourable men and degraded slaves: a social history of trade unionism among the
       Lanarkshire miners, 1775-1875; with particular reference to the Coatbridge and
       Larkhall districts.
       Ph.D., Warwick, 1976.

2285. CARTWRIGHT, J.A.
       A study in British syndicalism: the miners of South Wales, 1906-1914.
       M.Sc.Econ., University of Wales Institute of Science and Technology, 1969.

2286. CHALLINOR, R.C.
       Trade unionism in the coal industry until 1900 with particular reference to Lancashire.
       Ph.D., Lancaster, 1970.

2287. DAVIES, P.
       Syndicalism in the Yorkshire coalfields, 1910-1914.
       M.Sc., Bradford, 1977.

2288. EVANS, E.W.
       William Abraham, 1842-1922.
       M.A., Wales (Aberystwyth), 1953.
            /Official and for a period President of the South Wales Miners' Federation.7

2289. GARSIDE, W.R.
       The Durham Miners' Association, 1919-1947.
       Ph.D., Leeds, 1969.

2290. JOHNSON, W.H.
       A north-east miners' union (Hepburn's Union) of 1831-32.
       M.Litt., Durham, 1959.

2291. JONES, R.M.
       The trade union and political activities of the North Wales slate quarrymen in
       relation to their social and working conditions, 1870-1905.
       Ph.D., Warwick, 1976.

2292. MACHIN, F.
       Labour organisations of miners of South Yorkshire from 1858 to 1914.
       B.Litt., Oxford, 1930.

2293. ROGERS, E.
       The history of trade unionism in the coal mining industry of North Wales up to 1914.
       M.A., Wales, 1928.

2294. SCOTT, I.F.
       Lancashire and Cheshire Miners' Federation, 1900-1914.
       D.Phil., York, 1977.

2295. SMITH, D.B.
       The rebuilding of the South Wales Miners' Federation, 1927-39: a trade union in its society.
       Ph.D., Wales, 1976.

2296. WEBSTER, F.
       Durham miners and unionism, 1831-1926: a sociological interpretation.
       M.A., Durham, 1973-74.

2297. WILLIAMS, J.E.
       The political, social and economic factors influencing the growth of trade unionism
       among the Derbyshire coal miners, 1880-1944.
       Ph.D., Sheffield, 1959.

2298. WILLIAMS, J.R.
       The life and work of William John Parry, Bethesda, with particular reference to his
       trade union activities among the slate quarrymen of North Wales.
       M.A., Wales (Bangor), 1953.

2299. WILSON, G.
       The miners of the West of Scotland and their trade unions, 1842-74.
       Ph.D., Glasgow, 1977.

Post Office Workers

2300. SMITH, L.M.
Some aspects of staff organisation of the postal service with special reference to:
(a) the general history and development of the movement since 1895
(b) the struggle for official recognition
(c) the efforts to secure full rights
(d) the working of Whitleyism.
B.Litt., Oxford, 1931.

Pottery Industry

2301. WARBURTON, W.H.
The progress of labour organisation in the pottery industry of Great Britain.
B.Litt., Oxford, 1928.

Printing

2302. GILLESPIE, S.C.
A hundred years of progress: the record of the Scottish Typographical Association, 1853-1952.
Ph.D., Glasgow, 1954.

2303. MUSSON, A.E.
A history of trade unionism in the provincial printing industry during the nineteenth century.
M.A., Manchester, 1950.

2304. RICHARDS, J.H.
Social and economic aspects of combinations in the printing trade before 1875.
M.A., Liverpool, 1956.

Seamen, Dock-Workers and Allied Industries

2304A. FISHER, J.P.
The Transport and General Workers' Union and the Devlin modernisation programme in the port transport industry with particular reference to Southampton.
Ph.D., Southampton, 1976.

2305. HIRSCH, M.G.
The Federation of Sailmakers of Great Britain and Ireland, 1889-1922: a craft union in crisis.
M.A.*, Warwick, 1975-76.

2306. LENG, P.J.
The Dock, Wharf, Riverside and General Labourers' Union in South Wales and Bristol, 1889-1922.
M.A., Kent, 1973-74.

2307. LINDOP, F.J.
A history of seamen's trade unionism to 1929.
M.Phil., L.S.E., 1972.

2308. LOVELL, J.C.
Trade unionism in the port of London, 1870-1914.
Ph.D., L.S.E., 1966.

2309. SCHNEER, J.
Ben Tillett: the making and un-making of a British labour militant.
Ph.D., Columbia, 1978.
DA 39 2475A
/Founder and first secretary of the Dockers' Union.7

Textile and Clothing Industry

2310. CUTHBERT, N.H.
A study of trade unions in the British lace industry.
Ph.D., Nottingham, 1962-63.

2311. LERNER, S.
A history of the United Clothing Workers' Union: a case study of social disorganisation.
Ph.D., L.S.E., 1956.

2312. TURNER, H.A.F.
Labour organisation in the cotton trade of Great Britain.
Ph.D., Manchester, 1960-61.

2313. WEATHERHEAD, J.F.
The history of the trade unions in the Yorkshire woollen and worsted industries.
B.Litt., Oxford, 1925.

Transport Workers

2314.   GUPTA, P.S.
        The history of the Amalgamated Society of Railway Servants, 1871-1913.
        D.Phil., Oxford, 1960.

2315.   PHILLIPS, G.A.
        The National Transport Workers' Federation, 1910-27.
        D.Phil., Oxford, 1969.

"White Collar" Workers; and Professional Organisations

2316.   ADAMS, R.J.
        Union behaviour as a factor in union growth: a comparative study of white-collar
        unions in Great Britain and Sweden.
        Ph.D., Wisconsin, 1973.
        DA 34 6774A

2317.   BAIN, G.S.
        The growth of non-manual workers' unions in manufacturing industries in Great Britain
        since 1948.
        D.Phil., Oxford, 1968.

2318.   BARON, G.
        The secondary schoolmaster, 1895-1914: a study of the qualifications, conditions of
        employment and professional associations of masters in English secondary schools.
        Ph.D., Institute of Education, London, 1952.

2319.   BLACKBURN, R.M.
        Unionisation and union character in banking.
        Ph.D., Liverpool, 1965-66.

2320.   CHRISTIAN, H.
        The development of trade unionism and professionalism among British journalists:
        a sociological enquiry.
        Ph.D., L.S.E., 1977.

2321.   COATES, R.D.
        Organisations representing school teachers, as interest groups within the educational
        system of England and Wales.
        D.Phil., Oxford, 1970.

2322.   ELLIS, V.A.
        Some sociological dimensions of unionisation among technical and supervisory employees.
        Ph.D., Leeds, 1970-71.

2323.   HAILSTONE, D.B.
        The Hull Association of Elementary Teachers: some aspects of the Association's local
        activities and interests from 1871 to 1892.
        B.Phil., Hull, 1974.

2323A. HERITAGE, J.C.
        The growth of trade unionism in the London clearing banks, 1960-70: a sociological
        interpretation.
        Ph.D., Leeds, 1978.

2324.   HUMPHREYS, B.V.
        The development of clerical trade unions in the British Civil Service.
        Ph.D., L.S.E., 1953-54.

2325.   JONES, K.L.
        The growth and development of white collar trade unionism in the British steel industry.
        Ph.D., L.S.E., 1977.

2326.   McFARLANE, B.A.
        The chartered engineer: a study of the recruitment, qualification, conditions of
        employment and professional associations of chartered civil, electrical and mechanical
        engineers in Great Britain.
        Ph.D., L.S.E., 1960-61.

2327.   McMULLAN, G.
        The development of clerical trade unionism in the North of Ireland during the twentieth
        century.
        Ph.D., Queen's University, Belfast, 1971-72.

2328.   PHILLIPSON, C.M.
        A study of the attitudes towards and participation in trade union activities of selected
        groups of non-manual workers.
        M.A., Nottingham, 1964-65.

2329.   RIDEALGH, W.
        The history of the Hull and District Schoolmasters' Association from 1919 to 1935.
        M.Ed., Hull, 1975.

2330.   RIORDAN, P.J.N.
        The Association of Secondary Teachers, 1909-1968: some aspects of its growth and
        development.
        M.Ed., National University of Ireland (Cork), 1975.

2331.   ROY, W.
         The National Union of Teachers: a study of the political process within an association
         of professional workers.
         Ph.D., L.S.E., 1963.

2332.   SWABE, A.I.
         The Association of Teachers in Technical Institutions, 1904-1945: white collar
         unionism among professional people.
         M.Phil., London, 1977.

WOMEN-WORKERS

2332A.   LEVENHAK, S.T.
         Trade union membership among women and girls in the United Kingdom, 1920-1965.
         Ph.D., L.S.E., 1971.

NATIONAL AND REGIONAL STUDIES

Ireland

2332B.   BLEAKLEY, D.W.
         Trade union beginnings in Belfast and district with special reference to the period
         1881-1900 and to the work of the Belfast and District Trades' Council during that period.
         M.A., Queen's University, Belfast, 1955.

2332C.   D'ARCY, F.
         Dublin artisan activity, opinion and organisation, 1820-50.
         M.A., National University of Ireland, 1965.

2333.   DAURA, M.
         Structural problems of the Irish trade union movement.
         M.S.A., Trinity College, Dublin, 1968-69.

2333A.   DIGNAM, J.J.
         Organisational structure of trade unions and the trade union movement in Ireland.
         M.S.A., Trinity College, Dublin, 1967-68.

2334.   DOYLE, M.G.
         The development of industrial organisations amongst skilled artisans in Ireland, 1780-1838.
         M.Phil., Southampton, 1973.

2335.   GIBLIN, P.J.
         The origins and development of trade unionism in Ireland.
         Ph.D., National University of Ireland, 1964-65.

2336.   HILLERY, B.J.P.
         Trade union structure and organisation in the Republic of Ireland.
         Ph.D., National University of Ireland, 1972-73.

2337.   HOLOHAN, P.
         Daniel O'Connell and trade unions.
         M.A., National University of Ireland (Cork), 1968.

2338.   JUDGE, J.J.
         Organisation of trade unions in the Republic of Ireland.
         M.A., National University of Ireland, 1951.

2339.   KEOGH, D.F.
         The Dublin trade union movement and labour leadership, 1907-1914.
         M.A., University College, Dublin, 1975.

Scotland

2340.   EVANS, G.
         Trade unionism and the wage level in Aberdeen from 1870 to 1920.
         Ph.D., Aberdeen, 1951.

Wales

2341.   DONOVAN, P.W.
         Unskilled labour unions in South Wales, 1889-1914.
         M.Phil., Birkbeck College, London, 1969.

2342.   THOMAS, P.S.
         An outline of the activities of some trade unions of South Wales with reference to the
         question of compulsory membership.
         M.A., Wales, 1930.

England: Regional Studies

2343.   HOLTON, R.J.
         Syndicalism in Britain, 1911-20 with particular reference to Merseyside.
         D.Phil., Sussex, 1973.

2344.   LAYBOURN, K.
         The attitudes of the Yorkshire trade unions to the social and economic problems created
         by the 'Great Depression' of 1873-1896.
         Ph.D., Lancaster, 1973.

2345.   WALTON, J.
        History of trade unionism in Leicester to the end of the nineteenth century with special
        reference to the hosiery workers' union.
        M.A., Sheffield, 1952.

TRADES COUNCILS

2346.   BATHER, L.
        The history of the Manchester and Salford Trades Council.
        Ph.D., Manchester, 1956.

2347.   CLINTON, A.M.
        Trades councils from the beginning of the twentieth century to the Second World War.
        Ph.D., Chelsea College, London, 1973.

2348.   FRASER, W.H.
        Trades councils in England and Scotland, 1858-1897.
        D.Phil., Sussex, 1968.

2349.   MADDOCK, S.
        The Liverpool Trades Council and politics, 1879-1918.
        M.A., Liverpool, 1959.

UNEMPLOYMENT

2350.   AIAD, A.A.
        A study of some aspects of government policy with regard to regional unemployment
        in Great Britain, 1934-62.
        M.A.(Econ.), Manchester, 1964-65.

2351.   AWBERY, S.L.
        Self-help and unemployment in Gwynned.
        M.A., Wales (Aberystwyth), 1961-62.

2352.   BEVERIDGE, W.H.
        Unemployment in Britain with special reference to the period from 1909 to the present time.
        D.Sc., L.S.E., 1930.

2353.   BEVINGTON, S.M.
        Factors in occupational maladjustment: a comparative study of the careers of employed
        and unemployed lads in a typical London district.
        Ph.D., London, External, 1933.

2354.   BOOTH, A.E.
        The timing and content of government policies to assist the depressed areas, 1920-39.
        Ph.D., Kent, 1975.

2355.   BROWN, K.D.
        Labour and unemployment, 1900-1914.
        Ph.D., Kent, 1969.

2356.   CHAMBERS, J.F.
        The problem of unemployment in English social policy, 1886-1914.
        Ph.D., Cambridge, 1970.

2357.   COLLINGE, H.
        The problem of unemployment in Merseyside.
        M.A., Liverpool, 1953-54.

2358.   DAWE, C.V.
        A study of juvenile unemployment in West Ham.
        M.Com., Leeds, 1933.

2359.   EDDY, G.W.
        The problem of unemployment in relation to the industrial revolution and the depression
        of 1819-21.
        Ph.D., Ohio, 1932.

2360.   ELLIOTT, B.J.
        The social and economic effects of unemployment in the coal and steel industries
        of Sheffield, 1925-1936.
        M.A., Sheffield, 1969.

2361.   ENDERSON, R.E.
        The influence of unemployment upon the development of Thamesmead.
        M.Sc., Strathclyde, 1971-72.

2362.   FLETCHER, R.C.T
        A study of post-war regional cyclical sensitivity and structural unemployment in the
        U.K.: some policy implications.
        M.A.*, Lancaster, 1971.

2363.   FREEMAN, A.J.
        An investigation into the causes that render large numbers of boys unable to obtain
        employment on reaching early manhood with special reference to the conditions of boy
        life and labour in Birmingham.
        B.Litt., Oxford, 1914.

2364. GAYER, A.D.
Unemployment in British industries, 1815-50.
D.Phil., Oxford, 1931.

2365. HANCOCK, K.J.
The problem of unemployment in the United Kingdom, 1919-1929.
Ph.D., L.S.E., 1959.

2366. HAYBURN, R.H.C.
The responses to unemployment in the 1930s with particular reference to South East
Lancashire.
Ph.D., Hull, 1970.

2367. HIRST, J.D.
The role of the labour colony in English unemployment policy, 1886-1911.
M.A., Manchester, 1972.

2368. IRVINE, R.J.
Unemployed labour as a pressure group in Great Britain, 1919-32.
B.Litt., Oxford, 1951.

2369. JOLL, C.
The working class, unemployment and the state: an examination of working class attitudes
towards and action in promoting measures to deal with the problem of unemployment in
Britain and America, 1870-1914.
M.A., Sussex, 1977.

2370. LEHMANN, P.J.
Unemployment and the opportunity cost of mining labour.
D.Phil., Sussex, 1971-72.

2370A. LOVATT, D.A.
Unemployment and public policy in Britain, 1970-76.
M.Phil., University College, London, 1978.

2371. MEARA, G.
Juvenile unemployment in the South Wales industrial region: an economic and
statistical enquiry.
Ph.D., Wales, 1935.

2372. MILLER, F.M.
Work or maintenance? Unemployment policy in Great Britain, 1931-1936.
Ph.D., Wisconsin, 1972.
DA 33 5099A

2373. MONAGHAN, W.
Redundancy: a study of its incidence impact and causes, together with the reactions
of some employers and trade unions to redundancy situations.
M.Sc., Strathclyde, 1971-72.

2374. MORETON, P.W.T.
Labour turnover and its relationship to levels of employment and unemployment in
some sectors of British manufacturing industry since 1948.
Ph.D., Hull, 1970-71.

2375. OPIE, L.M.
Voluntary effort to help the unemployed in the 1930s.
M.A., Manchester, 1974.

2376. POPE, R.
The unemployment problem in North East Lancashire, 1920-38.
M.Litt., Lancaster, 1974.

2377. ROSAMOND, F.J.
The social and economic effects of unemployment in Manchester, 1919-26.
M.A.(Econ.), Manchester, 1970.

2378. SALT, J.
A consideration of some post-war unemployment problems in the Merseyside and
Manchester conurbations.
Ph.D., Liverpool, 1966-67.

2379. SALT, W.E.
Industrial combination and unemployment.
M.A., Sheffield, 1924.

2380. SHINTON, D.A.
Post-war regional unemployment and development.
M.A., Exeter, 1965.

2381. SHIPLEY, E.T.
Unemployment in Canada, Great Britain and the U.S.A.
M.A., Acadia, 1946.

2382. SHOWLER, B.
An analysis of the characteristics of adult unemployment in the sub-region of Humberside
since 1951.
M.Sc.(Econ.), Hull, 1969.

2383. TAYLOR, J.
       Unemployment and wage inflation in Britain and the U.S.A.: a post-war study.
       Ph.D., Lancaster, 1971.

2384. THIRLWALL, A.P.
       Regional unemployment and public policy in Great Britain, 1948-1964.
       Ph.D., Leeds, 1968.

2385. TILNEY, R.H.
       Aids to reducing unemployment in Great Britain between 1957 and 1967.
       M.Phil., Nottingham, 1972-73.

2386. WALSH, J.J.
       Employment and unemployment in the 26 counties.
       M.Econ.Sc., National University of Ireland, 1941.

2387. WATMOUGH, P.
       The politics of unemployment in London, 1892-1895.
       M.A.*, Warwick, 1974-75.

2388. ZEISEL, J.S.
       The structure of unemployment at full employment in Great Britain and the United States.
       Ph.D., The American University, 1968.
       DA 29 0722A
           (contemporary study)

UNREST, POPULAR DISTURBANCES AND REVOLUTIONARY INFLUENCES

2389. AMOS, S.W.
       Social discontent and agrarian disturbances in Essex, 1795-1850.
       M.A., Durham, 1972.

2390. ANDERSON, G.D.
       Public order and civil liberties, 1931-1937.
       Ph,D., Iowa, 1973.
       DA 34 5849A

2391. BAILEY, V.
       Social order and popular disturbance in Victorian England, 1867-1900.
       Ph.D., Warwick, 1975.

2392. BAXTER, J.L.
       The origins of the social war in South Yorkshire: a study of capitalist evolution
       and labour class realization in one industrial region, c.1750-1855.
       Ph.D., Sheffield, 1977.

2393. BEAMES, M.R.
       Peasant disturbances, popular conspiracies and their control· Ireland, 1798-1852.
       Ph.D., Manchester, 1976.

2394. BELOFF, M.
       Public order and popular disturbances in England, 1689-1714.
       B.Litt., Oxford, 1937.

2395. BENJAMIN, H.W.
       The London Irish· a study in political activism, 1870-1910.
       Ph.D., Princeton, 1976.
       DA 37 5284A

2396. BOYD, L.G.
       The role of the military in civil disorders in England and Wales, 1780-1811.
       Ph.D., University of Tennessee, 1977.
       DA 38 0956A

2397. BROOKS, H.F.
       English reactions to the continental revolutions of 1848.
       Ph.D., Nebraska, 1948.

2398. BURTON, V.C.
       Popular unrest in South East Lancashire and North-East Cheshire during the Luddite period.
       M.A.*, Lancaster, 1976.

2399. CAMPBELL, J.W.
       The influence of the revolutions of 1848 on Great Britain.
       Ph.D., Georgia, 1963.
       DA 25 1167

2400. COLSON, A.M.
       The revolt of the Hampshire agricultural labourers and its causes, 1812-1831.
       M.A., King's College, London, 1937.

2401. DOAK, J.C.
       Rioting and civil strife in Londonderry during the nineteenth and early twentieth
       centuries.
       M.A., Queen's University, Belfast, 1978.

2402.   DONNELLY, F.K.
        The general rising of 1820: a study of social conflict in the Industrial Revolution.
        Ph.D., Sheffield, 1975.

2403.   DONNELLY, F.K.
        Popular disturbances in Sheffield, 1790-1820.
        M.A.*, Sheffield, 1971.

2404.   DUTT, M.
        The agricultural labourers' revolt of 1830 in Kent, Surrey and Sussex.
        Ph.D., Birkbeck College, London, 1967.

2405.   FISHER, C.
        The Forest of Dean miners' riot, June 1831.
        M.A.*, Warwick, 1974-75.

2406.   GASH, N.
        The unrest in rural England in 1830 with special reference to Berkshire.
        B.Litt., Oxford, 1934.

2407.   GROSSHANS, H.P.
        The European revolutionaires in London, 1848-1870.
        B.Litt., Oxford, 1950.

2408.   GRUMBLING, V.O.
        John Thelwall: romantick and revolutionist.
        Ph.D., University of New Hampshire, 1977.
        DA 39 1586A

2409.   HAWKINS, D.W.
        The Gordon riots of 1780 in the context of the public order problem in late
        eighteenth-century London.
        M.A., Wales (Swansea), 1977.

2410.   HAYTER, A.J.
        The army and the mob in England in the generation before the Gordon riots.
        Ph.D., L.S.E., 1973.

2411.   HEARN, G.L.
        The politics of violence in the nineteenth century.
        Ph.D., London, 1954.

2412.   ISAAC, D.G.D.
        A study of popular disturbances in Britain, 1714-1754.
        Ph.D., Edinburgh, 1953.

2413.   JONES, D.J.V.
        Popular disturbances in Wales, 1792-1832.
        Ph.D., Wales (Aberystwyth), 1966.

2414.   KAMERICK, J.J.
        Great Britain and the continental revolutions of 1848.
        Ph.D., Iowa, 1950.

2415.   KELLER, L.
        Public order in Victorian London: the interaction between the Metropolitan Police,
        the government, the urban crowd and the law.
        Ph.D., Cambridge, 1977.

2416.   LOGUE, K.J.
        Popular disturbances in Scotland, 1780-1815.
        Ph.D., Edinburgh, 1977.

2417.   MUNGER, F.W.
        Popular protest and its suppression in early nineteenth-century Lancashire, England:
        a study of historical models of protest and repression.
        Ph.D., Michigan, 1977.
        DA 38 6951A

2418.   RANDALL, H.C.
        Public disorder in England and Wales, 1765-75.
        Ph.D., North Carolina, 1963.
        DA 25 4676

2419.   RICHTER, D.C
        Public order and popular disturbances in Great Britain, 1865-1914.
        Ph.D., Maryland, 1965.
        DA 26 1620

2420.   RUDKIN, O.D.
        Thomas Spence and his connections.
        M.A., London, 1924.

2421.   SEAL, G.
        Pre-political protest in English agrarian communities.
        M.A., Leeds, 1978.

2422.   SHELTON, W.J.
        English hunger and industrial disorders: a study of social conflict during the first
        decade of George III's reign.
        Ph.D., British Columbia, 1971.
        DA 32 6906A

2423.   SMITH, M.H.
        Conflict and society in late eighteenth-century Birmingham.
        Ph.D., Cambridge, 1978.

2424.   STEVENSON, J.
        Disturbances and public order in London, 1790-1821.
        D.Phil., Oxford, 1973.

2425.   URWIN, G.G.
        The standard of appreciation shown by the public during the conclusion of the
        Napoleonic War of the period of depression and insurgence, 1800-1830.
        M.A., London, External, 1947.

2426.   WILLIAMS, M.
        The Rebecca riots in Wales.
        M.A., Wales (Aberystwyth), 1913.

        WAGES AND INCOMES

2427.   ADAMS, R.M.
        A comparative study of the occupational wage structures of the iron and steel
        industries of Great Britain and the United States in the last seventy years.
        Ph.D., L.S.E., 1958.

2428.   ADDISON, J.T.
        The effect of productivity agreements on patterns of wages in a local
        labour market in the period 1960-1970.
        Ph.D., L.S.E., 1971.

2429.   ALI, M.A.
        Inter-industry differences in the rates of change in earnings in the post-war British
        manufacturing sector: a study using time series and cross-section statistics.
        Ph.D., Strathclyde, 1969-70.

2430.   ARMSTRONG, E.G.A.
        The operation of minimum wage legislation in Birmingham.
        Ph.D., Birmingham, 1965-66.

2431.   BARNES, S.E.
        Individual, local and national bargaining for teachers' salaries in England and
        Wales: a study of the period 1858-1944.
        Ph.D., King's College, London, 1959.

2432.   BARRATT, J.M.
        The remuneration and prospects of the elementary school teacher, 1914-1939.
        D.Phil., Hull, 1974.

2433.   BAYLISS, F.J.
        The history and working of British Wages Councils.
        Ph.D., Nottingham, 1959-60.

2434.   BERCUSSON, B.
        A comparative analysis of attempts at regulation of wages in government contracts
        in the United Kingdom and the U.S.A.
        Ph.D., Cambridge, 1974.

2435.   BOWERS, P.H.
        The level of earnings of manual workers in Burnley and its effects on migration.
        M.A.*, Lancaster, 1969.

2436.   BOWLBY, R.L.
        The statutory regulation of minimum wages in Great Britain.
        Ph.D., Texas, 1958.
        DA 19 0973

2437.   BRENNER, Y.
        Prices and wages in England, 1450-1550.
        M.A., Queen Mary College, London, 1960.

2438.   BURKITT, B.
        A study of inter-industry wage determination: 1924-1938.
        Ph.D., Leeds, 1972.

2439.   BURNS, E.M.
        Wages and the State.
        Ph.D., London, 1926.

2440.   CABLE, J.R.
        Methods of wage-fixing in a soap and chemical plant: a case study.
        M.A.(Econ.), Manchester, 1968-69.

2441. CORINA, J.G.
       The British experiment in wage restraint with special reference to 1948-50.
       D.Phil., Oxford, 1960-61.

2442. DEVINE, P.J.
       Inter-regional variations in the degree of inequality of income distribution:
       the U.K., 1949-65.
       M.A.(Econ.), Manchester, 1967-68.

2443. DORFMAN, G.A.
       British incomes policy and the Trades Union Congress.
       Ph.D., Columbia, 1971.
       DA 32 3382A

2444. DUGGETT, M.J.
       A comparative study of the operation of the sliding scale in the Durham and South Wales
       coalfields, 1875-1900.
       Ph.D., Wales (Swansea), 1977.

2445. ECCLESTON, B.
       A survey of wage rates in five Midland counties, 1750-1834.
       Ph.D., Leicester, 1977.

2446. EDELBERG, V.G.
       Wages and capitalist production.
       Ph.D., L.S.E., 1935.

2447. EMBLEY, P.
       Trade unions and wages: a re-examination of the Hines thesis.
       M.A., Keele, 1973-74.

2448. FELS, A.H.M.
       The British Prices and Incomes Board: the N.B.P.I. as an instrument of incomes
       policy administration.
       Ph.D., Duke, 1972.
       DA 34 0957A

2449. FINCH, C.D.
       Some problems in wages policy.
       Ph.D., L.S.E., 1949.

2450. FISHER, A.G.B.
       Some problems of wages and their regulation in Great Britain since 1918.
       Ph.D., London, 1924.

2451. GILL, C.M.
       Wage earnings in Great Britain: the case of manual workers, 1960-70.
       M.A.*, Lancaster, 1971.

2452. HARRISON, H.A.
       Perceptions of pay: a study of hourly-paid paper mill workers.
       M.Phil., Birkbeck College, London, 1971-72.

2453. HEALY, M.
       National guilds as wage-systems.
       M.A., National University of Ireland, 1920.

2454. HINDMARSH, N.M.
       The regulation of wages in England under the Statute of Artificers.
       Ph.D., London, External, 1932.

2455. HUNT, E.H.
       Regional wage variations in Britain, 1850-1914.
       Ph.D., London, External, 1971.

2456. HUNT, N.C.
       A critical examination of methods of individual remuneration with special
       reference to the requirements of British industry.
       Ph.D., Edinburgh, 1948.

2457. ISLES, K.S.
       Wages policy and the price level.
       M.Sc., Cambridge, 1934.

2458. JONES, A.B.
       Some contributions to a study of work, wages and prices in Wales in the sixteenth century.
       M.A., Wales, 1933.

2459. JONES, W.D.
       Problems of wages and wage regulation.
       M.Sc., London, External, 1936.

2460. KAHN, H.R.
       Salaries in the public services in England and Wales, 1946-1951: a vertical and
       horizontal analysis.
       Ph.D., Bedford College, London, 1958.

2461. KELLY, T.H.
       Wages and labour organisations in the brass trades of Birmingham and district.
       Ph.D., Birmingham, 1930.

2462. KNIGHT, K.G.
       Operatives wages and work group behaviour in the baking industry of England and Wales:
       two case studies.
       M.A.(Econ.), Manchester, 1968-69.

2463. LALOYE, A.O.
       Wage drift in British manufacturing industries, 1956-1968.
       M.Sc., Bristol, 1968-69.

2464. LENTON, J.H.
       Wages in the Leeds area, 1770-1850.
       M.Phil., Leeds, 1969.

2465. LEWIS, P.N.
       An examination of British incomes policy.
       M.A., Liverpool, 1968-69.

2466. McCARTHY, A.C.
       Wage theories in the nineteenth century with special reference to Thornton.
       M.Econ.Sc., National University of Ireland, 1941.

2467. McDOUGALL, M.M.
       Wage policy in the British electric supply industry (1964-68).
       Ph.D., Columbia, 1969.
       DA 30 4091A

2468. McGILLIVRAY, A.
       Regional differentials in the average earnings from employment in manufacturing industry.
       B.Phil., Dundee, 1971-72.

2469. MALIK, M.A.
       Some economic effects of minimum wage regulation in the U.S.A. and Great Britain in
       the post-war period.
       Ph.D., Michigan, 1963.
       DA 25 1616A

2470. MASON, W.H.
       An analysis of wage-rates in Britain in relation to employment levels since 1920.
       M.Sc., London, External, 1949.

2471. MERCER, E.J.
       Wage structures with particular reference to the engineering industry in the south-west.
       M.A., Exeter, 1973-74.

2472. NOMVETE, B.D.
       British wages policy, 1940-1950: a study of the decisions of the National Arbitration
       Tribunal.
       M.A.(Econ.), Manchester, 1954-55.

2473. NUTTALL, T.
       Changes in the wage structure of the coal industry since nationalisation.
       M.A., Leeds, 1966.

2474. PANITCH, L.V.
       The Labour party and the trade unions: a study of incomes policy since 1945 with
       special reference to 1964-1970.
       Ph.D.(Econ.), L.S.E., 1974.

2475. PAPWORTH, H.D.
       The determination of teachers' salaries with particular reference to secondary
       schools, 1870-1919.
       M.A., London, Institute of Education, 1964.

2476. PEITCHINIS, S.G.
       The determination of the wages of railwaymen: a study of British experience with a
       comparative study of Canada since 1914.
       Ph.D., L.S.E., 1960.

2477. POLKINGHORN, B.H.
       The British incomes policy, 1964-1970: its impact on the low paid workers.
       Ph.D., California, Davis, 1972.
       DA 33 5366A

2478. PRESLAND, G.J.
       Personal income from work and property with particular reference to the United Kingdom
       during the period 1951-61.
       M.A., Liverpool, 1965-66.

2479. PRIMORAC, E.
       A study of the division between pay and profits of the product of British manufacturing
       industry, 1924-1958, with special reference to short run variations, 1948-1958.
       Ph.D., L.S.E., 1966.

2480.   QUINN, E.
Trade unions and incomes policy: a study in the attitudes and behaviour of a pressure group.
M.Sc., Strathclyde, 1972-73.

2481.   REED, S.K.
An investigation into wage incentives and their effect on production with
comparisons between Great Britain and the United States.
Ph.D., Edinburgh, 1950.

2482.   RONDEAU, C.
The autonomous influence of the institutional determinants of the movements of money
wages in the United Kingdom, 1862-1938.
Ph.D., L.S.E., 1969.

2483.   ROUTH, G.G.C.
A study of the factors determining the level of pay in the British Civil Service since
1875, with particular reference to the General and Minor Post Office Manipulative and
Engineering grades.
Ph.D., L.S.E., 1951-52.

2484.   ROWE, J.W.F.
Changes of wage rates in certain industries during the last thirty to forty years, and
in particular, the relations between changes in rates and changes in earnings and their
causes.
M.Sc., London, 1923.

2485.   SAXENA, C.J.N.
Wages boards in Britain and the application of their procedure in India.
M.Sc.(Econ.), L.S.E., 1959-60.

2486.   SEMPLE, W.
Wages and prices in Belfast, 1914-23.
M.Com.Sc., Belfast, 1923.

2487.   SHAPIRO, J.C.
Inter-industry wage determination: the post-war United Kingdom experience.
Ph.D., L.S.E., 1966.

2488.   SHEPHERD, E.C.
The settlement of wages in government employment.
B.Litt., Oxford, 1923.

2489.   SMITH, P.M.
Prices and incomes policies, 1964-70.
M.A.(Econ.), Manchester, 1970-71.

2490.   STEINER, H.
The attitudes of the T.U.C. and the O.G.B. towards incomes policy.
M.A.*, Warwick, 1974-75.

2491.   STEPHENS, C.H.A.
Wage rates, 1750-1800.
B.Litt., Oxford, 1931.

2492.   THOMSON, C.M.
Cost of living indexation agreements in wage bargaining with special reference to
Great Britain since 1945.
M.A.(Econ.), Manchester, 1972-73.

2493.   UEHARA, N.
Comparative analysis of prices, wages and labour market structures in Britain and Japan.
M.Litt., Glasgow, 1971-72.

2494.   VERNON, K.
An economic study of wage and price inflation in the United Kingdom for the post-war period.
Ph.D., L.S.E., 1970.

2495.   WHELAN, P.
Alfred Marshall as an economist with special reference to wages and the working class.
M.Econ.Sc., National University of Ireland, 1945.

WOMEN IN SOCIETY: FEMINIST MOVEMENT

2496.   BILLINGTON, R.H.C.
The women's education and suffrage movements, 1850-1914: innovation and institutionalization.
M.A., Hull, 1976.

2497.   BRADY, N.
Shafts and the Quest for a New Morality: An examination of the 'Woman Question' in the
1890s as seen through the pages of a contemporary journal.
M.A.*, Warwick, 1978.

2498.   CRAWFORD, F.W.
Some aspects of the political and economic problems of woman in English society, 1884-1901.
Ph.D., New York University, 1956.
DA 17 0348

2499.   McCRONE, K.E.
The advancement of women during the age of reform, 1832-1870.
Ph.D., New York University, 1971.

2500. MORGAN, D.R.
       The politics of women suffrage in Britain and the United States of America, 1906-20.
       Ph.D., Cambridge, 1967.

2501. RILEY, L.W.
       The opposition to women's suffrage, 1867-1918.
       B.Litt., Oxford, 1977.

2502. ROVER, C.M.
       The women's suffrage movement in Britain, 1866-1914.
       Ph.D., London, External, 1966.

2503. SAYWELL, R.J.T.
       The development of the feminist idea in England, 1789-1833.
       M.A., King's College, London, 1936.

2504. SCOTT, J.C.
       Bradford women in organisation, 1867-1914: an introductory study of their contribution
       to social, political and economic development.
       M.A., Bradford, 1970.

2505. SOFTLEY, P.
       Changes in the social status of women in England: an analysis of the married women's
       property and divorce controversies, 1854-7.
       M.A., Leicester, 1962.

2506. STOBAUGH, B.P.
       Women candidates for the British Parliament, 1918-1970: statistical analysis and three
       case studies.
       Ph.D., Boston University Graduate School, 1975.
       DA 35 7824A
            /Case studies include Ellen Wilkinson._7

2507. WALTON, R.G.
       The place of women in the development of social work, 1860-1971.
       Ph.D., Manchester, 1971-72.

2508. WATSON, H.F.
       British women writers and the origin of the feminist movement in England in the latter
       half of the 18th century.
       M.A., Manchester, 1963.
            (See also entry no. 1782.)

        PROSTITUTION

2509. WALKOWITZ, J.R.
       "We are not beasts of the field": prostitution and the campaign against the
       Contagious Diseases Acts, 1869-1886.
       Ph.D., Rochester, 1974.
       DA 35 2202A

2510. WARE, H.R.E.
       The recruitment, regulation and role of prostitutes in Britain from the middle of the
       19th century to the present day.
       Ph.D., London, 1969.

        WOMEN WORKERS

2511. AINSWORTH, E.H.
       Changing attitudes to the employment of women and children on the land between the 1830s
       and the 1870s with particular reference to the county of Sussex.
       M.A., Sussex, 1969.

2512. ANGUS, E.Y.
       The higher education and employment of women in the twentieth century.
       M.A., L.S.E., 1931.

2513. BILLINGHAM, J.
       Women's work and wages in the West Riding of Yorkshire 1760-1830.
       M.A.*, Sheffield, 1977 (Department of Economic and Social History).

2514. BRAYBON, C.G.
       Attitudes to working women in British industry, 1914-1920.
       M.Phil., Sussex, 1977.

2515. CREIGHTON, W.B.
       The development of the legal status of women in employment in Great Britain.
       Ph.D., Cambridge, 1974-75.

2516. DALE, M.K.
       Women in the textile industries and trade of fifteenth century England.
       M.A., London, 1928.

2517. DAVIDOFF, L. (Mrs Leonore Lockwood)
       The employment of married women in England, 1850-1950.
       M.A., L.S.E., 1956.

2518. DAVIES, R.G.
Aspects of married-female employment in Cray Valley industry, Bromley borough.
M.A., Sussex, 1968-69.

2519. DONNISON, J.E.
The development of the profession of midwife in England, 1754-1902.
Ph.D.(Econ.), L.S.E., 1974.

2520. FLORECKA, J.
A comparative study of the economic position of women in Great Britain and Poland in
the inter-war period.
Ph.D., Edinburgh, 1945.

2521. HEWITT, M.
The effect of married women's employment in the cotton textile districts on the
organisation and structure of the home in Lancashire, 1840-80.
Ph.D., L.S.E., 1953.

2522. HOGG, S.
The employment of women in Great Britain, 1891-1921.
D.Phil., Oxford, 1968.

2523. HOLCOMBE, L.
Middle-class working women in England, 1850-1914.
Ph.D., Columbia, 1962.
DA 23 1004

2524. HUANG, F-S.
The role of women workers in the British textile industry, 1780-1850.
M.Litt., Cambridge, 1972.

2525. HUTTON, C.R.
Married women on full-time shiftwork: some domestic and social consequences.
M.A., Bedford College, London, 1961-62.

2526. JOHN, A.V.
Female life and labour in British coal-mining communities, 1840-90.
Ph.D., Manchester, 1976.

2527. KHAIRY, A.H.F.
The employment of women: evolution, pattern and composition with special reference to the
United Kingdom.
B.Phil., St. Andrews, 1972-73.

2528. LEWER, S.
Impact of the First World War on women's employment.
M.A.*, Warwick, 1973-74.

2529. MAPPEN, E.F.
Women workers and unemployment policy in late Victorian and Edwardian London.
Ph.D., Rutgers University, 1977.
DA 38 2986A

2530. MORGAN, D.H.J.
Theoretical and coneptual problems in the study of social relations at work: an analysis
of the differing definitions of women's roles in a northern factory.
Ph.D., Manchester, 1968-69.

2531. NEFF, W.F.
Victorian working women: a historical and literary study of women in British industries
and professions, 1832-1850.
Ph.D., Columbia, 1929.

2532. PINCHBECK, I.
Women workers and the Industrial Revolution, 1750-1850.
Ph.D., L.S.E., 1930.

2533. PINCHBECK, I.
The work of women in agriculture in the late eighteenth and early nineteenth centuries
and the influence of the agrarian revolution thereon.
M.A., London, 1927.

2534. ROWLING, M.
The study of women's employment with reference to the social and economic consequences.
B.Com.*, Leeds, 1934.

2535. SCOTT, R.J.
Women in the Stuart economy.
M.Phil., London, 1973.

2536. STANES, D.F.
The employment of women in supervisory and managerial positions in the cotton, clothing,
biscuit and cocoa, chocolate and sugar confectionery industries in England· with a
historical introduction from 1900.
M.Sc.(Econ.), L.S.E., 1954-55.

2537. TAYLOR, P.
Women domestic servants, 1919-1939· the final phase.
M.A., Birmingham, 1976.

2538. THOM, D.
Women munition workers at Woolwich Arsenal in the 1914-18 War.
M.A.*, Warwick, 1974-75.

WORK

2539. HUNDERT, E.J.
The conception of work and the worker in early industrial England: studies of an ideology in transition.
Ph.D., Rochester, 1969.
DA 30 3378A

2540. TRAVERS, T.H.E.
Samuel Smiles and the Victorian work-ethic: the rise and decline of the ideal of self-help, 1830-1890.
Ph.D., Yale, 1970.
DA 32 0372A

WORKERS' PARTICIPATION: WORKER CONTROL AND CO-OWNERSHIP

2541. CAREW, A.
Rank and file movements and workers' control in the British engineering industry, 1850-1969.
M.Phil., Sussex, 1971-72.

2542. COTE, A.
Legal regulation and workers' participation in the enterprise.
Ph.D., L.S.E., 1974.

2543. GOODRICH, C.L.
The frontier of control· a study in workshop politics.
Ph.D., Chicago, 1919.

2544. HADLEY, R.D.
Participation and common-ownership: a study of employee participation in a common ownership firm.
Ph.D., L.S.E., 1971.

2545. HILL, M.J.D.
Worker self-management in Western capitalist countries.
M.Sc., Sussex, 1973-74.

2546. McKINLAY, H.
Formal joint consultation: a study of the Works Council scheme in a chemical factory.
B.Litt., Glasgow, 1958-59.

2547. MARX, E.
Contemporary trade union attitudes to workers' participation: industrial democracy in Great Britain and Western Germany: a comparative study.
M.Phil., Sussex, 1970-71.

2548. POOLE, M.J.F.
A power approach to workers' participation in decision making.
Ph.D., Sheffield, 1969.

2549. PRIBIĆEVIĆ, B.
The demand for "workers' control" in the coal mining, engineering and railway industries, 1910-1922.
D.Phil., Oxford, 1957.

2550. REID, M.L.
Workers' councils; do they offer a solution for the present day industrial problem?
M.A., British Columbia, 1923.
        (A comparison between Great Britain, Canada and U.S.A.)

2551. ROSENSTEIN, E.
Ideology and practice of workers' participation in management: experiences in Israel, Yugoslavia and England.
Ph.D., California, Berkeley, 1968-69.

2552. TYSON, R.E.
The Sun Mill Co. Ltd.: a study in democratic investment, 1858-1959.
M.A., Manchester, 1962-63.

2553. WEINBERG, R.L.
"Workers' control": a study in British socialist thought.
Ph.D., L.S.E., 1960.

WORKING-CLASS: LITERACY AND READING HABITS

2554. THOMPSON, A.R.
An enquiry into the reading habits of the working classes in Scotland from 1830 to 1840.
B.Litt., Glasgow, 1961.

2555. WEBB, R.K.
The challenge of the working class reader in Great Britain, 1790-1848.
Ph.D., Columbia, 1951.
DA 12 0547

2556.   WILD, D.W.
The emergence of literacy: 1780-1860.
Ph.D., Washington, 1972.
DA 33 2349A
(Examines how Blake, Cobbett and Dickens reflected the changes England was
undergoing between 1780 and 1860 and especially concerned with the new
working class readership.)

WORKING-CLASS COMMUNITIES AND LIFE

2557.   ARMBRUSTER, G.H.
The social determination of ideologies· being a study of a Welsh mining community.
Ph.D., L.S.E., 1940.

2558.   BARNSBY, G.J.
Social conditions in the Black Country in the nineteenth century.
Ph.D., Birmingham, 1969.

2559.   CAPPER, T.E.H.
The rise and decline of the industrial colonies at Blackbarrow, Cark-in-Cartmel,
and Lowwood between the eighteenth and twentieth centuries.
M.A.*, Lancaster, 1969.

2560.   CROSSICK, G.J.
Social structure and working class behaviour· Kentish London, 1840-80.
Ph.D., London, 1976.

2561.   DAVIES, C.
The development of industries and settlements between Merthyr Tydfil and
Abergavenny from 1740-1840.
M.A., Wales, 1949.

2562.   DAVIES, W.H.
The influence of recent changes in the social environment in the outlook and habits of
individuals with special reference to mining communities in South Wales.
M.A., Wales, 1933.

2563.   EVANS, G.
Onllwyn· a sociological study of a South Wales mining community.
M.A., Wales (Aberystwyth), 1960-61.

2564.   EVISON, J.E.
The opening up of the "central" region of the South Yorkshire coalfield and the
development of its townships as colliery communities.
M.Phil., Leeds, 1972.

2565.   GORDON, A.
The economic and social development of Ashington: a study of a coal mining community.
M.Com., Durham, 1953-54.

2566.   GRIFFIN, C.P.
The economic and social development of the Leicestershire and South Derbyshire coalfield,
1550-1941.
Ph.D., Nottingham, 1969.

2567.   HELM, M.H.
The development of the industrial communities of Galgate and Dolphinholme mainly in the
nineteenth century.
M.A.*, Lancaster, 1969.

2568.   HENRYSON, M.M.
Factors in the informal and formal social relationship of inner city working-class
households: a study of three local authority housing estates in Central London.
M.Phil., Bedford College, London, 1969-70.

2569.   HOPKINS, E.
The working classes of Stourbridge and district, 1815-1914.
Ph.D., London, External, 1972.

2570.   JONES, A.G.
The economic, industrial and social history of Ebbw Vale during the period 1775-1927,
being a study in the origin and development of an industrial district of South Wales
in all its aspects.
M.A., Wales, 1929.

2571.   KAIJAGE, F.
Labouring Barnsley, 1816-56: a social and economic history.
Ph.D., Warwick, 1975.

2572.   KNIGHT, E.M.
A geographical analysis of the effects upon selected communities of closure and re-
organisation of collieries in the Northern coalfield since 1957.
M.Litt., Newcastle, 1968-69.

2573.   ROBERTS, E.A.M.
The working-class family in Barrow and Lancaster, 1890-1930.
Ph.D., Lancaster, 1978.

2574.   SEELEY, J.Y.B.
         Coal mining villages of Northumberland and Durham: a study of sanitary conditions and
         social facilities, 1870-80.
         M.A., Newcastle, 1974.

2575.   STONE, B.R.
         Down pit: a study of the work, the life style and the community of the British coalminer.
         Ph.D., Missouri Columbia, 1972.
         DA 33 5309A
            (Based on North Midlands mining villages.)

2576.   TAYLOR, I.C.
         A social geography of the working-class area of Liverpool, 1780-1864.
         Ph.D., Liverpool, 1976.

2577.   TODD, F.A.
         The living and working conditions of the workers in the Preston area, 1750-1850.
         M.Litt., Lancaster, 1975.

2578.   VARLEY, E.H.
         Wakefield and district as a traditional area in the Yorkshire, Derbyshire and
         Nottinghamshire coalfield.
         M.Sc., Birkbeck College, London, 1935.

2579.   WEETCH, K.T.
         The Dowlais ironworks and its industrial community, 1760-1850: a local study in the
         economic and social history of the late eighteenth and early nineteenth centuries.
         M.Sc., L.S.E., 1963-64.

2580.   WHITING, R.C.
         The working class in the 'new industry' towns between the wars: the case of Oxford.
         D.Phil., Oxford, 1978.

WORKING CONDITIONS

2581.   HANSON, H.
         The social and economic condition of canal boatmen in England, 1760-1914.
         M.A., Manchester, 1972.

2582.   SCHMIECHEN, J.A.
         Sweated industries and sweated labour: a study of industrial disorganisation and
         worker attitudes in the London clothing trades, 1867-1919.
         Ph.D., Illinois (Urbana-Champaign), 1975.
         DA 36 0495A

2583.   TOORN, K. Van der
         Labour conditions in the coal mining industry in the 19th century.
         B.Com.*, Leeds, 1935.

ACCIDENTS AND SAFETY

2584.   BALLANTYNE, R.D.
         Industrial accidents in Birmingham.
         M.Soc.Sc., Birmingham, 1969-70.

2585.   BENSON, J.
         The compensation of English coalminers and their dependants for industrial
         accidents, 1860-1897.
         Ph.D., Leeds, 1973.

2586.   MOORE, I.R.
         The incidence and prevention of industrial accidents in Ireland.
         M.A., Trinity College, Dublin, 1956-57.

2587.   RAYCHAUDHURI, S.
         Industrial injuries schemes in India and Britain: a comparative study.
         Ph.D., L.S.E., 1959-60.

2588.   REDMOND, P.W.D.
         History of the responsibility of a master at common law for the safety of his servants.
         LL.M., Liverpool, 1953-54.

2589.   SMITH, H.
         The responsibilities of employers and others for the maintenance and support of injured
         workmen and their families, including the families of deceased workmen, during the half
         century before 1840.
         M.A., London, External, 1964.

2590.   SMITH, H.
         Personal injury claims in Victorian Britain.
         Ph.D., London, 1970.

2591.   STEVENSON, J.
         The economic effect of industrial accidents with special reference to Northern Ireland.
         M.Sc.(Econ.), Queen's University, Belfast, 1958-59.

HEALTH AND DISEASE

2592. EDMONDS, O.P.
The coalminer and industrial dermatitis.
M.D., Leeds, 1958.

2593. ERDOGAN, V.
Ill health as a social problem: a case study in the pottery industry, 1910-1946.
Ph.D., Keele, 1974.

2594. HOLMES, J.G.
Epidermophytosis in coalminers.
M.D., Cambridge, 1954-55.

2595. JAMES, W.R.L.
Clinico-pathological evidence relating to problems on the medico-legal aspects of
coal-workers pneumoconiosis.
M.D., Wales, 1954-55.

2596. LUDKIN, S.
Tuberculosis in an urban mining community.
M.D., King's College, Durham, 1956-57.

2597. MAULE, H.G.
A study of the laundry industry: the general conditions of work and management which
may influence the health and well-being of laundry operators.
Ph.D., London School of Hygiene and Tropical Medicine, 1949.

2598. MEACHAM, G.
Medical aspects of lead-smelting.
M.D., Cambridge, 1957-58.

2599. WILLIAMSON, D.M.
The problems of industrial dermatitis in the coalmine worker.
M.D., Leeds, 1961.

2600. YEKUTIEL, M.P.
The history of pulmonary tuberculosis in the boot and shoe industry and its relation
to social conditions, including a comparison with other industries.
D.Phil., Oxford, 1953-54.

HOURS OF WORK: HOLIDAYS

2601. BIENEFELD, M.A.
A study of the course of change in the customary and in the specified or normal hours of
work of manual workers in certain British industries and of the factors affecting changes
in the specified or normal hours from the eighteeth century to the present day.
Ph.D., L.S.E., 1969.

2602. BOOTH, N.H.
Hours of work in the coal mining industry of Great Britain since the early part of the
nineteenth century with special reference to Northumberland and Durham and with an
account of certain movements connected therewith.
M.Litt., Oxford, 1930.

2603. HODGSON, J.S.
The movements for shorter hours, 1840-75.
D.Phil., Oxford, 1940.

2604. HODGSON, M.C.
The working day and the working week in Victorian Britain, 1840-1910.
M.Phil., Birkbeck College, London, 1974.

2605. MARTIN, G.C.
Some aspects of the provision of annual holidays for the English working classes down
to 1947.
M.A., Leicester, 1968.

2606. SALLIS, H.
Overtime in electricity supply in the period, 1954-1964: its incidence and subsequent
control.
M.Phil., L.S.E., 1971.

JOURNEY FROM HOME TO WORK

2607. DALTON, M.
Slough: a study of journey to work in the outer metropolitan area.
M.Phil., University College, London, 1973.

2608. HOLME, J.
An analysis of patterns of journey to work in a part of the Yorkshire, Nottingham and
Derbyshire coalfield. 2 vols.
M.A., Sheffield, 1968.

2609. HOUGHTON, D.S.
The separation of home and workplace in West Cumberland.
M.A., Hull, 1965.

2610.   LEIGH, R.
        The journey to work to central London, 1921-1951: a geographical analysis.
        Ph.D., L.S.E., 1968.

2611.   LIEPMANN, K.K.
        The daily ebb and flow of labour between home and workplace in English industrial areas.
        Ph.D., L.S.E., 1942.

2612.   OPSTAD, C.T.
        The journey to work in the London region.
        M.Phil., University College, London, 1969-70.

2613.   RANKIN, D.G.
        Journey to work movements and labour supply areas in the Nottingham-Derby district
        with specific reference to industrial firms.
        Ph.D., Nottingham, 1970-71.

2614.   WARNES, A.M.
        The increase of journey to work and its consequences for the residential structure
        of towns, with special reference to Chorley, Lancashire.
        Ph.D., Salford, 1969-70.

WORK DISCIPLINE AND ORGANISATION

2615.   HEDLEY, R.A.
        Freedom and constraint: a study of British factory workers.
        Ph.D., Oregon, 1971.
        DA 32 3443A

ADDENDA

2616.   BEECHEY, F.E.
        The Irish in York, 1840-75.
        D.Phil., York, 1977.

2617.   DUNCAN, N.O.
        British party attitudes to immigration and race with particular reference to special
        areas, 1955-1971.
        Ph.D., Manchester, 1977.

2618.   HUZZARD, S.J.
        The role of the certifying factory surgeon in the state regulation of child labour
        and industrial health, 1833-1973.
        M.A., Manchester, 1976.

2619.   LATHAM, P.A.G.
        Theories of the labour movement: a critique of existing theories in the context of
        an empirical study of building trade unionism.
        Ph.D., Goldsmith's College, London, 1978.

2620.   MACHIN, L.
        A critical survey of the mechanics' institutes of the Staffordshire Potteries.
        M.Ed., Liverpool, 1978.

2621.   ROCKEY, J.R.
        The ideal city and model town in English utopian thought: 1849-1902.
        D.Phil., Oxford, 1977.

2622.   RUSHTON, P.
        Housing conditions and the family economy in the Victorian slum: a study of a
        Manchester district, 1790-1871.
        Ph.D., Manchester, 1977.

2623.   WAINWRIGHT, R.W.
        Moral change and the growth and establishment of respectability: a study of cultural
        segregation within the London labour market with special reference to the writings of
        Francis Place and Henry Mayhew.
        M.Phil., Bedford College, London, 1978.

2624.   WILLIAMS, D.M.J.
        Vinyl chloride-related disease in a South Wales P.V.C. factory, 1968-1976.
        M.D., Welsh National School of Medicine, Cardiff, 1977.

2625.   HAMILTON, I.W.
        Education for revolution: the Plebs League and Labour College movement, 1908-1921.
        M.A.*, Warwick, 1972.

2626.   BOWES, N.
        The People's Convention.
        M.A.*, Warwick, 1976.

INDEXES

There are four indexes:
Index of persons
Index of places
Subject index
Index of authors
Reference is to item numbers

INDEX OF PLACES

County names and boundaries are as before the Local Government reorganization of 1974. References to ENGLAND and GREAT BRITAIN are not included, as they would have been too numerous.